Personal
Financial Survival

PERSONAL FINANCIAL SURVIVAL

A Guide for the 1980s and Beyond

David M. Brownstone

Jacques Sartisky

A Wiley-Interscience Publication

JOHN WILEY & SONS   New York • Chichester • Brisbane • Toronto

Library of Congress Cataloging in Publication Data:

Brownstone, David M.
    Personal financial survival.

    "A Wiley-Interscience publication."
    Includes index.
    1. Finance, Personal. I. Sartisky, Jacques.
II. Title.

HG179.B75   332.024   81-1796
ISBN 0-471-05588-3   AACR2

Printed in the United States of America

10 9 8 7 6 5 4 3 2 1

Preface

Sometimes a book grows to be larger in life than it was in conception—even when the conception itself was quite wide.

This is such a book. We set out to do a broad book on financial planning, capable of being used to lifelong advantage by people trying to do effective personal financial planning—and we have done that book. But, very early in the process, it became clear that a book on financial planning would be inadequate if it did not also face up—squarely and from the start—to the fact that the lives of all of us have been dramatically altered in recent years by the twin impacts of much-increased life expectancy and long-term inflation that will not go away, wrapped around a stagnant economy. Under these conditions, much previously standard lifetime planning advice becomes outmoded, and both accumulation for retirement and retirement itself may easily become myths. Long life can and should bring a wonderful new set of opportunities for all of us; but for many of us there is an excellent chance it will become a time of poverty and great sadness. In truth, effective financial planning under these new conditions becomes a matter of sheer survival, and of necessity a matter of career and lifestyle planning, along with the financial planning.

This book is intended to be a guide to lifelong personal planning for anyone and everyone—including people just starting out, those nearing retirement, and those in the middle planning years; people working for others and those independently employed; and people spanning the whole income range. We think it as necessary as a book can be.

Our thanks to Thurman Poston and Richard P. Zeldin, our editor and publisher, respectively, at John Wiley & Sons; to Alfred Stieber of Kurz-Liebow & Company; to Anita Handel, Robert

Madow, Leona James, and Rebecca Siegel of Pensions For Business, Inc.; and to our expert typists Shirley Fenn and Mary Racette. Special thanks to Irene M. Franck, whose insights inform every aspect of this book, and to Ruth Siegel, who gave us warm support and good counsel throughout the project.

DAVID M. BROWNSTONE
JACQUES SARTISKY

Chappaqua, New York
New York, New York
July 1981

Contents

Personal
Financial Survival

PLANNING YOUR FUTURE

1

Lifelong Personal Planning

Any book on lifelong personal planning is, by its very nature, "futurist." That is, it has at the heart of its analyses and recommendations a set of assumptions about the shape of our future, both as individuals and as part of an increasingly interconnected world economic system. To make this book most useful to you, we want to state these assumptions clearly and explicitly.

Given the extraordinary work now being done in biology and medicine, we can reasonably expect our already unprecedentedly long lifespans to lengthen dramatically. If so, we will also need to support ourselves for far longer than anyone might have predicted only a few generations ago. In practical terms, it is entirely possible that anyone now 60 years old and looking forward to retirement in a few years will live past the year 2000 and will need to be self-supporting for 20 or 30 years past retirement.

For someone now 40 years old, lifelong planning becomes a matter of attempting to look forward to the middle of the next century. We have every reason to believe that, short of a nuclear catastrophe, people who are now 40 and living in "advanced" industrial nations such as the United States can expect to live beyond the year 2030, and in some instances considerably longer. For someone born now, life may be very long indeed, with some seeing the dawn of the twenty-second century. Planning for one's loved ones can be a very long-term project.

The first assumption we make, then, is that we will tend to live increasingly longer.

Our second assumption is that, although the rate of inflation will vary during our lifetimes, a constant tendency toward inflation is built into our economic system. Savings, pensions, and other resources that seem quite substantial now may turn out to be pathetically inadequate as inflation and longevity erode current resources. Inflation is, after all, a historic long-term trend, only more apparent and damaging in periods of sharply rising prices and quick dollar-value debasement. Even the moderate and much sought-after inflation rate of 3 to 6% per year, pursued by one national administration after another without much success in recent decades, would badly erode the value of resources and pension payments 20 to 30 years after cessation of gainful employment. In fact, inflation rates have been far higher.

The third assumption we make is that we must largely plan to support ourselves throughout our extended lifespans. Although existing social insurance provisions, such as Social Security and Medicare, will probably be expanded during our lifetimes, we can reasonably count on government help only at or near the subsistence level. Therefore, the overwhelming majority of us will find it necessary to continue productive economic activity as long as we can; the combination of inflation and long life will so badly erode whatever resources we have at "retirement" that, well before the end of our lives, we will tend to slip into poverty and be unable to provide for those we care about most, unless we have accumulated very substantial private assets or plan to continue some kind of productive economic activity far beyond the traditional retirement age—and we may find we need to do both.

The fourth assumption that we must make is that our economic system will remain basically the same, a mixture of public and private ownership of the means of production and distribution, with a constant tendency on the part of government to move into more and more areas of life, but continuing in its present basic form.

Our fifth assumption, and the basis for this book, is that sound personal planning can take us all a long way toward many of life's major personal satisfactions—toward fulfilling work, lifelong personal independence, a reasonably comfortable lifestyle, and the ability to provide decently for our loved ones during our lives and after we are gone. Such planning may even contribute to a longer personal lifespan, made possible by a lessening of life's tensions, which are often enormously magnified by seemingly insoluble money and responsibility problems.

When approaching the question of lifelong financial planning, you should keep in mind some very basic personal approaches:

- Fight your way through to a total understanding of your current financial picture and where you seem to be headed; keep that ever-changing picture in your mind and on paper at all times.

- Try as hard as you can to know your goals and to understand where you want to go and how you want to go about getting there; then develop several alternative major ways to proceed along the financial and career paths you have outlined.

- Continually update your short-, medium-, and long-term goals and plans, just as you would watch and work with a specific set of investments.

- Assume that you *can* know what you are doing in the financial area, and learn as much as you possibly can about every investment, insurance, retirement, estate, and tax move you are contemplating, before you make it.

- Always consider the income tax implications of any use of your money. In evaluating any savings or investment transaction, focus on your *net* return after calculating the impact of the graduated income tax and of inflation. Obtaining tax-deferred or tax-exempt income will allow your monies to grow at a higher rate, often without additional risk.

- Get as much informed professional help as you can in making plans and decisions, changing your financial advisors as often as your feelings dictate, always seeking the integrity, personal concern, and expertise that meet your standards. But rely ultimately on your own knowledge and judgment, based on what you have learned from professionals, publications, and your own developing experience. No one will watch your interests as single-mindedly and skillfully as you will, if you take the time and trouble to become an increasingly well-informed person.

The essence of financial planning is to find the best possible answer to the question "How can I earn the most on my assets with the least possible risk?" That is a short-term question, to be asked every day; but it is also a long-term question, to be asked every day for decades—actually for the rest of your life. For every financial act you are considering, balance the risk and the rewards that are appropriate for you and your objectives. Fearing to take reasonable risks and taking risks too great for your situation can both be self-defeating.

This is a chaotic time in American economic history. The United States is no longer the world's police officer, banker, broker, granary, and industrial base—if it ever was. It may have seemed to be all or most of those things for a short while after World War II, but it is clear now that such an illusion is but an interesting footnote to the history of the twentieth century. The United States is now one nation among many, in economic terms. Not the boundless source of wealth it once seemed, the country is facing the hard economic facts of energy costs, inflation, unemployment, and impoverishment; and because of changing worldwide economic and political relationships, the American economy is unlikely to again reach the prosperous peaks of the past. Neither "fine tuning" nor "free enterprise" seems able to solve economic problems that will not go away. The American dream is far from a nightmare—if it were, people would not still want to come to the United States from all over the world—but it is a dream tempered by late-twentieth-century realities.

For investors and savers, it is a time when no pat formulas apply—again, if they ever did. There are only opportunities and risks to be continually evaluated, rather than fixed views to be embraced. In a fluid, considerably adverse investment climate, it is so imprudent as to be foolish to put your assets wholly or mainly into a single kind of investment—such as "the stock market," the money market, real estate, commodity futures, mutual funds, gold, collectibles, or what have you—and to leave it there untended. Today's perfectly sound investment or investment approach is tomorrow's loser or losing technique. In this period, investors and savers must carefully and continually evaluate investment vehicles, be ready to move from one kind of vehicle to another, anticipate the development of new techniques and transactions, and continually watch liquidity and safety more than ever before.

The central matter in financial planning in the late twentieth century in the United States is the protracted, usually only partly successful, attempt to beat inflation by growing one's assets through savings and investment at or better than the rate of inflation. We focus on that key aim throughout this book, always remembering that it is only part of every person's broader aim to live a full and meaningful life. It is to some of these broader questions that we turn first.

Wants, Needs, and Goals

"If I knew then what I know now . . ."

"I was young. I didn't know."

"It looked like a sure thing."

"We thought there was no tomorrow."

We have all made such comments—who hasn't? Our hope is that, after you have read and absorbed the contents of this book, you will never again have to say such things about your own financial life.

Everyone has wants and needs. The young couple starting out together in their twenties without a thought in the world about their future financial needs and plans are going to encounter the same needs as the young couple who pay significant attention to the nature of their wants and needs and who develop short-, medium-, and long-term goals. But there is a real difference between those two couples. Those who let their wants and needs develop "naturally" are those who go through life living from crisis to crisis, crushed by the weight of unwanted and unmet responsibilities. In contrast, those who analyze their wants and needs, make choices, develop goals, and set courses of action aimed at achieving those goals are more often life's "winners," moving through their lives with seeming ease and finding a large measure of the fulfillment that seems to elude many others.

But life is long, and we often have more than one chance to shape our lives. Many who later in life realize the need for sound planning get a second and even a third or fourth chance. Just as we have room for more than one career in our lives, if we wish, so we also have a chance to plan our lives and successfully work out those plans, starting in our forties, fifties, and even our sixties.

People *do* have substantial needs that are often hard to satisfy, a matter all too evident in a period of runaway inflation and currency debasement, when savings seem to melt away day by day in the struggle to make ends meet. All of us need adequate food, clothing, shelter, and transportation; most of us consider adequate education and some leisure-time activities almost equally necessary.

Many of us are in truth victims of a consuming society. To a considerable extent our wants have become our needs, much as is the case in any kind of addiction. Showy houses, expensive automobiles, private schools, costly vacations, expensive clothes, the "best" colleges—the consuming lifestyle is just as addictive and often just as damaging as alcohol or heroin. It all too often traps those addicted to it in work they hate, creating a debt structure that topples and destroys them economically, and often emotionally, if they are jobless or out of business for even a relatively short time.

We live in a society in which personal planning and all other private sector economic planning depends on the accumulation of capital, which is invested to yield net returns at least as high as the net of inflation over a period of decades. That is a central understanding for all of us. However, the consuming lifestyle is often the death of any effective personal planning. It guarantees that there will not be enough capital to use to meet the main expenses of life and that what should be the savings of the later, most lucrative years of work become only debt repayments and more fuel for the consuming addiction.

To some extent, people in their own businesses often have capital accumulation thrust upon them. With development, their businesses become worth more and become sources of capital on eventual sale. In a very real sense, their businesses are stores of value they build over the years, which become available for investment in their later years. Of course, if they have only that and nothing more, they may often have too little for their later years. They also have all their eggs in one basket then; if anything goes seriously wrong with the business, they are left high and dry in later life.

Those who work for others all too often depend on company benefit and retirement plans to see them through, not saving and investing on their own. They do not think about what might happen if their seemingly invulnerable companies go out of business, make enormous cutbacks to stay alive, merge with others who ruthlessly embark on wholesale firings, have pension plans that are not actuarially sound, or simply fire them when they are in their fifties and unlikely to find other jobs at anything near current income levels. Even if they stay with a solid company to retirement, such people often find that their pensions, which seemed more than adequate years before, now prove to be grossly inadequate in light of the current purchasing power of the dollar.

Take, for example, John and Ellen Smith. They met at college, back in the late 1950s, and married right after graduation. He had majored in marketing, she in journalism. He headed straight for the corporate world, starting as an executive trainee in the home office of a Chicago-based corporation. She worked for a couple of years as a reporter for a local newspaper in the suburb in which they found an apartment and gave that up when she had the first of their three children.

John has done all right. He may never be the president of a major corporation, but in his mid-forties he is well established in the home office marketing department of a substantial New York City-based corporation, with a yearly salary in the $35,000 plus range. Ellen has done all right, too. When her youngest child started school, she went back to work. It was hard, but she finally broke into New York publishing, on the editorial side, and for the past 10 years has combined satisfying work with increasing responsibility. Of course, publishing, being a "glamour" industry, does not pay all that well, so her yearly salary, though a good one in her trade, is in the $20,000 range. Both John and Ellen have good insurance benefits and pension plans and even company-aided savings and stock option plans.

They are successful people, by any reasonable definition. Now in their mid-forties, they live in a nice house in an affluent New York suburb, plan to send their three teenagers to good colleges—and graduate schools as necessary—in a few years, live well on their $55,000 joint yearly gross, and plan to retire and live the good life at age 65. There are some debts, and inflation is always worrisome, but they are both very promotable in their companies and can look forward to excellent future incomes and retirement benefits.

They do not have much in the way of savings, of course. Children, taxes, heating bills, cars, household help to take care of growing children while both parents work, and the annual vacation all seem to conspire to build debts up a little every year—but nothing that cannot be handled in the long run. After all, real estate values are rising swiftly, and the appreciation in the value of their home has more than kept up with any increase in total debts outstanding. In the short term, that may not be entirely true—to buy their current home a few years ago, they had to take out a second mortgage, but that will be paid off in less than 10 years, and with the pace of inflation the amounts actually being paid back in real dollars are less and less each year.

John and Ellen are not big spenders. Far from it—they entertain modestly; have no second "vacation" home, as so many of their neighbors do; and eat out only occasionally. Paying off two mortgages at once is a little difficult, with all the other necessary expenditures, but they have been able to handle it all quite well, with the help of the ubiquitous credit line. They often joke about how many credit cards they have been offered with credit lines attached—which they invariably accept and use.

It is quite an ordinary American success story. But the truth is that—like so many others—they are broke. Walking bankrupts. Economic basket cases. At this rate, John and Ellen are going to have to work as hard as they can all their lives to meet their obligations, hoping that neither one encounters long-term illness or unemployment; they will wind up in the sunset of life as impoverished wards of the state, in fact if not in formal designation.

They have saved nothing, have nothing growing for them that is really their own. The only thing they have that is worth much is their home, and the value of that, over the first mortgage, is more than canceled out by their second mortgage and their credit line balances combined. Before their second mortgage is paid off, they will face the absolute necessity of remortgaging to pay the truly enormous costs of sending three children to college—especially if they stick to their announced intention of sending their children to "good," meaning expensive, colleges. When their children are partway through undergraduate school, by the way, they will most likely run out of money and force their children to borrow heavily in order to stay in college. In effect, they will be forcing their children to mortgage their own futures because of the parents' status strivings as expressed through their choices of colleges for their children.

John and Ellen are so vulnerable that any of several quite possible events, which they should be capable of handling, can damage them enormously. If either of them loses a job and has difficulty in finding equivalent work quickly, they may lose what little they have. If either of them is unable to work for an extended period, the loss of current income will sink them economically. Should their marriage break up—as so many American marriages do—their children may be robbed of important educational opportunities, and John and Ellen will have a hard time making an economic go of it separately.

In the long run, their dependence on their employers for retirement income may prove to be the worst personal mistake of all. Today's seemingly excellent pension plan may turn out to be ludicrously inadequate 20 years further on, given the long-term pace of inflation. Today's pension plan may also turn out to be pathetically underfunded when the time comes to pay today's corporate employees; today's profit-sharing plan may be a victim of bad investments. And today's strong company may be tomorrow's horse-and-buggy maker, long out of business or bankrupt, with pension funds impaired, and unable to meet its solemnly incurred obligations to its employees in the year 2005, when John and Ellen plan to retire.

In an even deeper way, their personal plight is worse than it seems, for both of them, like most of us, are "hooked" on freedom and personal independence. Ellen wanted to be a journalist and then try her hand at some serious nonfiction writing—perhaps some fiction as well. John wanted to go into business and exercise his developing skills and judgment as an increasingly independent "entrepreneurial" type. He saw himself heading up a substantial corporate operation, perhaps going into business on his own and developing his own regional or national organization.

Now John and Ellen are trapped. She is a skilled editor, but is increasingly bored and limited by her constricted corporate, profit-oriented environment. She cannot really do anything about it, as things now stand—or so she thinks. He is mobile, but only within his corporate world and set of skills. He has changed jobs several times on the way up and may move once or twice more—but only to jobs in similar organizations. For him, freedom and independence are only childhood dreams.

Perhaps so, perhaps not. Had Ellen and John seen it more clearly when they were younger, they might have planned quite differently. More precisely, they might have *planned*—for that is what they did not do. Instead, they optimistically rode on the wind of seeming success; for, after all, they were Americans and America was the greatest country in the world, wasn't it? Nothing could really go wrong.

For them, it has gone wrong. But if they see that now, while they are in their mid-forties, they have a chance to recover. They can still move toward freedom and independence and away from the ultimate prospect of being unofficial wards of the state, while at the same time meeting their current obligations and not forcing their children into debt before they are even started in life.

It all starts with thinking through one's goals—as early as possible, but as late as necessary. No matter when, the act of thinking through long-, medium-, and short-range goals is the real beginning of the move toward freedom and independence, toward "winning." That means career and other personal goals, as well as purely financial goals. Ellen and John Smith, for example, might have made quite different arrangements if they had thought through their aims better and earlier.

Right at the start, they might have thought through the question of children differently. They had three children, essentially because that seemed like a nice number to have, without substantial regard for the direct and hidden costs of doing so. Had they thought the matter through, they might have had children later, giving themselves a modest opportunity to do a little saving—that is, to start capital accumulation. Or they might have had fewer children, or no children at all. There is no basic error in having children in any desired number, but there is an enormous error in having even one child without considering the impact of that decision upon your lives and those of your children. Ellen and John had three children rather quickly, substantially setting the economic conditions of their subsequent lives, including how long Ellen would be out of the job market, what kinds of housing accommodations they would need, what they would spend for many necessities, and the minimum they would probably have to pay for educating their children.

Had Ellen thought about the possibility of being trapped in a rather uninteresting and nonlucrative job in her mid-forties, she might have tried some career alternatives, even while having children. For example, she might have begun to write free-lance magazine and newspaper articles while she was in her twenties and at home with her children, graduating to books while still in her thirties. By so doing, she might have developed a considerable second income for the family, long before full reentry into the job market. Today, she might be both an editor and a writer. Or she might be the full-time writer she always thought she might like to be, earning a great deal more than she does as a corporate employee.

Had John considered the possibility of being trapped in a not very fast corporate career track, he might have organized his career quite differently. Entrepreneurially minded people with considerable marketing skills have the whole world of business open before them. Business opportunities of all kinds are always available to those who are thoughtful enough to grasp them. Many a corporate marketing person has moved into a distributorship or agency, directly marketing the same kinds of goods that he or she had been marketing for a major corporation. Other corporate people have found their skills transferable to quite dissimilar lines of business as well.

The error is never the end result, in this instance entrapment in dead-end careers, with a mountain of financial responsibilities and no resources. The error occurs earlier, in the failure to think through where you want to go and how to get there. "Losers" are not the only ones who drift through life. Many seeming "winners" have not taken the trouble to try to see beyond the goals drilled into them by the society around them and are thus often the worst losers of all, deluded by their apparent success. Putting it a little differently, losers are not the only people who find that their versions of the American dream are nightmares. To really win, you cannot rely entirely on hard work and upward job mobility. You must carefully think through what you want to do with your life, understanding that all decision making requires choices between available alternatives, to develop a set of careful, flexible, workable, personal plans aimed at taking you in the directions you want to go.

There are some basic precautions to take along the way. They are quite standard, but almost invariably ignored. It is foolish to have too many children too soon. It is right to seek second and alternative incomes, no matter how well you seem to be doing in the early years. It is dead wrong to move into a larger house, especially a showy one in an affluent area, if that means taking a second mortgage or even a very large first mortgage—either can be a large, long-term capital drain. It is absolutely necessary to get into the habit of saving and investing in some way, shape, manner, or form—and it is important to start doing so early, in the hope that saving and investing will become lifelong habits.

Horatio Alger was always largely a myth, and you will not become J. Pierpont Morgan by opening a grocery store and saving and investing your pennies wisely. But saving and investing, within the context of a thoroughly thought-through set of personal career and financial plans, can make it possible for you to reach your goals and to move out into clear air economically.

Effective planning requires defining needs—and distinguishing between needs and desires. We all share basic needs for food and shelter, but too often we treat our desires as needs and thoughtlessly limit our lifetime choices. Ellen and John Smith, for example, live in a far too expensive house in a far too expensive suburb, surrounded by people who are also living beyond their means. Such people are consuming far more food and shelter than they need—and are paying for them not only with money, but more important, with their personal freedom.

Effective planning requires looking forward to future needs and desires. On the most basic level, a young couple may want to plan for the possibility of forming a family. They want to be able to educate their children, pay debts they know they will incur in the future, plan careers or changes in careers, and develop adequate retirement funds.

All elementary, certainly. So elementary that this kind of common sense is taken for granted. Unfortunately, it is precisely these "givens" that are most commonly ignored by people who know they should be planning, but who instead float through their lives, hoping that upward mobility will somehow solve all of their economic and career problems.

Sound personal planning has very little to do with belt tightening and crash budgeting, not any more than dieting has to do with self-starvation. It is far more a question of long-term choices. Here is where many of the questions of lifestyle are raised.

All of us reach for an acceptable living standard—the ability to feed, clothe, and house ourselves and our families, if any, at least adequately. For most of us, that means owning a house, cooperative, or condominium and living on a level considerably better than subsistence. To live far more expensively than at a reasonably acceptable level of consumption may be a legitimate choice for a few; however, most people who adopt a too-expensive lifestyle do so not by choice, but as a capitulation to the pressures of a consuming society. The adoption of such a lifestyle means that it will be very difficult, and often impossible, to adopt many other planning choices that may be desired. If one is living at a higher-than-necessary level of consumption and wishes to make other personal choices, the remedy lies in a change of lifestyle. It is rare that anything less than that will even begin to do.

For many millions of Americans, of course, the question of what constitutes an "acceptable living standard" is moot. Their lives are bounded by economic necessity, in the attempt to make ends meet on what amounts to little more than a subsistence level. But even for them, the injunction to save and invest has relevance—it makes sense to evaluate the question of need and to relate perceived needs to savings and investments at every economic level. Millions of poor immigrants came to the United States during the last two centuries, worked for very little, saved enough to bring over members of their families one by one from the old countries, and continued saving and investing—very often through the medium of a small business. People who are poor today face some of the same choices and possibilities.

For most people reading this book, however, the question of acceptable lifestyle has very real relevance and involves immediate possibilities for choice, in terms of the seemingly mandatory expenditures that form the bulk of individual and family obligations.

One of the main choices is where to live. Most families reach for the most expensive home they can manage, with down payments often using up both cash reserves and long-term credit and with mortgages and taxes guaranteeing that current income will be deeply encumbered for many years. The rationale for doing so usually includes good schools for children, resale values, and enough space for the family to live in comfortably. The unannounced reason that often accompanies this rationale has to do with the prestige of living in an expensive house in an expensive community. That has not changed very much as a reason for home buying since the turn of the century, even in a period in which houses are unprecedentedly expensive, mortgage rates are in the 12 to 15% range, and down payments on resale houses are in the 20 to 30% range.

An expensive house purchase is, under these conditions, an absurd error, except for those few whose financial circumstances make such a purchase a relatively minor expenditure. A house costing $150,000, requiring a 25% down payment, and carrying a 13% mortgage requires a down payment of $37,500 and a mortgage of $112,500. In an affluent and child-conscious community, it probably carries taxes in the $7000- to $9000-per-year range. With high fuel and other utilities costs, the monthly carrying charges often are far higher than can be wisely carried. Regrettably often, the owners must carry a second mortgage or other debt obligation as well, to pay off part of that huge down payment.

Quite often, a house just as sound, perhaps a little smaller but still adequate, and located in a community with schools not as desperately competitive as those of the affluent community shows startlingly different numbers. For example, a house or condominium in a nearby community with some industry and considerably different tax factors may cost $110,000—still a very great deal, but more than 20% less than the $150,000 house. The 25% down payment becomes $27,500, a full $10,000 in cash less than the down payment needed for the $150,000 house—and sometimes the difference between available cash and a second mortgage or other credit use. Taxes are likely to run considerably lower than those in the affluent community and, applied to the less expensive house, should come in at about $4000 yearly. Fuel and other utilities might be about 10% less for a slightly smaller house. The net difference in payments over the years can be enormous. For many people, that money alone can mean the difference between the availability of modest funds for savings and investment and an ever-growing mountain of debt.

Sound planning is often a question of taking the time and trouble to make an informed, planned decision on major questions, rather than floating with the prevailing consuming stream in the culture in which we find ourselves. Unthinking participation in a consuming society is a major financial trap. Food, clothing, transportation, shelter, and education are needs. It is when we go far beyond real need into the desires sold by the consuming society that we fall into traps.

Unthinking participation in a status-oriented set of college choices is a second major financial trap. The predictable costs associated with college education constitute a major area of choice in economic planning. During the last decade, literally thousands of articles and many books (one of them coauthored by one of the authors of this book)* have dealt with the question of constantly

*Gene R. Hawes and David M. Brownstone, *How to Get the Money to Pay for College*, McKay, New York, 1978.

escalating college-going costs. It has become startlingly clear that college costs have become the second—sometimes the first—largest expenditure incurred by millions of American families.

There are many ways to soften the truly massive impact of college costs. There are part-time work programs, several kinds of federal and state grant programs, advanced placement courses in high school, college credits available by examination, early admissions plans, and work-study plans. There are loan programs through which students mortgage their futures at lower rates than those at which their parents routinely mortgage theirs. There are other loan programs through which parents can borrow money at the customarily enormously high interest rates commercially available. There are remortgages available through which parents can give up whatever equities they have built up in their homes for the privilege of paying back what are in essence college loans at high rates of mortgage interest right up to the time when they might otherwise have retired or at least moved to less exacting forms of work.

Means of lessening college costs are limited, if available at all, for most college-bound students and their families. The facts are these: In the early 1980s, assuming no real financial relief from federal, state, and work sources—and that is a fair assumption for most middle-class and upper-middle-class families—it costs more than $10,000 a year to send a student to a top-rated (that means, among other things, most expensive) large or small private college, such as Harvard, Yale, Columbia, Amherst, Williams, or Bard. The same is true for graduate schools. Therefore, if John and Ellen Smith stick to their resolve to send their children to the "best" schools, they are going to spend $40,000 or more to send each of their three children through undergraduate school and probably $30,000 more in graduate school. That's $150,000 in all!

Impossible? No, not really. Such families will not even realize how much they are spending. The parents will use up whatever cash reserves, college funds, and credit lines they have, all intermixed with their other family expenditures. There may be modest legacies from their own parents—some of all of that will go, too. The children will borrow, at "favorable" rates, and will wind up coming out of school broke and deeply in debt for the next 10 years or more. Why? Because they went to expensive colleges, when they could have done just as well, and sometimes better educationally, at less expensive schools.

For a few—but only a very few—top students headed for fast graduate school and career tracks, the top-rated private colleges can make sense and may be justified both academically and financially. Often these are also students who can qualify for meaningful financial aid. But for the overwhelming majority of American college students, the meaningful investment for career purposes is not the undergraduate school at all—it is the graduate or professional school investment that matters. Even then, it is only the highest-ranked graduate and professional school graduates for whom the name of the school matters much in the world of work.

It makes just as good career sense for most students to go to public colleges and some less expensive private colleges as to go to expensive private colleges—and it makes much better economic sense. The total average cost of an undergraduate education at an in-state, publicly supported college will be in the area of $4000 per student per year, varying to some extent with the state in which the student lives, as in-state students are often given admission preferences and tuition breaks over out-of-state students.

Although $4000 per student per year is still a great deal to handle and will very often require substantial borrowing on the part of both parents and students, the difference between $10,000 per student per year and $4000 per student per year is truly enormous. For the Smiths, for undergraduate school alone, it is the difference between $120,000 and $48,000, or $72,000 saved! That's not $72,000 they have, either—it is money they would otherwise have to borrow. In financial planning terms, that $72,000, or whatever sum it might be, is often the difference between a real retirement fund and no retirement fund. For parents, the difference is between using their most productive mature years to pay off obligations and building their current lives and future independence. For young people, it is the difference between starting independent lives as substantial debtors and entering adult work life as people free of debt.

That is the kind of net difference that can result from a small and timely planning decision—to run against the consuming society stream, and to handle college costs as sanely and sensibly as possible. A substantial noneconomic side benefit of making such a choice in education as well as in housing can be the removal of children from damagingly competitive school and community situations. Superachievers seldom achieve without substantial personal cost; those who are not superachievers but who are in an environment that forces corrosive competition upon them often do not achieve as much as they could in a less competitive environment and may experience very great personal costs.

For the great majority of students, there are no very good reasons, aside from status striving, to spend $40,000 on undergraduate education. Many public colleges and universities are at least the academic equals of far more highly touted private schools according to every available standard measure of academic excellence, including such measures as graduate school admissions, class size, and faculty salaries. Only the status is different—and the cost.

There are other areas of need and desire where choices can—and should—be made. Insurance to cover ourselves and those we care about against the specifically unpredictable, but statistically predictable, crises of life is a real need. So is some kind of capital accumulation program, which, at the very least, should provide funds aimed at preventing one from becoming a ward of the state late in life and, at most, should provide real financial independence as early as possible and funds with which to provide some of the same kind of independence for one's survivors. Dealing with such defensive and accumulative needs and desires is a major goal of this book; we devote much of the balance of it to discussing how best to meet those needs and desires. But make no mistake about it: the entirely predictable and avoidable financial traps set by a consuming society—traps that most middle-class and upper-middle-class Americans fall into—must be avoided if planning is to have any real meaning. Those who have no resources and who have mortgaged their futures, no matter how seemingly successful, will, unless they change now, live much of their lives in an increasingly nightmarish continual financial crisis.

It is always too late for "walking bankrupts" like Ellen and John Smith—unless they begin to think through their personal choices, to change their unthinking participation in a consuming society, and to take their lives, hopes, and careers into their own hands. It is almost never too late when you begin to do that in a consistent, long-term way. There are no reasons, aside from inertia and status striving, to continue to live far more expensively than is necessary or desirable. Yes, moves can somewhat disrupt the lives of parents and children—but moves because of job changes do that all the time, and a massively beneficial change in lifestyle is far more important than most corporate promotions.

Ellen Smith need not consider her career options closed, just because she and John need her salary desperately, as they do his. It is not at all too late to start writing the articles and books she always wanted to write—part time, while holding down a full-time job. Writers do it all the time. She may be able to spend decades as a writer, earning at least as much as she earns as an editor and perhaps developing royalty-yielding book properties that will, later in life, provide funds far in excess of any pensions she might have received from her present employer.

Of all the Smiths, it may be most difficult for John. From the start, he, like so many other American men, has been the family's money machine. The role may no longer suit him well, but now he has a great many obligations, no capital, and needs to maintain at least his current level of income without a substantial break. A move to a different lifestyle will help, as will sane decisions on education, but prior debts, coming major expenses, and a tax system that much favors business owners over employees are all real obstacles. He has spent a lot of time with the same company and has meaningful pension arrangements, which cannot be dismissed lightly. He may be trapped; even if he is not, he may need years to work his way out of the current set of economic problems. He may find a career shortcut along the way; for example, a smaller company might bring him and his big-company skills into its operations and pay him in both salary and equity, giving him a chance to accumulate some capital rapidly though he will be starting rather late. Such situations are often chancy, though; John would have to look hard and weigh career changes very carefully—far more carefully than would have been necessary had independent, effective career and financial planning been part of his thinking from the start.

That kind of timely, effective planning is done every day by individuals and families of all ages and all walks of life, often with the help of astute professional advisors. It starts with the need for a sober, careful assessment of one's true financial position and joins that assessment with soundly thought-through personal and financial goals. Such assessments and goals are entirely individual, varying widely from person to person; however, the materials in Chapter 3, on organizing the financial side of life, should help you begin to put your financial house in order and to make some basic decisions about your future.

The rest of the book will help you clarify these decisions and put them into practice. Part II covers the basic approaches, techniques, and instruments of financial planning. Part III presents 20 practical financial plans for a wide variety of personal financial planning situations. Part IV covers the language of financial planning, with a series of brief commentaries on key terms and phrases aimed at demystifying financial and investment jargon. Part V presents a selection of sources of financial planning information, which will help you keep current in those areas that concern you most. Finally, the Index will be useful for later reference, to help you locate discussion of topics as needed in your personal financial planning.

3

Organizing the Financial Side of Life

It is axiomatic that effective planning requires organization. We know that to be true of all planning, and it is no less true for lifetime financial planning. However, what constitutes effective organization is often not so clearly understood. All too often, in business as well as personal life, mere paper shuffling substitutes for the continuous identification and reevaluation of goals and resources, the securing of qualified advisors, the proper illumination of available alternatives, and the rounded development of sound planning processes.

Effective planning adds up to the ability to understand your own financial and career positions at every step along the way; to constantly reassess your personal situation in terms of general economic changes, new legislation, and other factors that may affect you; and to move fluidly from short-term to long-term goals, making the moves look easy, as does a top-notch professional athlete. Such assessments require self-discipline, but it is important to remember that *no* decision is still a decision. Failure to act means that you are deciding to retain the status quo—which may well be a guarantee of failure in financial planning in a changing world.

As in all planning, the main thing is not the paper you shuffle, but the people you pick to work with. Forms can be useful; the right professional advisors and sources of information are crucial.

Some widely perceived problems are connected with the securing of sound professional advisors. First, none but the wealthy can afford to hire full-time or even substantially part-time people to advise them in financial planning areas. Second, it is always difficult to evaluate the extent of the self-interest of people who render such advice, when they themselves directly benefit when you follow that advice, as do insurance sellers, stockbrokers, and real estate brokers. Third, it is often difficult to evaluate the competence of those rendering such advice when you yourself are not very knowledgeable in financial areas.

These are real problems, which are not easy to solve and which can serve to turn you away from the hard, time-consuming business of finding good professional advisors. Difficult or not, however, the finding of such advisors is of prime lifelong importance to you, just as if you were going into business and needed to staff up with both inside and outside professionals. In every important sense, personal financial planning is a business—your personal business—and must be treated that way.

When you do not have enough money to directly hire a lot of professional help, when you are worried about the motives of some of those who should be sources of such help, and when you are not sure that you are capable of realistically evaluating the quality of help you are offered, what you need is a starting place. In most parts of the United States, that starting place is likely to be a Certified Public Accountant (CPA); in a few states, it may be a public accountant; and in some rural and semirural places, it may be an attorney. For the somewhat more affluent, it may be a Certified Financial Planner or a bank financial planning organization.

Why a CPA? Because, for most of us, the accountant—and you have a large stake in getting and keeping a good one—is that person who best knows your whole financial, career, and personal situation; is equipped by training and daily activity to deal with financial questions; and is paid by you and you alone to handle financial matters. Where an attorney fulfills those functions, then that attorney naturally takes the role of financial advisor.

A sound, experienced accountant with financial planning experience can be a great deal more to you than a tax preparer. It is not a very long stretch from tax return preparation to tax planning, and from tax planning to total financial planning. More and more accountants today actively reach for the financial planning role. You can get a tax return from an accountant and leave it at that, in which case you may as well go to a relatively inexpensive tax return service. Or you can get a tax return, invest a little more time and money, and get a yearly review of your whole financial picture, with tax planning recommendations that can very well save you a great deal more money than the additional fees you spend for the advice.

Traditionally, bankers have performed similar functions. In smaller places, they sometimes still do, but that is increasingly rare. The friendly bank branch manager who dispenses sound financial planning advice may indeed be friendly, but is highly unlikely to be equipped by training and experience to render very good advice. Early in his or her career, a banker may be that accessible to you, but be too inexperienced to be really helpful; later on, that banker will be involved with the bank's larger clients and with running the bank and will often prove inaccessible. On the other hand, many large banks have developed financial planning departments, staffed by Certified Financial Planners or other trained personnel. You should assess banks with the same criteria you use in assessing any personal financial advisor.

Lawyers can be sources of sound financial advice; however, the main business of the law is not finance, but rather the interpretation of the law and the drafting of legal documents to confirm and support clients' personal and economic activities. Fifty years ago, when lawyers handled most personal financial matters, acting as general family counselors while conducting general law practices, many lawyers did tax returns and rendered associated financial planning advice. But tax laws and regulations have become enormously complex in the last half century, and accountants have largely taken over tax preparation and planning functions—and with them the main financial planning functions.

Bankers and lawyers, like accountants, are people who are paid by you to render advice; however, they also are sometimes involved in selling products and may benefit in ways other than receiving your fees for their advice. As with anyone else, you should be alert to potential conflicts of interest in assessing these advisors and their advice.

Accountants will, in most instances, be your main tax and financial advisors, although bankers and lawyers have roles to play as well. Many accountants and lawyers, recognizing the need for other planning professionals, will often bring in someone who specializes in insurance, investments, or both, to help advise clients on financial planning moves. Some people who sell insurance and investments can make very significant contributions to your financial planning, although their objectivity should be assessed with some caution. You may have some difficulty in assessing, on your own, the reliability of financial planning professionals, but your accountant or attorney should have much less difficulty. In general, the better the accountant or lawyer, the better the other people who will be brought in to advise you. Such advisors will, in most instances, be people your accountant works with consistently in similar situations, forming part of an informal financial planning "team." That is one of the reasons you have a considerable stake in securing a good accountant.

How do you find a good accountant or other professional financial advisor? The same way you find a good doctor, plumber, or auto mechanic—you ask everybody you respect to recommend one, stressing financial planning; ask them why they recommend certain professionals; and then go ahead and try the most likely of the lot. As with a doctor, plumber, or auto mechanic, you will be wise to opt for experience and the soundness of judgment that comes with it. The doctor who "tries" a new medication on you has an almost exact counterpart in the accountant who "tries" the newest wrinkle in tax avoidance on you—and the results can often be equally damaging.

In the end, nothing will substitute for your own evaluation of your professional advisors. The most highly recommended accountant, attorney, banker, financial planner, insurance seller, or investment broker in the world may prove, after some contact, to be somebody with whom you feel personally uncomfortable or for whom you have no respect. Then you must move to someone else. You may try four successive accountants in successive years before you come up with someone you want to work with for the long haul. That is unlikely, but it can happen—if it does, so be it. It is very much worth the effort to find a fully satisfactory key advisor. When evaluating financial advisors, you should look for several things, but primarily three: integrity, competence, and concern for you as an individual.

First, to put it simply, search for advisors you can trust. When in doubt, change advisors. This does not, however, mean that you should take advice without question. Rather, search for someone who has soundness of thought, steadiness, and a willingness to share his or her thinking with you. Avoid any advisor who wants you to make financial moves largely on faith, rather than carefully discussing the reasons for the move being recommended, no matter how good the specific advice may be; in the long run, you will become merely dependent, rather than informed and independent. Much of what you should gain from a sound financial advisor is the ability to think through financial plans and moves yourself, checking your developing thinking against advisory thinking, rather than depending on advisors.

You should, of course, make a routine check on the background of any advisor who is new to you, as you would with a potential employee. For example, professional associations, such as the American Bar Association, the International Association of Financial Planners, or the American Institute of Certified Public Accountants, though not giving you an evaluation of a professional's quality or integrity, will at least give you any gross negative information, such as current expulsion proceedings or other serious charges.

The second primary factor, competence, is difficult to assess until you have worked with an advisor for some period of time. Certainly you want an advisor who has been well trained and who keeps current. In recent years, many parts of the financial and academic communities have been actively training financial planners. Many colleges and universities provide courses, seminars, and degree programs integrating the many subjects, approaches, and methods that are involved in financial planning. Major financial institutions, securities firms, and insurance companies have joined the legal and accounting professions in providing internal courses and seminars to train and update their personnel in financial planning techniques. The International Association of Financial Planners and institutions like the College for Financial Planning offer a large number of courses and inter-disciplinary training programs attended by a wide variety of professionals, including attorneys, accountants, bankers, insurance and real estate agents, and stock brokers.

The result has been that many more people from a variety of professions have been trained in financial planning areas. Although degrees and titles certainly do not guarantee quality or professional competence, they may help you assess the training and current knowledge of any potential financial advisor.

Third, you should expect your financial advisor to be concerned about you as an individual. Broad financial advice, computer studies, and other advanced training and techniques can play an important role in financial planning, but only when applied with attention to your individual case, not with a broad brush. Search for financial advisors who will understand your needs, relate to your objectives, and integrate your desires in your own financial planning. You expect such concern from your medical physician—it is not too much to expect from your "financial physician."

Whoever you choose as your financial advisors, you should keep one obvious, but often-ignored, point in mind: Someone who is primarily concerned with selling you a given product cannot be relied on for overall advice. For example, you can get excellent securities purchase and sale advice from some securities brokers, but you may not receive a fully balanced set of financial advice from them. It is not a question of advice dishonestly tendered—that happens, but is rare—but rather a question of focus. A good salesperson must believe in what he or she has to sell, and that skews judgment. It does not make sense to expect a securities broker to advise you to get out of the stock market and move your assets into bank accounts and local real estate. Aside from the fact that such a move generates no commissions for the broker, that broker cannot be expected to believe that doing so is a proper course of investment action—even when it is. Similarly, you cannot reasonably expect most life insurance sellers to tell you that, within the total context of your financial goals,

plans, and resources, you have more life insurance than is desirable and that you should cut the amount in force. You may get
excellent advice from both securities and life insurance sellers.
The key is to know enough to evaluate that advice yourself; having one or more other independent professionals available with
whom to check your thinking can be very useful.

Some Certified Financial Planners have broad training and are
skilled enough to be excellent sources of financial advice. Many
have several things to sell, and a few may stress what they have
to sell rather than developing a balanced, long-term financial
plan. But the best of them can help you build the kind of long-
term plan you want to develop. Some limit their activities to the
handling of only large bodies of assets, but more and more are
handling the assets of middle-class and upper-middle-class people. A real plus is the focus of many Certified Financial Planners
upon the tax aspects of financial transactions.

Accountants and lawyers are the traditional disinterested parties from whom to seek financial advice, at least to the extent of
checking your thinking and information against theirs. Accountants, especially, because of their constant involvement in tax
and business matters, are often trusted and much-used financial
advisors. It is quite normal and a very good idea to check the tax
aspects of a projected move with your accountant and, in the
process, to better assess the value of this transaction to your specific situation.

In a wider sense, you should continually assess potential conflicts of interest regarding any financial advisor. Those who do
not sell products may still have a vested interest in the advice
they offer. For example, an attorney may not sell a product, but,
in return for recommending a given securities firm or insurance
broker, may receive legal work or referrals from those parties as
a token of gratitude; similarly, accountants, who solely advise on
or prepare taxes, may obtain a "finder's fee" for referring a tax
client to a real estate company.

Ultimately, you must assess on your own the overall integrity,
competence, and concern for you shown by the financial advisors
you choose. The key is full disclosure—it is important that you
be as aware as possible of all the facts as to how your potential financial advisor is reimbursed for his or her services.

Seeking good financial advisors is itself a long-term project, as is constantly evaluating and reevaluating the quality of the advice offered. Anyone, no matter how skilled and committed to your interests, can give bad advice on occasion, and staying with the "devil you know" is sometimes better than striking off into the unknown. When you do find sound professional advisors, cultivate them; they are some of the most important people in your life.

Over the years, you and your professional advisors will work with some basic and necessary forms and documents. Your accountant will work with your tax reporting and financial transaction forms. Your lawyer will work with your will and any trust documents, as well as with property transfers and documents related to business transactions. Your banker will work with your credit, savings, and some investment transactions. Your insurer and investment advisor will work with a surprisingly large number of insurance and investment transactions.

In assessing your personal financial status, you will rely very heavily on the records you keep and the changing goals you develop—which goals depend considerably on the real facts of your financial life. Sometimes those facts seem hard to ascertain and to hold clearly in mind for planning purposes as life proceeds. All too often people have no real idea of their net worth, their real liquidity, their potential tax liability, or the extent to which they should be insured in view of their circumstances and goals. In trying to establish these basic financial facts, it is useful to take a lead from standard business practice.

In business, a series of well-established and widely used financial statements indicate the current status and financial health of enterprises. The balance sheet, showing current assets and liabilities as of the time of its preparation, acts as a still photograph of an enterprise's financial status. The cash flow statement illuminates the movement of cash and cash equivalents in and out of the enterprise during a given period. The profit and loss statement shows the net, plus or minus, of business activities for a given period. The budget or forecast shows anticipated cash flow and projects profit and loss for a given period. Most of the very same tools can and should be adapted to our personal businesses; these are the best tools yet devised to help us see our real finan-

cial situations and can enable us to do effective financial planning
on the basis of real information and realistic objectives. We explore some simplified, personalized versions of some of these
statements shortly.

Most of the data we need for personal financial statements and
realistic budgets is developed yearly for tax preparation purposes. Just as an accountant should be far more to you than a tax
preparer, so the process of doing a yearly tax workup should be
even more. It should be a time not only for summation of the
previous year's economic activity, but also for reassessment of
that year's planning and the preparation of the next year's plan.
No less than once a year should you evaluate how well the previous year's economic plan worked out and consider any new factors that may cause you to revise your financial plans for the next
year.

Even your monthly bank statement reconciliation should not
be just a time to discover whether you forgot to enter a check or
a time to check your arithmetic skills. Except for payment of bills
and monthly reconciliation of the checkbook, many people look
at their financial status only at tax preparation time. However,
you should plan to assess your standing monthly. Use this time
to do such things as allocate money you plan to add to your investment and savings account, check on investments, or see if a
bank certificate or dividend payment is coming due. You may
find that an investment was not wise or that it can be improved
upon; a monthly review will allow you to make changes prompt-
ly.

The main elements of your tax workup should be in place before the turn of each year, assuming that you are a calendar year
taxpayer; this should be early enough—often in October or No-
vember—to enable you to make any possible advantageous tax
planning moves, with counsel from your financial advisors, for
the current year before that year ends. Your main financial reevaluation should occur then, too. Most accountants and other financial advisors understand very well the value of such tax and
financial planning; they will be happy to meet with you every au-
tumn to review your plan and wish that more of their clients
would call on them for that kind of help. An alert financial advi-

sor may suggest a number of transactions, prior to year-end, that may reduce your taxes without fundamentally changing the nature of your financial situation or your portfolio. Always remember that the less you pay in taxes in a given year, even if you "recapture" that tax payment in later years, the more favorable to you, since you can put those tax savings to work, earning for you.

If, however, your accountant turns out to be the rare one who does not want to participate in this kind of planning with you, you should seriously consider changing accountants. This kind of yearly tax and financial workup and planning session is central to the health of your personal financial business. To try running your financial life without it is extraordinarily unwise, much like running a business without financial statements of any kind—a sure prescription for financial disaster.

It is not very easy to assess your own financial progress. You are earning, consuming, investing, and borrowing, while the value of the dollar continues to erode because of inflation. The answer to the question "How am I doing?" is often "I don't really know" or "I'm not quite sure."

One useful way to approach the matter is to attempt to estimate yearly, as closely as you can, the value of your assets. This estimate would not include all of your assets, as would be included in the balance sheet of a business, because your consumable personal property, aside from certain collectibles, disappears as it is consumed, ultimately to be resold, if at all, for something very close to its scrap value. Nor would your estimate include your Social Security and employee corporate pension plan shares, for these are things over which you have no control, unless you are a small company owner who is using a pension plan to accrete assets. Your estimate *should* include all substantial assets of continuing, if fluctuating, value. The Yearly Asset Growth Estimate—Table 1—gives one simple form you can use in making this estimate; you may wish to modify it to suit your individual needs.

The Yearly Asset Growth Estimate will take a little time to calculate, especially the first time, but it is relatively simple and should take less time in succeeding years, becoming more valu-

TABLE 1.   YEARLY ASSET GROWTH ESTIMATE

	Start of Year	Year-end	Change
Asset value			
Savings accounts			
Short-term			
Long-term			
Securities			
Stocks			
Bonds			
Other			
Own business			
Real estate			
Personal			
Business			
Insurance			
Own pension and profit-sharing plans			
Other (gold, collectibles, etc.)			
Total			
Debts			
Mortgages			
Personal			
Business			
Other business			
Personal			
Total			
Net apparent yearly asset growth			
Impact of inflation			
Net real asset growth			

able as your experience develops. You should start by entering the value of your assets and debts at the beginning of the year; the calendar year is an easy period to use, since your tax workups will serve as partial bases for these computations, but any 12-

month period will do. Then enter the current values of your assets and debts at the end of the year, and find the net gain or loss in each category. Total the net gains and losses for your assets and also for your debts. Finally, subtract the net debt change from the net asset change, and you have an estimate of your net *apparent* gain in asset value. To make that figure a meaningful comparison, you must then adjust it, by subtracting the annual rate of inflation, to find your net real asset growth.

Note that no attempt is being made to further adjust for the ultimate tax consequences of transactions made, because many kinds of offsetting transactions and tax-bracket differences would need to be estimated many years before they may occur. For example, a house that appreciates 15% in value in one year must ultimately be sold—but will it be sold and will tax be paid on the gain? Or will it be sold with the seller's taking advantage of a large, one-time tax exemption, as is now the law? Or will it be sold after the death of its present owner by an heir operating under entirely different tax laws, after passing tax free, or very nearly tax free, because of deductions available under estate and inheritance tax laws? Will a tax-sheltered investment result in substantial taxes on deferred taxables later on? Or will those potential taxes be forever avoided by the use of offsetting devices and the operation of estate and inheritance tax laws? Such questions are far too complex and unpredictable to be included in this general estimate; the estimate can, however, be a useful guide for you and your financial advisors in assessing what tax moves might be advantageous and how your long-term capital accumulation is progressing.

Note that this approach measures only asset growth, not investment return (that measurement is taken up a little later), and that for individual items, only change in asset value is being measured.

Note also that we have not computed "net worth" here, feeling that it is not a very useful personal financial planning concept. Should you want to estimate your net worth, you would add an estimate of the value of your personal property and of your vested pension and profit-sharing plans.

Once you have your financial status laid out before you, you can make some basic decisions, in consultation with your financial advisors, about what changes would allow you to grow your assets at a faster rate.

Just as you estimated your yearly asset growth, you can estimate the yield of a specific investment or kind of investment. Only one essential modification is necessary: the splitting apart of growth and cash yield, so that you can estimate the aftertax cash income resulting from an investment during a period.

Aftertax cash yield on investment is often very difficult to estimate, because a number of factors must be taken into account, including the proportion of income that is derived from such primary sources as employment or ownership of one's own business, the amount of investment income that is tax sheltered, and the proportions of consumption and investment occurring within a body of discretionary spending. Therefore, it is safest to estimate the impact of income taxes at the level of the top tax brackets in which your taxes are paid, while in practice you attempt to reduce that as much as possible.

For example, a common stock worth $100 might pay 4% in dividends and grow 4% in a given year, a year in which the impact of inflation is 10%. A rough estimate of the resulting net investment return to a taxpayer in a 50% bracket is as follows:

Value of stock 12/31	$104		
Value of stock 1/1	100		
Gain from 1/1 to 12/31		$4	
Aftertax value of 4% cash			
dividends in 50% bracket		2	
Net apparent gain			$ 6
Impact of 10% inflation			(10)
Gain or *loss*			($4)

In this case, the 10% inflation rate multiplied by the $100 value of the stock at the beginning of the year caused an apparent $6 gain to be a real $4 loss. The loss here might be even larger, because whenever the stock is sold, taxes will have to be paid on that apparent gain.

Here is another instance, which makes the same assumptions, except that the asset is a parcel of real estate that has appreciated in fair market value by an estimated 15%—an estimate only, which can be put to reality's test only on eventual sale, if that should occur.

Value of house 12/31	$115,000		
Value of house 1/1	100,000		
Net apparent gain from 1/1 to 12/31		$15,000	
Impact of 10% inflation		($10,000)	
Gain or loss			$5,000

Here the net gain is 5%. These are, of course, rough estimates, far from what would be acceptable for planning purposes in large corporations. For individuals, they meet the tests of rough accuracy and ease of use in planning, supplying a "bird's-eye view" of individual investment and asset growth progress.

Effective budgeting is an essential financial planning tool. A budget is merely a forecast, yet it is such an essential management tool that large companies spend enormous amounts of highly compensated executive time making the guesses that go into budget forecasts, and whole departments are devoted to the development of computerized forecast models and the forecasts themselves. Businesses estimate both cash flow and profit and loss. Forecasts are detailed at least month by month for a year, and forecasts for a full year ahead are often revised every quarter. Often much longer-term plans are also developed, as a context within which to develop shorter-term plans and forecasts.

Individuals, whose economic lives are very much like small businesses, are best advised to pay careful attention to the development of yearly cash flow forecasts, as the context within which to run their economic lives most effectively and with the least possible personal strain. Why say "cash flow forecast" instead of "cash budget"? Because the word "budget" conjures up in all too many minds a series of nit-picking arguments as to whether or not to buy a steak, a chuck roast, or a can of beans. To many people "budgeting" means hard times, and to others it means retreat from the unrestrained consumption thought to be such an important part of the American dream.

But that is not what budgeting, or cash flow forecasting, is really about. Budgeting is, to a large extent, seeing long- and short-term choices clearly, taking alternative courses of action, and fighting your way free of entrapment in a consuming society. Oddly enough, budgeting does not straitjacket, as so many think; it creates freedom by making financial independence more than a dream and rational asset growth something that can occur in the here and now, not out somewhere in the indefinite future. When you are creating savings for investment, which is what budgeting makes possible, you can take advantage of opportunities and have a chance to beat inflation. As a trapped consumer, whether employee or business owner, you are free only to worry about an increasingly uncertain future.

Table 2 gives a form you can use for developing your cash flow estimates for each month. If you make such estimates every 6 months for the 12 months ahead, you will have included in a self-adjustment technique. Record the anticipated major expenditures in the months in which they occur; do not forget such special matters as tax payments or refunds, expensive vacations, lump-sum education payments, insurance premiums, and the impact of inflation. This recording is done most easily by spreading out all 12 months on a large sheet of accounting paper, which can be purchased in any stationery store. It provides a model to use each month.

This kind of cash flow forecasting can be as helpful to you as it is to businesses. It can tell you well in advance when you will need more cash than you are currently generating. If you have a cash buildup from previous months or years, it can tell you when to hold that cash for coming short-term needs and when to invest for the longer term; by matching current needs and available cash, you can maximize the productive use of investment money. It can tell you when you will need to tap current assets for anticipated cash needs or to borrow to meet those needs, giving you ample time to convert longer-term holdings into cash or to look for financing, if necessary. The quick cash emergency sale is very often a sale at a loss or at less profit than could have been realized; the emergency loan is usually harder to get than the timely loan and is often more expensive as well. In the long run,

TABLE 2. CASH FLOW FORECAST

	Projected	Actual
Cash in		
Direct compensation (each full-time job, part-time job, or business salary separately)		
Dividends and interest (each source separately)		
Rental and royalties (each source separately)		
Alimony and child support		
Other*		
Total		
Cash out		
Mortgage repayments or rent		
Other fixed monthly payments		
Utilities (each separately)		
Taxes		
Insurance		
Alimony and child support		
Education		
Medical and dental		
Food		
Clothing		
Transportation		
Household maintenance		
Personal care		
Contributions		
Recreation		
Major purchases		
Other		
Total		
Net cash flow for month		
Net cumulative cash flow for year to date		

*Note: Possible additional sources of income this month (bonuses, gifts, sales of assets, second job not yet held, tax refunds, etc.)

the matching of projections with actual results, month after month, then year after year, develops the habit of extremely effective cash management, a skill that is central to the development of a healthy financial future.

Financial transactions generate paper. That paper must be kept and should be filed so as to be easily retrievable; some paper, in the form of valuable documents, must be kept safe. Therefore, effective financial planning requires two very obvious physical things—a good place to work and a safe-deposit box. If at all possible, you should have an office at home, or at least a portion of a room separate from all other household activities, which should include adequate worktable space and sufficient, well-organized file space, with some files being lockable. Even if no children are about—and in many households they are—other people are often present, including guests, the children of guests, and sometimes cleaning people. It is worth setting yourself up properly for an activity that will extend throughout your lifetime.

You will want to keep careful, detailed, and long-term records of financial transactions, often far beyond the minimum times necessitated by tax law. For tax purposes, you should hold all materials relating to items on your tax returns for at least four years—three years to satisfy the normal statutory requirements and one year more, because the facts embodied in your return stem from the year before the return was actually filed. On the other hand, there is no statute of limitations on tax fraud, and in certain complex tax situations your accountant may advise you to keep some kinds of tax-related documents indefinitely.

Personal financial statements and the worksheets used to develop those statements should be held indefinitely. They constitute a running record of the financial side of your life and can be quite valuable financial review tools later on.

No matter how much paper is involved—and it can be a good deal—be very sure to hold indefinitely all materials relating to investments, pensions, insurance, estate planning, and tax planning. How and when a pension plan contribution was handled can be a matter of considerable tax and benefit significance 30 years later. What you originally paid for a collectible can be of great tax significance to you or your heirs when taxing authorities are trying to set a realistic basis for computing gain on eventual sale decades later. Knowing precisely when a financial transaction took place can save you a lot of money in future years. Receipts for valuable personal items should also be kept to indicate the value of objects in case of fire or casualty loss for which you are filing an insurance claim.

Some papers, such as deeds, copies (not originals) of wills, stock certificates, and contracts, are best kept in a safe-deposit box, often with copies in your possession at home or business for day-to-day checking purposes, if necessary. The original, witnessed copy of your will should be kept in some other safe place, such as in the office of the lawyer who prepared it. Your personal safe-deposit box will, on your death, be sealed in anticipation of estate settlement, and if your will is sealed with it, unnecessary legal difficulties may result for your executors and heirs.

In general, overplan and overkeep. Ask your professional advisors just a few more questions than you need to ask, rather than several fewer; you will learn and keep learning that way. When in doubt as to whether or not to keep papers, keep them; you can always throw them away later, but you cannot recover them once they are gone.

Organizing the financial side of life is prosaic and time consuming and involves constant questioning and paperwork. In the course of pursuing a busy life, often full of other personal chores and business-related paper of all kinds, it is very easy to let personal affairs slide, to let the papers pile up, to send your tax preparation work up to your accountant by mail and miss a yearly tax and financial planning conference, and to find years later that your personal affairs are in a mess. Try not to let that happen; the lifestyle you desire depends on the state of your finances, and in an increasingly uncertain world, organizing the financial side of life is a must, an essential part of long-term personal financial planning.

THE TECHNIQUES AND INSTRUMENTS OF FINANCIAL PLANNING

CHAPTER

4

Some Basic Approaches

One classic advertising come-on starts, "Are you sincerely interested in making money . . . ?" Another, usually delivered as part of a fast-paced telephone sales pitch, is, "I think you can make a quick killing in_____, but only if you act right now!" You fill in the blank. However, the only quick killing you can look forward to making is the death of your own investment.

In financial slang, a "lamb" is a terribly unwary investor who makes investment decisions on the basis of "advice" from the unscrupulous—promoters, con artists, uninformed sellers—who fleece the lambs, lining their own pockets with the money. A lamb is also someone who invests money on the basis of rumors, tips, alleged trends, and advice tendered by other equally unknowing investors. Together these lambs form a herd, which is led to financial slaughter. One of these lambs may be you, unless you understand some financial planning basics and apply them consistently throughout your life.

"Wait a minute," says the lamb. "Isn't making money what this is all about? And don't people make money, real money, if they can hit it right? Look at gold, silver, collectibles of all kinds. Anyway, I can't possibly make what I need to make on the little I can save; I need to hit it big."

We have some sound advice for those who truly feel so. Close this book, take or send it back to its seller, and try to get a refund. If that refund is secured, bet the money on the daily double at the nearest available racetrack. We firmly believe that people who hold to those views are incurably obstinate lambs and beyond financial redemption.

People who are not willing to be lambs should ask several basic questions about any contemplated investment move.

The first and most important of them is, "Am I making an investment move of my own, to fit *my* financial plan, based upon my knowledge of a specific investment, or am I buying management of my funds, feeling that the investment decisions made by those investing my funds will be better than mine?" The purchase of the common stock of a company you know extremely well, perhaps one that is your employer, is a move of your own. So is the purchase of a piece of local real estate, alone or with others. But the purchase of a mutual fund of any kind is the purchase of management for a fee, however stated, as is the purchase of a unit in a real estate syndicate. If you buy someone else's investment management skills, you will usually have to pay something for them, whether that payment is in the form of a management fee or in some unstated form.

A second key question is, "Am I buying a specific investment, geared to my own needs, or am I following a trend?" Both are, at different times, valid investment approaches. During the great bull market of the 1960s, investors quite properly tended to follow trends as well as to analyze specific investment possibilities. In the 1980s, however, with erratic market behavior quite usual, it is vital to analyze a specific investment on its own merits, rather than to follow a seemingly wide trend. For example, many investors bought gold-mining common stocks early in the 1980s solely because they seemed attractive during a gold price boom. But each gold mine or group of mines is a discrete economic entity; some were good investments, some quite poor. The error was not in buying that kind of stock, but rather in buying it indiscriminately, without proper research and analysis of the specific stock being purchased.

A third key question is, "What is likely to be the net aftertax yield of the investment?" Closely related to this is a fourth key question: "What is the likely change—growth or decline—in the value of the investment during the same period?" We took a brief look at that in Chapter 3, where we estimated the growth in value of a single asset. Here, let's examine the question more closely, looking first at some basics of investment growth.

Effective long-term financial planning depends largely on an understanding of the mechanics of compound interest and on applying that understanding to the relationship between net after-tax (not pretax) earning and growth and the rate of inflation. "Net aftertax" is the key phrase. The comparison must be between everything you net from savings and investment, including what you have and what you add every year, and the rate of inflation. If you can add substantially to your real assets every year, after taking into account the rate of inflation, no matter how high it is, you are going in the right direction, moving ahead in the strength of your financial position—in a sense, in the growth of your own personal business. If you fall behind again and again, or gain a little in some years and lose a little or more than a little in other years, it's reevaluation time.

The heart of the matter is the way interest compounds—for you as your investments grow and earn, against you as inflation takes down the value of the dollar. Table 3 illustrates how $1 compounds over 50 years at different interest rates. That is for just $1. If you can add $1 every year and have that compound, too, so much the better. Table 4 shows how interest accumulates, assuming you start with $1 and add $1 each year, reinvesting all interest.

Your actual gain in interest is far smaller than it seems to be in Tables 3 and 4 because of the progress of inflation, which erodes the value of dollars just as inexorably as the mechanics of compound interest cause them to grow. The essence of the matter is to have some dollars working for you, and, if at all possible, netting after taxes enough to keep up with or even surpass the rate of inflation.

In the 1970s and early 1980s, 3% has not been a high rate of inflation or a high net aftertax return. Yet for many, 3% is all that is netted, after taxes, on a savings account paying 6%, while inflation has moved at a double-digit yearly rate often in this period. The figures do tell a good deal of the story in this instance.

TABLE 3. THE VALUE OF $1 OF PRINCIPAL, WITH COMPOUND INTEREST ACCUMULATED OVER 50 YEARS AT VARIOUS RATES

No. of Years	Interest Rate					
	3%	6%	9%	12%	15%	18%
1	1.0300	1.0600	1.0900	1.1200	1.1500	1.1800
2	1.0609	1.1236	1.1881	1.2544	1.3225	1.3924
3	1.0927	1.1910	1.2950	1.4049	1.5209	1.6430
4	1.1255	1.2625	1.4116	1.5735	1.7490	1.9388
5	1.1593	1.3382	1.5386	1.7623	2.0114	2.2878
6	1.1941	1.4185	1.6771	1.9738	2.3131	2.6996
7	1.2299	1.5036	1.8280	2.2107	2.6600	3.1855
8	1.2668	1.5938	1.9926	2.4760	3.0590	3.7589
9	1.3048	1.6895	2.1719	2.7731	3.5179	4.4355
10	1.3439	1.7908	2.3674	3.1058	4.0456	5.2339
11	1.3842	1.8983	2.5804	3.4786	4.6524	6.1759
12	1.4258	2.0122	2.8127	3.8960	5.3503	7.2876
13	1.4685	2.1329	3.0658	4.3635	6.1528	8.5994
14	1.5126	2.2601	3.3417	4.8871	7.0757	10.1472
15	1.5570	2.3966	3.6425	5.4736	8.1371	11.9737
16	1.6047	2.5404	3.9703	6.1304	9.3576	14.1290
17	1.6528	2.6928	4.3276	6.8660	10.7613	16.6722
18	1.7024	2.8543	4.7171	7.6900	12.3755	19.6733
19	1.7535	3.0256	5.1417	8.6128	14.2318	23.2144
20	1.8061	3.2071	5.6044	9.6463	16.3665	27.3930
21	1.8603	3.3996	6.1088	10.8038	18.8215	32.3238
22	1.9161	3.6035	6.6586	12.1003	21.6447	38.1421
23	1.9736	3.8197	7.2579	13.5523	24.8915	45.0076
24	2.0328	4.0489	7.9111	15.1786	28.6252	53.1090
25	2.0938	4.2919	8.6231	17.0001	32.9190	62.6686
26	2.1566	4.5494	9.3992	19.0401	37.8568	73.9490
27	2.2213	4.8223	10.2451	21.3249	43.5353	87.2598
28	2.2879	5.1117	11.1671	23.8839	50.0656	102.9666
29	2.3566	5.4184	12.1722	26.7499	57.5755	121.5005
30	2.4273	5.7435	13.2677	29.9599	66.2118	143.3706
31	2.5001	6.0881	14.4618	33.5551	76.1435	169.1774
32	2.5751	6.4534	15.7633	37.5817	87.5651	199.6293
33	2.6523	6.8406	17.1820	42.0915	100.6998	235.5626

TABLE 3. *(Continued)*

No. of Years	Interest Rate					
	3%	6%	9%	12%	15%	18%
34	2.7319	7.2510	18.7284	47.1425	115.8048	277.9638
35	2.8139	7.6861	20.4140	52.7996	133.1755	327.9973
36	2.8983	8.1473	22.2512	59.1356	153.1519	387.0368
37	2.9852	8.6361	24.2538	66.2318	176.1246	456.7034
38	3.0748	9.1543	26.4367	74.1797	202.5433	538.9100
39	3.1670	9.7035	28.8160	83.0812	232.9248	635.9139
40	3.2620	10.2857	31.4094	93.0510	267.8636	750.3783
41	3.3599	10.9029	34.2363	104.2171	308.0431	885.4464
42	3.4607	11.5570	37.3175	116.7231	354.2495	1044.8268
43	3.5645	12.2505	40.6761	130.7299	407.3870	1232.8956
44	3.6715	12.9855	44.3370	146.4175	468.4950	1454.8168
45	3.7816	13.7646	48.3273	163.9876	538.7693	1716.6839
46	3.8950	14.5905	52.6767	183.6661	619.5847	2025.6870
47	4.0119	15.4659	57.4176	205.7061	712.5224	2390.3106
48	4.1323	16.3939	62.5852	230.3908	819.4007	2820.5665
49	4.2561	17.3775	68.2179	258.0377	942.3108	3328.2685
50	4.3839	18.4202	74.3575	289.0022	1083.6574	3927.3568

If you have $10,000 in savings accounts and leave that $10,000 in those accounts at 6% for 20 years, reinvesting all interest, and if at the top of your income you pay 50% in combined income taxes, you are netting 3% on those savings. You will have netted only $18,061 (from Table 3, $1 after 20 years at 3% is $1.8061, multiplied by $10,000) after income taxes at the end of those 20 years. That same $10,000 accreting at an aftertax net of 9% would have grown to $56,044; at 15%, to $163,665. At the 3% level, you would have lost much of the $10,000, measured in real value, because of inflation. At 9%, you might have stayed a little ahead or fallen a little behind, depending on the average rate of inflation over those 20 years—but you would, at least, have a far better chance of holding your savings. At 15%, your chances of making meaningful investment gains are rather good.

TABLE 4.   THE VALUE OF $1 OF PRINCIPAL TO WHICH $1 IS ADDED PER YEAR, WITH COMPOUND INTEREST ACCUMULATED OVER 50 YEARS AT VARIOUS RATES

No. of Years	Interest Rate					
	3%	6%	9%	12%	15%	18%
1	1.0300	1.0600	1.0900	1.1200	1.1500	1.1800
2	2.0909	2.1836	2.2781	2.3744	2.4725	2.5724
3	3.1836	3.3746	3.5731	3.7793	3.9934	4.2154
4	4.3091	4.6371	4.9847	5.3528	5.7424	6.1542
5	5.4684	5.9753	6.5223	7.1152	7.7537	8.4420
6	6.6625	7.3938	8.2004	9.0890	10.0668	11.1415
7	7.8923	8.8975	10.0285	11.2997	12.7268	14.3270
8	9.1591	10.4913	12.0210	13.7757	15.7858	18.0859
9	10.4639	12.1809	14.1929	16.5487	19.3037	22.5213
10	11.8078	13.9717	16.5603	19.6546	23.3493	27.7551
11	13.1920	15.8700	19.1407	23.1331	28.0017	33.9311
12	14.6178	17.8821	21.9534	27.0291	33.3519	41.2187
13	16.0863	20.0151	25.0192	31.3926	39.5047	49.8180
14	17.5989	22.2760	28.3609	36.2797	46.5804	59.9653
15	19.1569	24.7825	32.0034	41.7533	54.7175	71.9390
16	20.7616	27.2129	35.9737	47.8837	64.0751	86.0680
17	22.4144	29.9057	40.3013	54.7497	74.8364	102.7403
18	24.1169	32.7600	45.0185	62.4397	87.2118	122.4135
19	25.8704	35.7856	50.1601	71.0524	101.4436	145.6290
20	27.6765	38.9927	55.7645	80.6987	117.8101	173.0210
21	29.5368	42.3923	61.8733	91.5026	136.6316	205.3448
22	31.4529	45.9958	68.5319	103.6029	158.2764	243.4868
23	33.4265	49.8156	75.7898	117.1552	183.1678	288.4945
24	35.4593	53.8645	83.7009	132.3339	211.7930	314.6035
25	37.5530	58.1564	92.3240	149.3339	244.7120	404.2721
26	39.7096	62.7058	101.7231	168.3740	282.5688	478.2211
27	41.9309	67.5281	111.9682	189.6989	326.1041	565.4809
28	44.2189	72.6398	123.1354	213.5828	376.1697	668.4475
29	46.5754	78.0582	135.3075	240.3327	433.7452	789.9480
30	49.0027	83.8017	148.5752	270.2926	499.9569	933.3186
31	51.5028	89.8898	163.0370	303.8477	576.1005	1102.4960
32	54.0778	96.3432	178.8003	341.4294	663.6655	1302.1252

TABLE 4.   *(Continued)*

No. of Years	3%	6%	9%	12%	15%	18%
33	56.7302	103.1838	195.9823	383.5210	764.3654	1537.6878
34	59.4621	110.4348	214.7108	430.6635	880.1702	1815.6516
35	62.2759	118.1209	235.1247	483.4631	1013.3457	2143.6489
36	65.1742	126.2681	257.3760	542.5987	1166.4975	2530.6857
37	68.1594	134.9042	281.6298	608.8305	1342.6222	2987.3891
38	71.2342	144.0584	308.0665	683.0102	1545.1655	3526.2991
39	74.4013	153.7620	336.8824	766.0914	1778.0903	4162.2130
40	77.6633	164.0477	368.2919	859.1424	2045.9538	4912.5913
41	81.0232	174.9506	402.5281	963.3595	2353.0069	5798.0378
42	84.4839	186.5076	439.8457	1080.0826	2708.2465	6842.8646
43	88.0484	198.7581	480.5218	1210.8125	3115.6334	8075.7602
44	91.7199	211.7437	524.8587	1357.2300	3584.1284	9530.5770
45	95.5015	225.5082	573.1860	1521.2176	4122.8977	11247.2610
46	99.3965	240.0987	625.8628	1704.8837	4742.4824	13272.9480
47	103.4084	255.5646	683.2804	1910.5898	5455.0047	15663.2580
48	107.5407	271.9585	745.8656	2140.9806	6274.4054	18453.8250
49	111.7969	289.3360	814.0836	2399.0182	7216.7162	21812.0930
50	116.1808	307.7561	888.4411	2688.0204	8300.3737	25739.4500

Tables 3 and 4 can be very useful to you over the years as you make such analyses and comparisons between various investments. With those basics in mind, let us return to our third and fourth questions: "What is likely to be the net aftertax yield of the investment?" and "What is the likely change—growth or decline—in the value of the investment during the same period?"

Yield and growth expectations, measured together, with taxes subtracted, add up to the single aftertax number that you must estimate in order to evaluate the probable worth of an investment. In finance, "yield" is the measurable amount of value returned by an investment, not including the worth of the investment itself. If you put $10,000 in a savings account at 6%

yearly interest (without worrying about compounding for the purpose of this example), the yield is $600 in one year. If placed in a savings certificate carrying an interest rate of 10%, that $10,000 yields $1000 in one year. A bond worth $10,000 when originally issued and carrying a 9% interest rate, yields $900 per year. However, if the bond's value has declined to $9000 by the time you buy it, it still pays $900 per year; in that case your yield would be 10% of a $9000 investment, or $900.

Let's take a different example. Some common stock you bought for $10,000 pays after-tax dividends of $500, or 5%. Suppose that common stock goes up in market value to $11,000 one year from the time you buy it. If you sell it then, you have gained $1000 in growth and $500 in dividends, for a total gain of $1500, or 15% on top of your original investment. Part is growth and part is direct yield, which is money actually paid out. The two are sometimes lumped together for purposes of description. They are often taken together in business, to provide a single, very useful number—ROI, an abbreviation for "return on investment," a key tool for business investment analysis. In personal financial planning, however, the two should be distinguished; combining them confuses further analysis, particularly with tax factors in mind.

Yield and growth can thus be viewed very narrowly, as in the preceding examples, and usually are so viewed in investment analysis. However, we urge you to take a considerably wider view of yield and growth in your personal financial planning.

Take, for example, Peggy Jones, 35-year-old mother of two children, who has a bachelor's degree, but no marketable skills, and is going back into the job market. In purely financial terms, the best possible investment she and her family can make is in professional training of some kind. In financial terms alone, consider the yield. If Peggy Jones goes back to work in an unskilled job, she will probably make at least $5000 per year less than she would make as a beginning professional, with the gap widening to $10,000 to $15,000 per year as the years go by, as measured in current dollars; the gap will seem to widen even more as inflation continues. Assuming that her professional training takes two years and that it is undertaken while she lives at home and commutes to school and before she would have otherwise entered the job market, she and her family probably will have to make a cash investment in the neighborhood of $10,000. Make it even less favorable—assume that her training takes three years and costs $20,000. Now also assume that she works for 30 years at her profession and that she makes an average of at least $10,000 per year more during her working life than she would have made without that training, as measured in current dollars. That is a $10,000-per-year yield on a $20,000 investment, or 50%. For individuals, that is a key way to measure anticipated yield, not as precisely as in calculating a return on a specific investment, but indispensable for people who want to plan their financial futures.

Professional training can very easily be seen as one of the best investments an individual or family can make—and not only from a purely financial point of view. It is also usually true that professional training in an area of choice will lead to employment far more satisfying than unskilled work, but that is a separate, though vitally important, matter.

Other broad estimates of anticipated yield are far harder to make and therefore to include in lifelong financial planning. For example, the same $20,000 investment might have had a combined growth and dividends rate of 15% and, after taxes had been paid on the actual cash yield, might have returned a total of 10%. Compounded over many years, that would be a tidy sum, though of course nothing like the magnificent return available from professional training. But Peggy Jones might decide to use the $20,000 to go into a small business, figuring that here was a real chance to let the money grow into something very substantial, while deriving both income and satisfaction from the investment. That is perfectly good thinking. A successful small business can mean financial security and independence—if it is successful. But the truth is that most small businesses fail, for a wide variety of reasons, eating up savings and creating new debts.

Which leads us to the fifth basic question to ask when contemplating an investment move: "What is the degree of risk?" The degree of risk differs greatly among kinds of investments and very often conditions the possible yields available. At the most elementary level, a corporate bond's rate of return will directly relate to the amount of risk the bond rating services see in purchasing the bond, as expressed by their ratings of the investment qualities of such bonds. A stock in a small, lightly capitalized company may be a real "buy" if the company's new product takes off in its marketplace, but may be worth nothing if the company fails. Bonds issued by another country may pay a great deal more than their seemingly equivalent United States bonds, and an investment in them may be a good one—or that country may later default on its solemn obligations, leaving bondholders holding worthless paper. During a gold-buying boom, gold may be the best investment then available in the world—if it is bought at a low-enough price and even though it yields no current income. On the other hand, its price may drop as suddenly as it rose, causing catastrophic losses to those who bought it high. Risk is a matter to be assessed very carefully; one who does not do so can sometimes be an accidental and temporary winner, but ultimately becomes just another lamb.

A sixth basic question is, "How liquid is the investment?" In other words, "How quickly can I get my funds out if I want or need them?" Cash kept in a can buried in your backyard is very liquid indeed, but it is not an investment, because it yields nothing, grows not at all, and diminishes in value in direct proportion to the rate of inflation. Cash kept in a day-to-day savings account can be secured on demand or withdrawal in all but very exceptional circumstances, such as the bank holiday that occurred during the depths of the Great Depression of 1933 or under certain conditions of bank failure. Government bonds, most traded securities, most traded bonds, and many other financial instruments are readily convertible into cash, barring most exceptional economic or political circumstances. But equity in real estate may be hard to turn into cash quickly, either by sale or by mortgage borrowing; buyers may not be readily available at any acceptable price, and mortgage money may be tight or far too expensive. Money invested in one's own business or in education may yield or not, but it is very often entirely used up, having been turned into income potential rather than definable, and therefore salable, assets or assets that can be sold or borrowed against.

The seventh basic question that you should ask about any investment is, "What will be the tax impacts of the investment move being considered?" A corollary question is, "What are the best ways to handle taxes here?" Every financial move and strategy has tax impacts, and the nature of those impacts will very often determine which moves you should make and which strategies you should follow. For example, an owner-occupied house accretes value tax free until it is sold and carries a once-in-a-lifetime tax break on the gain in value it has accreted, up to a stated limit. As a result, a home can be one of the best investments most people can make in their lifetimes, even without the long-term upward trend in real estate values that has characterized the American real estate market since the end of World War II. In contrast, savings accounts' interest and dividends are taxed as ordinary income, except for the annual tax exemption of the first $200 of such income for individuals and $400 for married couples, thus effectively yielding only a little over half of what they seem to yield for a taxpayer in a 50% combined federal, state, and local tax bracket. Pension plans depend on favorable tax legislation; insurance plans often become desirable or undesirable depending upon tax considerations.

Financial planners pay a great deal of attention to the tax aspects of every business and personal move. For personal financial planning, it is important to have at least a basic knowledge of how taxes work and of the general tax consequences of each investment move contemplated. True, tax matters are handled best by professionals, but as a practical matter, only the rich can afford to consult tax advisors on every investment move.

These, then, are the seven basic questions you should ask about any financial move you are considering. Answering these questions will allow you to assess, independently, advice given to you by financial advisors. And you should seek such advice. Even though some financial advice, including advice on tax aspects, must be paid for in one way or another, getting it from good professionals must be a key objective of all who attempt to plan their financial futures. The world is too complex to try to do it all alone; as we discussed in Chapter 3, sound professional help can be hard to find—but it is a must.

Information and advice from publications form the context

within which you can use the advice of financial advisors to maximum advantage. Ultimately, there is no long-term substitute for your own informed decision making, and that, in turn, depends significantly on the extent to which you have taken the trouble to become and to stay informed over the years. A rolling, surging boom in a particular form of investment, such as commodity options, can be a real opportunity for alert, informed investors—and a deadly, disastrous trap for the unwary.

It is absolutely essential to stay abreast of the economic, political, and social contexts within which your investment decisions will be made. An oil crisis, in which economic and political factors are inextricably intertwined, and which causes short-, medium-, and long-term changes in the total economic environment, cannot be understood and acted upon by investors who rely on the evening news for all of their information. The investment implications of an enormously high rate of inflation cannot be understood without arriving at some prior estimate of how long that inflation can reasonably be expected to continue; that, in turn, depends on some long-range economic and political estimates.

Keeping informed starts with daily reading of the hard general news, along with all the economic and specific investment news and analysis you can find in such newspapers as the *New York Times* and the *Wall Street Journal*. For many, it also includes careful reading of one or more of the many investment-oriented periodicals and advisory services publications available. Part V of this book offers a selection of sources of financial planning information, with a description and ordering information on each. You should look over that list and identify which materials seem most appropriate for your purposes, either to subscribe to or to consult in the library. Subscribing to and reading such materials may seem to be a considerable expenditure of money and time, but such subscribing is tax deductible and is as essential as subscribing to a trade or industry periodical in your line of work. In fact, consistent investment success requires viewing financial planning as nothing less than a second line of work, with all the information-gathering and analytical obligations that that implies.

The investment climate always changes. It is not only that, to paraphrase J. Pierpont Morgan, the only thing that can be guaranteed about the stock market is that it will fluctuate, but that in our time, as in his, there are very many investment vehicles to consider in creating a coherent financial planning program. Such a program must take into account a number of factors, varying with each set of life circumstances, while at the same time recognizing similar desires and needs within fairly definable groups of people. For example, the Smiths of Chapter 2, corporate employees in their forties, will have very different financial plans than will a couple in their sixties retiring from a successful small business. Moreover, one couple planning to stay in business on a limited basis after retirement will plan quite differently from another couple planning to go out of business entirely and to live in a Florida retirement community.

Whatever the major currently available investment vehicles, however they may change, you must be sure never to put all your eggs in one basket. In your financial planning, you must provide for everything from short-term emergencies to lifetime income needs, always bearing in mind that today's opportunity may be tomorrow's trap. However, after all precautions, it is our view that most people can invest successfully and can indeed fight their way through to financial independence and a significant measure of freedom. The balance of this book is aimed at helping you do just that.

CHAPTER
5

A World Turned Upside Down:

Savings, Bonds, Stocks, and Mutual Funds

A popular English tune of the late 1700s was "The World Turned Upside Down," the tune played by an army band as the British troops who had surrendered to the Continental Army at Yorktown, Virginia, turned in their weapons, signaling the end of British colonial rule in what was to become the United States. That tune should probably be played at the opening of the New York Stock Exchange every day in these years, for in many ways the investment world has indeed turned upside down in the early 1980s.

It is a world in which several heretofore rather conservative, modest-yield investment vehicles have become not only the safest, but also some of the highest-yielding, fixed-dollar investments available; in which the United States dollar is worth comparatively little, and American common stocks are worth, at best, half of what they were worth in the late 1960s; in which speculation in high-risk vehicles is so common as to be routinely touted by quite reputable investment services and organizations; and in which such terribly old-fashioned vehicles as real estate, small businesses, government bonds, savings accounts, and some insurance policies can be seen as the excellent investments and long-term planning tools they were all along.

This chapter and the next cover specific kinds of investments. This chapter deals with the kinds of investments that have, in this century, become the classic investment vehicles used by most Americans in trying to provide for their financial well-being: savings, bonds, stocks, and mutual funds. The next chapter deals with a number of investment vehicles that have become better known to most Americans in recent years, although some have, in the past, been classic investment vehicles: gold and other precious metals, commodities, futures, options, collectibles, tax-sheltered investments, and at least one insurance policy that combines investment with conventional insurance features.

SAVINGS

During the 1950s and until the late 1960s, savings were viewed by many people thought to be "in the know" as a particularly foolish financial planning vehicle. Putting your money into a savings account at 6% interest, even if compounded hour by hour, could not possibly compare with the yields that seemed virtually guaranteed by hundreds of common stocks in the great bull market, that steeply rising market of the period. Further, interest was taxable as ordinary income, while stocks could be held and their gains in value cashed in at very favorable long-term capital gains tax rates.

It held true—as long as the great bull market continued to rise. But markets do not move in only one direction; stocks fluctuate. Eventually, many people who had bought and bought found themselves holding less in real dollars than they had put in over the years. The Dow Jones Common Stock Index, which had been in the 900-to-1000 range well over a decade earlier, was in the 700-to-1000 range in the late 1970s and early 1980s. That looks somewhat similar; it is not. The dollars in which the index's stock prices are measured were, in 1980, worth considerably less than half what they had been worth a decade before. As a result, stocks worth $1000 in the early 1980s are worth a little more than $400 in 1970 dollars, and average stock prices have really lost more than half their value in a decade. By the early 1970s hundreds of thousands of small investors had left the stock market, poorer but not necessarily wiser. They had purchased stocks high and had sold them low, as lambs always do. Increasingly trapped by inflation and the fast-eroding value of their savings, they moved into other investment vehicles, always seeking maximum gain at minimum risk, but constantly tending to sacrifice security for gain.

Savings as an investment vehicle did make a substantial comeback in the 1970s, however, spurred largely by very real fears about impending economic collapse. In addition to the standard savings account, at a legally required maximum 5½ to 6% yearly interest (compounded daily, it comes to a little more), banking institutions began to offer a variety of longer-term savings arrangements. Through these, banks were able to offer as much as 10 to 14% interest annually for a term commitment of funds on the part of the saver and with penalties for short-term withdrawal. The key security element in all these accounts, as it was and is in the straight 5½ to 6% savings account, is that the saver is protected by substantial amounts of Federal Deposit Insurance. This insurance applies to an individual account or to a joint account, as well as to accounts held by other family members, so that, for example, five accounts held in the names of five different family members in the same bank are each so insured, as are five accounts held by the same person in five different banks.

That is an enormously important plus for those deeply concerned about a possible economic collapse such as that of the Great Depression of the 1930s, when thousands of banks failed, and millions lost everything in those failures. For Federal Deposit Insurance, like federal government bonds, is backed by the "full faith and credit" of the United States government. That is a general promise to pay the interest and principal of those obligations, backed by the unlimited taxing power of the government.

Yet, financial systems do crash, and governments do default on their obligations. The United States has seen little of this, but many people who have themselves come from other countries, or whose parents or grandparents were immigrants, vividly recall the experience of financial and government collapse in the past century of war, revolution, dictatorship, and depression. In the kind of collapse that can come with worldwide economic crisis or war, very little financial planning is possible. Planning then is much like having an ineffectual fallout shelter in an atomic war— it doesn't hurt, but it may not help very much. A stock of canned goods and a few can openers, a fireplace and a supply of wood if possible, a few hundred dollars (in a currency that may be worthless) buried in a can somewhere accessible, and perhaps a few other things to barter would be the main necessities in such a period of collapse. Gold and other precious metals and stones are common mediums of exchange, but in the kind of social/economic/political collapse that so many are worrying about, food, shelter, heat, and water would be primary and worth far more than anything else.

Savings should not be viewed as that kind of catastrophe insurance, any more than should gold and other such stores of value. Savings are properly viewed on the one hand as short-term insurance against personal emergency, and on the other as an investment vehicle to which such normal evaluators as aftertax yield, risk, and liquidity are to be applied. Looking at it that way, demand deposits (deposits that may be withdrawn at any time) covered by Federal Deposit Insurance are, as they have been ever since Federal Deposit Insurance began in the 1930s, an important short-term personal funds vehicle. They yield little after taxes, but are as safe as the federal government can make them; that is true of the state government as well. The only substantial precaution to take is to be sure that your deposits are insured by the Federal Deposit Insurance Corporation (FDIC), the National Credit Union Association (NCUA), the Federal Savings and Loan Insurance Corporation (FSLIC), or a state insurance corporation at the current maximums, which change from time to time and can be expected to change somewhat more frequently in periods of rapid inflation and consequent debasement of the dollar.

One caution as to the liquidity of demand deposit funds, however: Demand deposits can generally be withdrawn at any time on the signature of their owner, the account holder. Under certain very special circumstances, they may not be so available, including the sort of national bank holiday Franklin Delano

Roosevelt declared in 1933, closing the nation's banks for a period in a successful attempt to save the country's banking system. That also may occur on failure of a single bank, but in recent years, the federal government has managed in all cases to maintain continuity of demand deposit payments, even in cases of bank failure. In case of failure, governments will guarantee payment to you, but under circumstances of widespread economic distress, that payment may take some time, and your demand deposit may not be entirely available on demand. A bank, savings and loan company, or credit union that fails may close its doors and leave you looking to the appropriate insuring body for payment. So far, that payment has been swiftly forthcoming—but nothing is immutable, and in times of deep trouble that payment may not come so quickly. People who are concerned about imminent collapse might be well advised to keep a little "rainy day" cash outside the banking system; to spread their savings among various large, well-established, deposit-insured banking institutions; and to stock up on some hard goods and commodities to see them through a temporary period of crisis.

In the early 1970s some Americans became aware of the possibility of putting their savings into Mexican accounts, which yielded far higher interest rates than those available in the United States. And so they did—until Mexico, without warning, revalued its national currency, causing the amounts deposited in its banks to lose about half their value immediately, as compared to United States currency. An amount of $10,000 yielding 10% in a Mexican bank suddenly became $5000 yielding 10%, or half of what it had yielded the day before. The moral of that story is not "Don't put your money in foreign institutions." It is "Put your money where you feel you should, but only after careful investigation." A foreign institution may carry hazards an American one does not. If you decide to take a risk in this area, make sure that you fully understand the economic and political risk and that the possible return is commensurate with that risk.

Savings and investments are closely related and thus often seem, for all practical purposes, the same, with any differences between them seen as important to economists, not to individuals trying to find ways to do effective financial planning. To some extent that is true, but as in all analysis, it is important to know the meaning of the terms used and of any analytical results obtained. In financial planning, one particular reason to examine savings and investments as separate concepts is the widespread use of the term "savings" as a selling point by some sellers of insurance and investments. For example, many insurance sellers point out the "forced savings" feature of straight life insurance, which we will discuss a little later, as a positive reason for buying that form of insurance. Positive or not, the fact is that, when you purchase that kind of life insurance policy, you are buying a combination of insurance and management of your funds by those who are managing the insurance company's investment portfolio.

The operative selling phrase is usually "Put your savings into." It is also used by people who want you to invest in a money market, municipal bond, or other kind of mutual fund, and it is usually put this way: "Why not put your savings into a_____?" You fill in the blank.

Take, for example, that "money market fund" that is doing so well. Doesn't "money market" mean the buying and selling of money, and isn't money what we mean when we talk about "savings"? No, not really. Money is several things, depending on the width of the view adopted. The national money supply is defined by the federal government in four progressively wider ways, but none of them includes investments. The widest of the four definitions, which embraces the other three narrower definitions, is that the nation's supply of money includes all currency, demand deposits, commercial bank time deposits, and savings held by institutions of all kinds. That definition does not include all the kinds of "money market instruments," such as government bonds, bankers' acceptances, and certificates of deposit, which are bought and sold on the "money markets" and which in many instances carry significantly higher risks than do federally insured savings. Your savings are insured by national policy—that is, by a set of legislative and regulatory actions taken following the 1929 Crash. If you convert those savings into investments, they may no longer be so insured; they may carry higher or lower net aftertax yields, but at least equal, and usually greater, risks. In the long run it is very important to understand that investments are generally riskier than savings, because national policy insures savings and does not insure investments.

By savings, we mean, in essence, earnings you have kept and can use in discretionary fashion. These funds need not be after-tax; you may, for example, be holding savings accreted over the course of a year and be planning to pay taxes out of them at tax time, or you may have found a way to shelter some of your savings from taxes through use of an appropriate tax-sheltering device.

Your savings may take the form of a deposit in a commercial bank, carrying no interest, with the money not working for you. A surprising number of people let that happen, not realizing that the "small" amounts thought to be involved are not really so small when seen over the course of a lifetime.

More often, you will have savings in an insured, interest-bearing, demand deposit account in a commercial bank, savings bank, or savings and loan association. National policy, as of this writing, continues to allow savings banks and savings and loan associations to pay slightly higher interest rates than commercial banks on such deposits, by about one-quarter of 1%. That may change at any time, but the difference is not terribly significant, since considerably more favorable and equally safe savings vehicles have been developed by the banking industry in recent years.

All major savings vehicles will compound interest, which means they will pay interest on the interest that accumulates, refiguring that interest rather frequently, often daily or weekly. The net effect may be another one-quarter to one-half of 1% paid on savings accounts. That is not terribly significant in the short run, but makes a real difference in the long run. Simple interest does not compound, so that 6% per year in simple interest paid on $100 is $6 per year; you will have $106 after one year, $112 after two years, and so on. Compound interest, at its simplest, will pay $6 the first year; 6% of $106, or $6.36, the second year; and so on. Compounded more frequently, the fractional increments go up somewhat more rapidly. Note very carefully, however, that you must pay taxes on such interest at ordinary income tax rates, after the modest annual tax-deductible amounts, and that the accreting funds the savings banks so proudly point to as part of their sales efforts are not, in terms of your total financial picture, accreting at anything like the claimed rates, once you take your tax payments into account.

In the late 1970s and on into the 1980s, banks have been offering an increasingly wide range of higher-paying insured savings vehicles in attempts to attract savings deposits. During this period the interest rates permitted on normal demand deposit savings accounts were far lower than the rates available in a wide variety of very safe investments, including at many times even United States Treasury bills, the utterly liquid and safe primary, short-term obligations of the federal government. Two major forms had been developed as of the time of this writing, but others can be expected in this very fast-moving area, in which the distinction between savings and investments increasingly has blurred, as inflation and extraordinarily high interest rates have turned safe, quiet savings vehicles into an area of major financial interest.

The first, and somewhat older, form is that of the time deposit, which is a deposit on which a savings institution will pay a considerably higher rate of interest than it pays on ordinary demand deposits in return for a minimum size of deposit—sometimes as low as $500—and somewhat less liquidity. These are not demand deposits, but rather funds that cannot be withdrawn without notice until a stated maturity date; when withdrawn with notice before the agreed-upon term, there is often a substantial forfeit of interest. A variation upon this form, more in name than in concept or practice, is the "consumer certificate of deposit," which functions, in essense, as a time deposit. Like the time deposit, it is offered under many names and with many quite minor variations in an attempt to make it as attractive as a combined savings/investment medium.

The second major form is that of the bank "certificate of deposit," a short-term, bank-issued financial instrument that pays interest at, or slightly higher than, the rates of interests being paid on United States Treasury certificates at the time of issue of the bank certificates—usually based on the previous week's Treasury certificate rate of interest. These certificates run for various periods of time, typically for 26 weeks, and are in minimum denominations, typically $10,000. However, minimum denominations, terms, and lengths of time are all very much in flux, as banks attempt to secure savings and investments funds in competition with government, corporations, and other institutions.

That competition for funds occurs in both bond and stock markets. It is to these massive, traditional investment vehicles that we now turn.

BONDS AND OTHER DEBT OBLIGATIONS

We are here using the term "bonds" to describe all those kinds of debt obligations offered for public sale by their public and private issuers. The instruments involved—and they are many—are thought of and described by most individual investors as bonds, even though they include a wide variety of debt obligations that are not technically bonds, but rather other debt instruments, including bills, certificates, and money market instruments. We are not here discussing instruments that are packaged into the many kinds of mutual and other investment funds managed by others—these are discussed in a separate chapter. We are not discussing "futures," those investment instruments that reflect estimates of the future prospects of several kinds of investment instruments, including debt instruments, nor are we discussing "options," sometimes called "rights"; these, too, are treated in a future chapter.

Savings are your assets, held by another and returnable to you. Their holder pays you for the privilege of holding and using your money. That, after all, is the essence of the banking business. Banks pay you for the privilege of holding your money and using it. The difference between what they realize from your money and what they pay you pays their bills and yields whatever profit they make from the aggregate of their activities. In contrast, when you buy bonds, the essential transaction that takes place is that you become a direct lender, performing the transaction that is at the heart of the banking business. Reaching through all the documents and varieties of instruments, you are passing your money to an entity, which, in turn, is promising to pay you back with interest, almost always at a specific time and usually at a fixed rate, although some variable interest rate bonds have been introduced in recent years.

As a bondholder, then, you are extending credit. As a potential creditor, you will want to exercise the same kind of prudence a bank loan officer must display when evaluating a potential borrower. That will require considering some, though not all, of the same matters a banker will consider as potential creditor, and some other questions besides.

A creditor must first consider the nature of the debt obligation's issuer. It is not wise to be dazzled by high rates of interest and favorable tax considerations; the issuer may be a poor risk, such as a poorly managed corporation in deep financial trouble or a municipality in serious danger of bankruptcy. Bond rating services—the main services are Moody's and Standard and Poor's—are helpful in evaluating the quality of bonds offered for sale to the public. You should not, however, regard them as a complete substitute for your own investigation of the relative degree of safety of a debt obligation.

The question of safety is, in some instances, settled by the nature of the issuer. A direct obligation of the United States government, backed by the "full faith and credit" of that government—which in translation is simply a promise to pay—is as safe as a debt can be. Governments default in many ways, and some people may prefer the security of burying gold in a backyard or in a vault somewhere, but our view is that, in the 1980s, federal government obligations of this kind will continue to be safe investments. As in any credit-granting situation, the question of safety can be fairly well settled by insurance coverage. A federally insured debt obligation should be considered a safe investment.

Collateral aids safety, too. A debt secured by specific physical assets will usually be safer than a general promise to pay, as any adequately secured loan is safer than an unsecured loan, other factors being substantially equal.

Circumstances are involved in the question of safety, as well. In a period of severe economic downturn, rapid inflation, or both, circumstances far beyond the control of the borrower or debt obligation issuer may materially affect the borrower's ability to repay; an otherwise quite financially stable municipality, for example, might be faced with several industrial plant closings coupled with tremendous and unanticipated municipal government cost increases due to inflation.

Beyond safety, but much intertwined with it, is the question of yield. Generally, that which is safest yields lowest, but tax factors may alter that equation to some extent. The interest rates paid by issuers to bond and other debt instrument holders depend very heavily upon the prevailing rates of interest paid by debtors to creditors throughout the economy at the time the debt instrument is issued. Putting it a little differently, borrowers have to meet prevailing interest rates in order to get their desired share of the loan money available at the time they enter the market looking for some, much as a consumer has to pay the "going rate" to borrow money at the bank. The "safer" the issuer and the instrument, or the more tax advantaged, the lower the rate of interest that must be paid to those who buy the debt instruments.

For example, a highly regarded, stable corporation, such as American Telephone and Telegraph, going to market in the mid-1970s with a bond issue backed by the corporation's full faith and credit, or promise to pay, might have had to pay 8% interest to bond buyers. At that rate, it would have sold its bonds easily and quickly, as the issue would have been top-rated by the bond-rating organizations and the interest rate would have been competitive in the money marketplace; that is, it was as good as purchasers might have received with equal safety elsewhere at that time. But in the early 1980s, with far higher interest rates throughout the economy, the same company might have had to pay 15% interest on its bonds in order to induce investors to buy those bonds—that is, to lend the company money.

At the same time, the American Telephone and Telegraph bonds sold at an 8% interest rate in the 1970s would be trading on the bond market at a discounted price that accurately reflected current interest rates, so that someone buying them during the high-interest 1980s would, in effect, be able to secure the current rate of 15%. For example, a single bond issue at a face, or stated, value of $100 for a 10-year period at an 8% yearly rate of interest, will pay $8 per year for 10 years, then $100 at maturity. If sold after five years, at a time when interest rates on new bonds of the same quality of safety are in the 15% range, it will sell for enough less than $100 to allow for 15% return on its selling price, taking into account the fact that $100 will be due on maturity of the bond after its original 10-year period is completed. Do not attempt the mathematics of yield yourself. Bonds are best bought and sold through brokers or sometimes bankers; let them do the mathematics for you.

The ideas behind the mathematics are simple enough. The main thing to understand is that the degree of risk or safety is closely related to the rate of interest available within the context of current "going" interest rates in the whole economy. Those going interest rates are, in turn, determined partly by federal manipulation, through the Federal Reserve system, of the amount of credit available and the interest rates that will be charged for that credit and partly by major economic trends affecting the demand for credit in the economy. An analysis of the national and international money and credit system, although it can be intensely interesting, is far beyond the aims of this book.

Bonds are not traded on organized exchanges, as stocks and some other investment vehicles are. The "bond market" and the "money market" are only convenient ways of describing a large, informal, international set of trading arrangements engaged in by many substantial banking and investment institutions, forming a worldwide web of bond and other debt instrument traders. New bonds and other debt instruments are originally brought to market either directly by their issuers, such as the United States government, or by groups of investment bankers organized into "underwriting syndicates," which generally buy whole bond issues from their issuers and then sell them directly to the public themselves or sell them as wholesalers to brokers, who in turn sell them to the public.

Before the 1970s, bonds were generally an institutional kind of trading vehicle, with millions of dollars usually involved in institutional trades. Some moneyed people also regularly traded in the bond market, especially in the municipal bond market, which afforded people in high income tax brackets substantial tax avoidance benefits. Only federal government savings bonds were routinely bought by small investors, yielding modest rates of interest and functioning much as did savings accounts. That situation changed dramatically as the stock market started its breakneck slide in the late 1960s, as hundreds of thousands of small investors left the stock markets, as inflation began to accelerate, as interest rates began to climb, and as small investors trying to keep up with the pace of inflation more and more desperately sought relatively high-yielding, safe investments. In the investment climate that then developed, sellers found ways to market debt instruments to small investors, much as they had marketed stocks for decades before.

In the 1970s investors turned to bonds and other debt instruments en masse—and for good reason. In difficult, uncertain times, with runaway inflation, energy crises, high interest rates, and a previously rocklike American dollar that was losing value every year, debt instruments proved to be a series of relatively high-interest, low-risk investments.

It was—and is—a period in which the standard, sound, conservative financial planning advice that had been offered since World War II no longer applied; the basic situation had changed for the first time in a quarter of a century.

The public had come into the financial markets in a big way in the early part of the century and had flooded into the markets during the 1920s. That all stopped after the Crash of 1929 and did not resume until 1945. But after 1945, savers began to become investors again and moved into the stock markets. The standard advice given by conservative advisors, all too often ignored, was to keep a fair amount of savings in savings institutions "for a rainy day," carry ample life and health insurance, own your own home as unencumbered by debt as possible, and put the rest into fairly conservative securities. The standing operating procedure of most small investors was to nod gravely, live as high as possible, carry fairly minimal insurance and very small savings, encumber themselves as much as possible with debt, and try to run up a fortune in moderately to highly speculative securities. Then, after the slaughter of the lambs in the stock market declines of the late 1960s and early 1970s, the speculative turn was toward whatever seemed to yield the highest possible returns, with commensurate risks.

But many had learned from the negative experiences of the 1960s and early 1970s and also were properly alarmed by the turn taken by the national economy. Many more had followed the sound, conservative advice of the period after World War II and had not been wiped out by the stock market declines. Many, many more continued to generate savings and therefore investment money from their main means of livelihood, money that could not be tucked away in savings accounts and forgotten. They understood that, when inflation is at a 10 to 15% rate, and your aftertax return on a 6% savings account is really 3 to 4%, you lose 6 to 12% of the value of your savings in a single year and a great deal more than that as the loss compounds. That is very simple arithmetic, and hundreds of thousands of small and medium savers and investors, knowing that arithmetic well, have turned to debt instruments that bear much higher interest, yet are relatively secure, at a time when stock yields have been far smaller than debt instrument yields. All of these people have turned to three basic kinds of debt instruments: United States government debt obligations, state and local debt obligations, and the debt obligations of privately owned organizations.

United States Government Obligations

The United States government is a truly enormous spender and borrower. Now, after decades of annual deficits, it is also an enormous interest payer, with carrying charges on past debts one of the largest items in every yearly federal budget. Political rhetoric set aside, it is highly unlikely that the basic situation in this area will change, at least for the balance of this century. Inflation, energy costs, continued and at times accelerated massive military expenditures, and a Social Security system that at some time in that period will run out of money and need to be financed out of general tax revenues will all see to that.

Governments repudiate debts, including those owed to their own citizens. They do not always do so directly—that can bring down a government and even change a whole social system. But very often they do so indirectly, by paying back debts in dollars that are worth a great deal less than those lent the government by unwary lenders in previous years.

That is clearly what has been happening—not through any grand conspiracy, but in fact—to long-term debts solemnly incurred by the United States government in the past and maturing in these years. Long-term federal govenment bonds issued many years ago and paying interest in the 3 to 6% range at a time when the rate of inflation was in the same range continue to pay those rates of interest to maturity, guaranteeing substantial losses for their holders. Federal savings bonds, which are nonnegotiable, can only be cashed in in order to cut losses. Negotiable long-term federal obligations can be traded on bond markets, but trade at far lower prices than those at which they were originally sold, reflecting the constant tendency of bonds to adjust their prices to current interest levels. Such bonds are as safe as they ever were in terms of receiving principal at maturity date, being backed by the full taxing power of the federal government, but they are worth a great deal less. Technically, that is not repudiation of debt; practically, it works just as surely as partial debt repudiation would.

That is why investors have, in the late 1970s and early 1980s, turned to short-term federal debt obligations and why the government has had to turn more and more to that kind of obligation to meet its enormous and growing cash needs.

You can buy some kinds of federal obligations from your bank, paying small service charges. Most kinds will be available through your broker. Some you can buy yourself, avoiding charges, if you are willing to take considerable time and trouble to do so. Information on direct purchasing is available from your bank or broker or directly from the Treasury Department in Washington, D.C. Such debt obligations are also part of many mutual fund and bank fund portfolios selling participations to investors; they are discussed under mutual funds.

Treasury bills are the most common short-term federal debt obligations. The United States Treasury issues 3-, 6-, and 12-month bills that pay fixed interest for the period of issue. The bills are discounted in advance, meaning that you will pay less than the face value of the bills and at maturity will be repaid the face value, the difference being your interest payment on the obligation. In periods of rapid inflation and great financial uncertainty, the three-month bills have been widely purchased by both institutions and individuals. In periods of somewhat greater stability, the longer-term Treasury bills may be somewhat more convenient to handle, necessitating fewer transaction fees and less attention. Interest can be lost on these and on all other short-term obligations if they are not "rolled over" quickly, meaning that, immediately upon sale of one short-term obligation, another must be bought with the proceeds of the first.

In more stable times, Treasury notes, which mature in 1 to 10 years, are a safe way to soak up surplus funds, although they do not necessarily have a high-enough yield. These bear coupons, as do many other kinds of bonds, which are clipped and presented for fixed payments at stated intervals; the term "coupon clipper," in fact, has come to describe someone living on the interest from his or her bonds. Like all longer-term debt obligations, these notes may appreciate in value if interest rates go down after purchase and may lose value if interest rates go up after purchase. If held to maturity, the fixed interest is paid periodically, and the principal is returned at maturity. Treasury notes and longer-term federal debt obligations are as safe as debt obligations can be in terms of interest and principal repayment, but during their lives are as sensitive to fluctuations in the interest rate as are other high-grade obligations.

Federal bonds are those federal obligations maturing in more than 10 years. Except for savings bonds, which are discussed subsequently, they are mainly traded in large blocks by institutions, rather than being proper instruments for personal financial planning.

In addition to Treasury-issued debt obligations, there are an increasingly large number of debt obligations issued by federal agencies of all kinds, such as the Government National Mortgage Association (GNMA), known as "Ginnie Mae"; the Federal National Mortgage Association (FNMA), known as "Fannie Mae"; the Federal Land Banks; the Small Business Administration; and the Tennessee Valley Authority. Federal agency debt proliferates very quickly. These agencies are funded by legislation, and their debt-incurring activities are carried out on their own. Therefore, although backed by the United States government's promise to pay, they are not direct Treasury issues and thus have, at times, been considered slightly less safe than Treasury obligations. As a result, they have sometimes paid somewhat higher interest than that paid by Treasury issues, making them attractive to those who realize that they are very good risks indeed. However, in uncertain, high-interest-rate periods, many have chosen to invest only in the shortest-term issues of these agencies, some of which run as little as three months. Agency debt obligations are purchased through brokers and banks.

Federal savings bonds were very popular during World War II, when purchasing them was the patriotic thing to do, and when their interest rate was only a little below that available from other vehicles. Even today, they are sold quite aggressively by the federal government. They are usually purchased by people who have only small amounts of dollars at a time to put into savings or investments, since they can be purchased through periodic payments of small amounts, as in a payroll deduction plan. We would certainly not advise anyone who wanted to buy them for patriotic reasons to hold back for a second. But anyone buying them for financial reasons should think very carefully before doing so in the economic climate of the 1980s. At this writing, they yield 7½%, but only after being held for five years; before that, they graduate upward from a little over 5½% during the early years. They are nonnegotiable and cannot be used as collateral. Their interest is fully taxable, but only at maturity, thus affording only a small tax break, which does not even come close to making up for their negative investment characteristics. For someone looking for tax breaks, state and local debt obligations may prove far more rewarding—if one is careful.

State and Local Obligations

State and local obligations are the debt obligations of all other governmental bodies in the United States outside the federal government. These include tens of thousands of state and local governments and their multifold agencies, which together form what is commonly called the "municipal bond market," even though they include many bodies that are neither municipalities nor in any way related to municipalities.

Their major financial attraction is that, as a matter of national policy, their interest is by law exempt from federal income taxes. Where a purchaser is a legal resident of an issuing locality, that interest is in many instances also free of state and local taxes, as a matter of state and local taxing policy. Tax rates vary widely and tax laws change continually, but the tax breaks provided by these state and local obligations offer a very substantial attraction indeed.

Wealthy people have long taken advantage of the tax advantages inherent in municipals. Even during the 1950s and 1960s, with stocks enjoying a historic boom and bonds paying relatively low interest rates, municipals offered real advantages for many high-income people. In that period, municipals tended to be quite safe, as well, with very few defaults or moratoriums. "Defaults" are failures to pay interest or repay principal when due, with bondholders getting some of their money back much later. "Moratoriums" are failures to repay principal when due, with interest payments extended. In either case, bonds tend to lose a good deal of their market value in such situations.

As individual investors tended to move out of the stock market in the late 1960s and early 1970s, and as interest rates began to soar, making bonds generally far more attractive investment vehicles, people in the upper-middle income tax brackets began to buy municipals. Some of those who began to buy might have advantageously invested in municipals long before, but neither knew nor were advised properly as to their net aftertax yield possibilities. As more and more investors began to be interested in municipals, however, brokers began to follow their customers in that direction. Some began to strongly recommend municipals; others began to form and aggressively market mutual funds composed of municipals—more is said about those funds a little later. What investors and brokers were learning about municipals was that, although the interest rates paid on them were almost invariably lower than the interest rates paid on corporate bonds, and even lower than the rates paid on most federal obligations, the tax exemptions they carried enabled some high-income investors to secure higher aftertax yields than were available with any other bonds.

The resulting rush to municipals unfortunately failed to take into account the fact that the same economic factors that had made the stock market unattractive operated throughout the economy and that many of those issuing municipals were in serious economic trouble. That oversight became common knowledge when New York City ran into enormous financing difficulties in the mid-1970s, as did many other issuers in the same period.

In the late 1970s and early 1980s, another problem became apparent. Medium- and long-term municipals, like all other bonds, declined sharply as interest rates rose, and those holding them suffered substantial paper losses. That is, if the municipals were sold before maturity, they had to be sold at a very substantial discount from their face value; if held to maturity, the municipals would pay their face value then, but would pay interest until maturity at rates considerably lower than those currently available. Either way, the municipal holder experienced a real loss in the long run.

Yet the tax break remains. Maturities shorten, lessening the risk of long-term interest rate rises. Insurance is placed on some municipal issues, lessening the risk of default or moratorium. Interest rates on new issues rise to meet the current level of interest in order to compete for buyer attention. Some issuers are still excellent risks and will continue to be so for the foreseeable future, such as some substantial localities in energy-rich Sunbelt states. What is necessary is to view municipals as discrete investments, rather than as a kind of tax break. It is just as unwise to invest in "municipals" as it is to invest in "the market." The wise investment is in the specific municipal issue, just as the wise investment is in the specific company. Although a municipal may carry insurance against default and moratoriums, there is no way to insure against market decline.

There are several kinds of municipal issues. Although they offer somewhat different degrees of safety, investors should, in deciding whether or not to invest in a specific issue, consider primarily the safety, or lack of it, afforded by the total economic situation and the ability to pay of the issuing locality.

Issues called "general" carry a direct and unlimited promise to pay on the part of the issuer and therefore are described as being backed by the "full faith and credit" of the issuer. These are backed by the taxing power of the issuer, which is subject to federal and state restrictions. Only the federal government can create an unlimited balloon of credit; that is not possible for municipals issuers, which is why such obligations, as a group, are not nearly as safe as federal obligations. The federal government can and routinely does raise its own debt limits; lesser governments in the United States cannot.

Short-term tax anticipation notes, sometimes called "warrants," are borrowings that pay interest for the privilege of using your money now, to be repaid in tax receipt money later, and that are intended to be used as smoothing-out devices for government income and expenditure. Tax receipts do not usually follow even collection patterns, with equal amounts collected each month. Instead, receipts wax and wane with tax collection due dates, whereas expenditures tend to be more regular. Since these notes usually carry a prior claim upon receipts and are relatively short term—usually six months or less—they are both relatively safe and less vulnerable to changes in interest rates than are longer-term debt obligations. They tend to be sold in very large denominations to institutional investors and not be directly accessible to individuals, but they are an important part of some mutual funds composed of "money market instruments" and are thereby accessible.

Revenue bonds carry a promise to pay interest and principal out of the revenue coming in from a specific source, for example, from bridge tolls in relation to a bond issued in order to raise funds to build the bridge. They are not backed by a general promise to pay on the part of the issuer. Making the point with an extreme case, the destruction of the bridge by earthquake might bring bridge tolls and bond interest to an end for many years, if not forever. Recently there has been a proliferation of revenue bonds to raise funds for purposes far less secure than bridges and roads. For example, a municipality may issue revenue bonds for an industrial park in order to attract new businesses into the community. The investor must be aware, however, that, while interest rates may be higher than those on other municipal bonds, they really pose a far greater risk, for the industrial park may fail in its purpose, leaving the investor with worthless revenue bonds even though the municipality may continue as a viable entity.

The special assessment bond is, in a sense, a kind of revenue bond, although it is usually classified separately. It carries a promise to pay interest and principal out of special taxes levied in connection with whatever is to be financed with the proceeds of the bond—for example, assessments to a group of homeowners for building a sewer system.

Municipals will continue to be interesting to savers and lenders in upper-middle and high income tax brackets for the foreseeable future. As a group, they are a trap for the unwary—but that may be said of almost any group of investment instruments. As individual investments coupling substantial interest rates with large tax savings, and therefore as proper vehicles for personal financial planning, some can prove quite attractive—as can some of the corporate bonds we discuss now.

Corporate Obligations

Private industry generates several kinds of short- and long-term obligations that may be directly or indirectly purchased by investors. The short-term obligations are "commercial paper"; the longer-term obligations are "bonds."

Short-term corporate debt obligations are traded on national and international money markets, take several forms, and may be secured or unsecured, usually the latter. As of this writing, these corporate debts usually run from 90 to 180 days, are the debts of well-known "blue-chip" companies, and are traded in minimum denominations of $100,000.

Until the late 1970s, investors could not participate in the purchase of such short-term obligations because of the $100,000 minimum size of the instruments, although rates of return and safety factors made these instruments attractive. In recent years, however, investors have been able to purchase participations in money-market mutual funds (of which more is said soon), which provide indirect participation, with the funds buying large participations and selling smaller participations to the public. In future periods of even higher interest rates and even lower stock market prices, companies may turn more directly to the public to satisfy short-term borrowing needs; but they may continue to satisfy those needs by issuing commercial paper bought by banks, mutual funds, pension plans, and other purchasers in large denominations.

Coming as they do from very highly rated major companies, these short-term corporate debt obligations can indeed be quite attractive, usually paying 1.5 to 2.5% more than federal short-term obligations, and carrying low risks. But, for those who are very concerned about the American economy and the possibilities of a major depression, it should be pointed out that there have been some—not many, but some—defaults on short-term corporate obligations in the 1970s and 1980s. Also, the size of the instruments makes it impossible to pick and choose the companies to which you will loan short-term money, since the small investor must buy them through mutual funds. At the same time, the fact that the individual investor buys these obligations as mutual fund shares spreads the risk and minimizes the size of potential default-related losses.

Bonds, on the other hand, are normally issued in denominations that make it possible for most investors to purchase them directly. They are the direct medium- and long-term debt obligations of privately owned companies, including industrial, transportation, utility, and financial organizations. Many of the investors who left the stock market during the 1970s and early 1980s moved into corporate as well as government bonds.

Corporate bonds pay fixed interest rates for specified lengths of time and repay principal at maturity. Like all bonds, they tend to fluctuate with changes in interest rates, declining in value as interest rates rise above their set amounts and increasing in value as interest rates decline below their set amounts. Many companies include call provisions in their bonds, allowing the companies to recall the bonds should interest rates decline below a specified point, so that the issuing company can issue new bonds at lower interest rates, thereby cutting company financing costs.

Corporate bond values, like all bond values, fall sharply when interest rates rise quickly, as they did, for example, in 1979 and 1980. That is a considerable hazard for investors. At the same time, bonds issued by highly regarded American corporations and rated at least "A" by both Moody's and Standard and Poor's are likely to be excellent risks throughout the 1980s. But again, you should not invest in "bonds," but in the debt obligations of specific companies—and you should learn enough about the companies and bonds you have invested in to be able to follow them over the years and make informed decisions about them as necessary.

There are several kinds of corporate bonds. One very special variety, which became popular in the 1960s, is the "convertible," which provides for conversion of the bond into common stock at the option of the bondholder, within bounds specified on issuance by the bond itself. The right to convert is exercised by a holder when the preferred or common stock into which it can be converted rises far enough to make it an attractive move. Until then, the market movement of the stock causes the bond itself to fluctuate somewhat more than other bond market factors, such as interest rates, might do by themselves. Convertible bonds have not been attractive in the 1970s and early 1980s because of the move away from the stock market and into other investment vehicles, although they may become attractive again, as the situation changes.

Corporate bonds may be unsecured by any collateral. In that case, they are often called "debenture bonds," or "debentures." They are then backed by the "full faith and credit" of their issuer, constituting a promise to pay based upon the future business prospects of the company. For some companies, that promise to pay may be enough to create an attractive investment possibility, if coupled with relatively high interest to make up for the lack of collateral. It is quite reasonable, for example, to suppose that

American Telephone and Telegraph will be able to honor its commitments in the foreseeable future. But for most companies some kind of collateral, securing the promise to pay, provides better security for bondholders, especially because many corporate debentures are "subordinated"; that is, they are not unlimited promises to pay, but, rather, promises to pay only after certain other kinds of debts, such as those owed banks and insurance companies, are paid in a business crisis situation, such as bankruptcy.

The collateralized bonds issued by corporations come in several forms. Most of them involve securing the debt instrument with corporate physical assets, such as realty, sometimes directly and sometimes through the creation of intermediary trust instruments, which hold the land and guarantee payment out of assets held. No matter what device is used, the thing to look for is a clear, unambiguous, unencumbered use of physical assets that are likely to hold their value in the event of corporate disaster. That is what any competent lender would look for when loaning you money with your property as collateral—so it should be when you loan money to others.

First-mortgage bonds can be good bond collateral if the property used to secure the mortgage will be able to withstand corporate troubles. For example, a large parcel of improved land in suburban Houston may be excellent security, with the underlying value of the property carrying the value of the bond issue easily. In contrast, a factory near the center of a depressed northern industrial town may be next to worthless, even an expensive white elephant, if closed, and hardly worthwhile security at all. In the latter instance, the bond is still a general promise to pay out of future corporate earnings, just as is a debenture, and should be treated for investment purposes as if it were a debenture, rather than a first-mortgage bond.

General mortgage bonds are often misnamed. They might better be called "second mortgages," for that is what they often are: mortgages on property that is already wholly or partly mortgaged. Often property has appreciated in value, if only because of inflationary factors, and a second mortgage—a borrowing against the additional value of the property—becomes possible.

Existing mortgages take precedence for payment, however, and general mortgage bonds should generally be viewed as if they were debentures.

The main thing to bear in mind when buying corporate bonds is that you are lending money to a corporation mainly upon your estimate of that corporation's current and future strength. If the corporation is strong now and in the future, you will be paid interest and will be repaid principal; if not, you are likely, one way or another, to lose all or some of your invested money. If you invest directly in bonds at all, that argues strongly for investing in the bonds of very strong, major companies with excellent future prospects. And it requires watching those companies, just as if you had bought shares in them. Bonds and other debt instruments are investments to be watched, not to be tucked away. There are not really any "annuity" stocks and bonds, or "widows' and orphans' " investments, to be bought and put away and to sit unexamined over the years, yielding safe, excellent interest and dividends for generations. There never were, but it is more apparent now, in this time of financial concern and chaotic financial market conditions.

STOCKS

Ah, "the stock market," the preoccupation of some millions of investors during the booming 1950s and 1960s, the source of enormous anguish in the late 1960s and early 1970s, and the target of repeated predictions of impending renascence in the early 1980s. For many professionals and most amateurs, a heart-quickening gambling game, no matter how soberly approached with all the jargon of finance and statistics.

"The market" is a place where today's selling language becomes tomorrow's impressive language of finance, where new jargon is coined daily to describe old phenomena, where those "in the know" usually know very little, and where many "professionals" exhibited a pronounced tendency to cling to their preconceptions and illusions during the 1970s, only later to follow their erstwhile "amateur" clients out of stocks and into several other higher-yielding investment forms.

Yet, although stocks have not been a terribly popular investment form in the early 1980s—at least as of the time of this writing—some stocks will turn out to have been excellent investment vehicles when we look back at them from 20 and 30 years on. Some stocks—not the stock market. For, once again, you are investing in a company, in an ownership share of a specific company, not in a kind of investment vehicle, and not in "the stock market." Because stocks are ownership shares, not debts, and are in no way insurable, it is even more vital to analyze their issuers with extreme care before buying them. When you buy a stock, you buy a piece of a company, with the hope of sharing, through dividends, in the current profits of that company and of sharing in the growth of total value of that company as reflected in higher market value for the shares you have purchased. What you hold is a certificate, embodying those hopes and your ownership equity. You are a stockholder, a shareholder, an equityholder—they are synonyms.

The standard form of stock ownership is "common stock," which is capital stock that is in no way limited and whose owner fully shares the risks and possible gains of the company. The owner of common stock votes in company affairs, although, as a practical matter, that vote rarely has any real impact on the conduct of those affairs. Common stock is freely negotiable and may be traded on a recognized stock exchange or over the counter—more on that soon.

A much less used form of stock issue and ownership is "preferred stock," which provides an equity position somewhat senior to that of common stock, in which the owner receives stated amounts of dividends before dividends are paid to common stockholders, sometimes has considerably greater voting rights than the owner of common stock does, and sometimes has the right to cumulative dividends, meaning the collection of dividends later, if no dividend is currently declared. At the same time, the owner of preferred stock does not share in dividends declared beyond the stock's stated amounts.

The stocks of substantial corporations are traded on recognized stock exchanges, including the New York and American Stock Exchanges and a number of regional exchanges in North America, as well as on major exchanges throughout the world. Thousands of stocks, sometimes of quite large corporations, are traded on no exchanges; these are traded "over the counter," through a national and international body of brokers, linked together by trade associations and computer networks. All brokers and traders together, on and off recognized exchanges, constitute the stock market, although in common usage "the market" often means the New York Stock Exchange. Even more narrowly, the question "What did the market do today?" usually means "What did the Dow Jones industrial average do today?" That is one of three stock averages maintained by Dow Jones and Company, the others being transportation and utilities stock averages, all being widely regarded as the most standard stock market indicators, even though such organizations as Standard and Poor's and the *New York Times* also maintain stock averages.

To understand how stocks may or may not fit into your financial planning, it is necessary to examine patterns of growth and yield in order to be able to make comparisons between stocks and between stocks and other investments.

When a corporation is "publicly held"—that is, when it has sold some of its ownership equity to the public—control of operations and policies is still in the hands of those who either hold a controlling interest or form a self-perpetuating management elite within that corporation. A corporation may have sold only 30% of its ownership to the public and be controlled by a single founding family owning 70%. Or it may have sold 80% to the public and be controlled by a group holding as little as 10% of its stock. Or its stock may be so widely held that no single group of stockholders control it, but management does. In any case, the smaller investors in that corporation most emphatically do not control it, and corporate policies will reflect attempts to grow the corporation and to make it more and more profitable, certainly paying dividends to stockholders, if only to maintain the market value of the stock, but with far more attention paid to the internal needs of the company than to the dividend desires of the stockholders.

Add to that the fact that corporate profits are taxable and that a prime corporate objective is to minimize taxes, an objective encouraged by tax laws encouraging reinvestment of profits in the corporation, and it is easy to see that there are some powerful reasons for corporate management to reinvest, show profit—but not too much—and keep dividends at an attractive, but "reasonable," level. Dividends voted by management to stockholders—always a matter of management's discretion in the case of common stock—vary considerably, but a time-tested rule of thumb is that they will average about 50% of aftertax profits. Of course, a specific corporation may profit greatly and vote a much-larger-than-average proportion of aftertax profits as dividends; that is a very important reason for buying pieces of specific companies rather than investing in "the market."

The result is a rather low profit share for stockholders. But stockholders have not usually expected more—most stocks are brought primarily not for their dividends, but rather for a combination of dividends and the increased values resulting from that constant reinvestment and company growth that is translated into higher stock prices. That is the way it worked in the great bull market of the 1950s and 1960s, and that is what stopped working in the late 1960s and has not worked at all in the 1970s and early 1980s, at least until the time of this writing.

The truth is that the general level of stock values has not gone up appreciably in more than a decade, while dividends have gone up, but not nearly as quickly as the rate of inflation, and yields on several other kinds of investments have gone up very much more than total aftertax stock yields, even including any minor increases in stock values; as a result there has been very little interest in investing in most stocks and very little reason to generate such an interest. When, in the late 1970s and early 1980s, interest rates and investment yields went up suddenly and sharply, there was even less reason to invest in most stocks, for the yield comparisons between most stocks and many other instruments became even less favorable to stocks.

But the stocks of some well-established, major, publicly owned firms do have a place in your financial planning, as they have had in the past and will have again. The combination of long-term growth and dividends stemming from purchase of a high-grade common stock—at the right price—can, in significant ways, provide better security and just as high earnings in the long run as money that follows the short-term swings of a high-interest-paying, but chaotic, bond market. We do not recommend specific stocks here; that would be exceedingly foolish in a book that is written long before it is published and perhaps years before it is read by a specific reader. However, in investing, you should look at long-term possibilities, such as those that are inherent in firms heavily involved in energy in an energy-poor world, in information in a world involved in an information explosion, and in medical technology in a world witnessing major breakthroughs in the health care field and life sciences. The specifics depend greatly on short-term trends and prices at the time you are ready to invest.

At a time when investment vehicles of a certain kind are unpopular, thoughtful investors will look even harder for specific investments of that kind. For example, the last time stocks were quite as unpopular as they are at the time of this writing was during the 1930s, after the catastrophe of the 1929 Crash and the Great Depression that followed. That was a time when a little long-term investment money went a long way, with the stocks of major, heavily capitalized corporations available at very low prices, compared to their dividend yields and reasonable growth possibilities. It was also a time when a very small "speculation" in the stock of a new firm, but one known well to the investor, might be lost or might yield very large profits later. Although we are not in the midst of another Great Depression, in some ways the situation is similar. There are "buys" in the stocks of some major firms. There are small firms starting now that will be big firms in a decade or two—there always are. There are always investment possibilities in the stock market and never more than when "the market" is unpopular with the great mass of investors.

It can be as simple as investing in the firm in which you are employed—if it's a good investment, not out of misguided loyalty. If it is a good investment, as an employee you are better qualified than most to find out; if it is not, the same is true. You may even have stock options available as a fringe benefit through your company, enabling you to buy company stock on favorable and somewhat tax-advantaged terms. A dividend reinvestment plan may be appropriate, through which you reinvest any dividends received from your company stock in more company stock, growing your stake even faster. You will have to pay taxes on those dividends, but the accretion of the stock plus reinvested dividends may help create a useful and quite sizable investment over the years. It is often well worth doing, if the company is as good an investment as any other you can find, if you can sell the stock without any kind of penalty when you will, and if you do not have to borrow high-interest money to buy the stock.

Finding the right stocks to buy at any time, and especially when stocks are declining, is real work. It may require considerable discussion with others, such as brokers, bankers, accountants; considerable reading about the company you are considering for investment; considerable thought about the medium- and long-term prospects of that company and the field or fields in which it operates. It requires bearing in mind that no matter how astute a broker you have, or believe you have, a broker is in business to do business; it is a rare broker indeed who will not have some recommendation to make, even though that recommendation will not be as good as something else a month or two later. The old saw is that nobody watches your business as carefully as you do yourself—and it is true.

We are not here suggesting anything remotely resembling speculation. If you feel that your total financial position is excellent, and you want to take a few thousand dollars and try to run it up in the stock market, or in commodities, precious metals, or some other kind of speculative investment, go right ahead. You may be doing some informed gambling, but it is still gambling; that has very little to do with the kind of financial planning we are discussing, which is total and for a lifetime. You can open a credit account with a broker, called a "margin account." You can buy and sell "short," meaning with borrowed money, in which the impact of gain or loss is magnified by the impact of further borrowing.

You can look for "special situations," meaning companies that afford particularly good profit opportunities, usually because they are in considerable trouble and are alleged by securities sellers to be about to "turn around," that is, to begin coming out of that trouble to profit and grow. These situations are rare, especially when encountered in a period of general economic difficulty and high interest rates, and usually are merely an opportunity to lose your money as the company in trouble keeps on going downhill.

You can look for "growth" stocks, those that pay little or nothing in dividends, but show a strong growth in business and stock values. If they are major companies, and if your dividend need at your time of life is small, sometimes that can turn out well. But beware the fashionable smallish company in a period in which stocks have regained some popularity; you may buy an upward trend stemming from that popularity, rather than anything real, and lose a good deal of your money.

A fund for these kinds of speculations has little or nothing to do with financial planning, any more than racetrack or dice table winnings or losings would. If you are so minded, though, be sure that you really are in a good financial position and have taken into account the impact of inflation and high interest rates. Do nothing that will force you to put good money in after bad, such as paying interest and repaying principal on borrowed money lost in speculation. Try not to get caught in gambling fever, for that is what stock market and other investment instrument speculation is. And do not confuse gambling fever with long-term financial planning, as so many did in the 1960s, to their intense and long-term sorrow.

MUTUAL FUNDS

A "mutual fund" is a company organized to invest the money of others; the term is synonymous with "investment company." It is not an individually direct kind of investment, such as stocks, bonds, real estate, commodities, or collectibles, but rather a pool of money used to invest in one or more kinds of investments.

When you buy a share in a mutual fund, you purchase a share in a pool of values managed by those managing the fund. The share purchased may be in an "open-end fund," which is a fund that will sell shares on a continuing basis to all comers, growing as large as possible through a combination of share purchases and hoped-for growth in the market value of the investment instruments held by the fund, whatever they may be; this is the most common form of mutual fund. Or the share purchased may be in a "closed-end investment fund," a less common form, which has issued a set number of shares on formation and tries to gain in value solely through investment instrument growth. Shares in many closed-end funds are traded freely, being treated like common stocks for trading purposes.

In either case, the fund's managers charge share purchasers fees for management of their money. These fees are variously computed, but in all instances must be large enough to cover management costs, profit, and, in front-loaded funds, quite substantial promotion costs. As always, there is no free lunch.

In the 1960s, when open-end funds investing mainly or wholly in stocks first became very popular, it was quite common for mutual funds to charge whopping "front-load" charges against investors' accounts, when they were investing periodically in "contractual" plans, meaning that substantial sums were deducted from initial investments to defray sizable selling costs. Under those circumstances, investors selling their mutual fund shares within a year or two of purchase sometimes found that they had dramatically decreased in value, even while the stock market was rising. But the mutual fund industry was competitive, with many sellers vying for buyer attention, and some sellers found it profitable to change modest fees for noncontractual plans or to do business in a "no-load" fashion, still charging management fees, but spreading them and cutting selling costs so that there was little start-up cost for the investor, who was then able to get out of a mutual fund when he or she desired, without the losses caused by front-load arrangements.

It is important to understand that the management of your investments by others always costs money. A mutual fund may be a perfectly fine idea, given your circumstances and interests and the possibilities opened up by getting professional help and pooling your money with that of others. You may be able to invest thereby in large-scale and highly profitable financial instruments that you would not be able to buy as a small investor. You may be able to diversify your holdings through participation in the fund's purchases and so avoid the "all-your-eggs-in-one-basket" risk. You may think very highly of the fund's management, feeling that, with its professional skills, it will do far better in the investment marketplace than you could.

But it will still cost you money, just as any professional investment management will cost you money. Mutual fund fees are really no different in principle than the fees paid by a trust to a bank that is managing that trust on behalf of its beneficiaries; they are no different than the fees paid an investment manage-. ment firm to handle all or part of your investments. The essence of the transaction is the same in all three instances. When you buy or sell an investment for your own account, you may pay a bank or broker a one-time fee for transacting your business; however, when you give your money to others to manage for you, by mutual fund purchase or in any other form, you are contracting to pay for that management for as long as that money is professionally managed, rather than on a one-time fee basis.

In truth, mutual funds do provide diversification and therefore diminish risk, although a mutual fund composed of volatile stocks in a dropping market or of municipal bonds in a period of soaring interest rates, offers nothing like the safety and profit available from short-term federal obligations. It is also true that money market funds investing in large-scale financial instruments can obtain somewhat higher returns than smaller individual investors can get on their own. These returns are somewhat offset by the management fees you will pay one way or another for management of the funds, and your investment is potentially at considerably greater risk if fund managers become adventurous in their search for higher yields—especially in a depressed economy.

On the other hand, although some mutual funds outperformed the general levels of common stock prices at times during the bull markets of the 1950s and 1960s, their professional managers did no better than the general level of stock prices during the period of great decline. Most fund managers exhibited a deplorable tendency to stay within their established investment patterns, at most moving their funds into more liquid positions rather than finding ways to move into better-yielding forms of investment.

Some investment managers developed an extraordinary investment theory—extraordinary in that it was so absurd. It was called "indexing," and it added up to an attempt to organize and weight portfolio holdings so as to duplicate as nearly as possible the performance of a major stock index, such as the Dow Jones industrial average. Investors were then presented with the spectacle of "professionals" who were trained and paid to make money on investments, but who instead made a virtue of trying to perform only as well as a stock average. It was a classic case of attempting to create virtue out of necessity as the stock market declined.

The quality of the professional management available is only one of the problems in mutual fund investment. At least as serious are the related problems of habit and established promise. Although some funds are "balanced," meaning that they are able and willing to invest in several kinds of investments at once, many mutual funds tend to invest in a single kind of investment vehicle. That is the nature of their charter in most instances and therefore the nature of the set of established promises held out to potential investors, as well as of the set of established investment habits of its managers. It makes for a peculiar kind of contradiction. Investors buy professional management when they move into mutual funds, yet, in an uncertain investment climate, investors tend to move to new investment vehicles faster than do most professional investment managers, whose commitments and habits make it more difficult to move. It is quite natural and even absolutely necessary for those managing a common stock fund to continue to invest in common stocks, while investors have begun to move in large numbers to money market instruments and real estate—but it is very bad investment management nonetheless, and nothing that anyone should be paying for. It is equally natural and even necessary for those managing real estate and money market funds to be slow and locked in when it is time to move back into common stocks. In both instances, however, the investor is paying for professional management and finding that it does not help and that it may even hinder proper investment timing, causing unnecessary losses. The original decision to put money into a mutual fund might have been a good one—but once again, it is clear that nobody can watch your interests as carefully as you do yourself, if you take the time and trouble to become—and to stay—informed. Those whose money is invested in mutual funds will do well to consider investing in "families" of funds, which allow you to switch from one kind of fund to another, for as little as a $5 fee, as market conditions and your own estimates indicate.

There are nearly as many kinds of mutual funds as there are investment goals, techniques, and vehicles. Some of the largest are the "balanced" funds, which move their resources relatively freely between several kinds of investment vehicles, normally holding resources in several kinds of investments at once and changing the mix held when fund managers feel that market conditions call for doing so. A "balanced" fund may have had by far the greatest bulk of its assets in common stock in the mid-1960s and, by the late 1970s and early 1980s, may have moved largely into bonds and short-term obligations. During the speculative 1960s, these kinds of funds were often described as "conservative," and so they were—compared with a number of get-rich-quick funds then popular and sold hard by investment "professionals." The ability to move in one investment direction and then another as conditions changed, however, proved extremely valuable in the chaotic late 1970s and early 1980s—and the "balanced" funds outlasted many more narrowly based funds.

Many other funds were popular then and may become popular again as investment climates change, although perhaps under different names. Common stock funds were widely sold. Investing solely in common stock, these funds sailed up in value with the booming stock market of the time, their investors happy with their gains, and their sellers and managers happy with the money they charged investors for successfully managing their money. Of course, most of them were front loaded and were sold for "long-term appreciation" rather than for current dividends. People bought them for the long haul, counted their paper profits, and then watched in disbelief as those paper profits evaporated, with their common-stock-based mutual fund shares sinking at least as fast as the market did at the end of the 1960s—and those were funds that were mainly invested in "blue chips." The funds that were mainly invested in more speculative stocks sank far, far faster and lost much, much more.

In addition, there were "growth" funds, heavily invested in common stocks that were moving up fast, whose company managements were putting all or almost all profits back in the business and paying little or no dividends. There were "hedge" funds, operating even more speculatively and failing even more spectacularly. There were "convertible" funds, investing in convertibles, which were touted as supplying enormous amounts of "upside" potential and very little "downside" risk—an assumption that proved less than correct in a decade-long stagnant market. There were also "index" funds, aimed at matching the performance of stock market indexes, and even "funds of funds," which invested solely in shares of other mutual funds. The "fund of funds" was a particularly damaging device. It added a second layer of selling and management fees to the layer that was characteristic of all funds, making it that much more difficult for even the best-invested "fund of funds" to do well in the investment marketplace.

In the early 1980s many of these kinds of common stock funds have disappeared, to be replaced by other kinds of funds better suited for the current investment climate. But although forms change, concepts change less quickly. The "special purpose fund" of the 1980s is first cousin to the common stock funds of the 1960s. These are funds investing in a narrow range of equities and debt obligations in which are thought of by their managers as fast-growing and particularly lucrative business areas, such as energy and oil. For the investor seeking to make a quick speculative profit, those kinds of areas may indeed prove lucrative—and can be invested in directly, rather than though a fund. Indeed, such areas really call for careful investigation of specific companies and opportunities, rather than for blanket investment in an area through a fund. For the investor trying to do some rational long-term financial planning, get-rich-quick special purpose funds can be the same kind of snare that the common stock funds were in the 1960s.

In the late 1970s one major new fund form did develop, as tax-advantaged "municipals" gained favor with investors disillusioned with the stock market and common stock fund performances. Municipal bonds and municipal bond funds in that period seemed to many to be excellent alternatives, with aftertax yields far higher than those offered by common stock funds, coupled with the greater safety of bonds, as compared to common stocks. Some were excellent, some weren't. Some are, some aren't. It soon became clear that, in periods of intense inflation, the already strained finances of many municipal bond issuers became overstrained. The New York City debacle of the mid-1970s was spectacular, but in many ways only a warning of what might happen to the values of bonds issued by near-bankrupt issuers.

In the early 1980s another problem emerged, one common to all medium- and long-term bonds in a period of disastrous inflation and soaring interest rates. Municipal bonds, and funds composed of municipal bonds, suffered sharp drops in value as interest rates went up, with money seeking the higher new rates and forcing existing bond prices down. It became possible for a municipal bond fund composed of sound, quite safe obligations to lose from 15 to 20% of its value in a very short time, as interest rates skyrocketed and investors moved into directly purchased short-term obligations and "money market" funds.

Money-market mutual funds invest solely in short-term debt obligations, those maturing in less than one year, and carry average maturities of less than 120 days. They are diversified, carrying no more than 5% of their assets in the obligations of a single issuer, except for those of the United States government. A child of the 1970s, the money market fund is an alternative worth considering for very many financial planning situations; such funds vary widely in terms of the contents of their portfolios, maturity of their instruments, and tax considerations. In periods of rising interest rates, they tend to invest largely in very short-term obligations, very often heavily investing, for example, in overnight loans to banks. In this way, they are able to take advantage of rising interest rates as soon as they occur. They are completely negotiable at any time. In periods of lowering interest rates, money market funds tend to invest in somewhat longer term obligations, but still within the previously cited bounds, in order to hold better-than-current interest rates as long as possible. Money market funds invest in a wide variety of short-term debt obligations, such as overnight loans, Treasury bills and other federal obligations, bankers' acceptances, the commercial paper of large companies, bank certificates of deposit, and Eurodollars. Some of the kinds of debt instruments they buy are fully insured, such as Treasury bills. Some are in no way insured, but are substantially recession-resistant, such as commercial paper. Some may be recession-resistant, but are partially dependent on international political questions, such as Eurodollars.

Alone among kinds of stock and bond funds, money market funds offer a kind of investment opportunity that less-than-wealthy investors cannot reach for on their own. Some kinds of short-term obligations, such as commercial paper and some government obligations, are issued in such large denominations that most individual investors cannot invest in them—and sometimes their interest rates are very attractive. The money market funds, pooling, as they do, large sums of money, can and do routinely buy obligations with minimum denominations of as much as $100,000, therefore providing their investors with a significant advantage.

On the other hand, money market funds should be investigated just as carefully as any other funds and should be watched just as carefully, as well. The same chaotic economic conditions that cause double-digit inflation and steeply climbing interest rates can bring about the undoing of substantial issuers of short-term money market instruments. That is particularly true of those funds that invest heavily in international debt obligations, which are subject to political and economic pressures that cannot be anticipated or controlled. It may not matter that the fund in which you have invested is diversified if diversification partially consists of many investments in a particularly shaky kind of issuer, with many issuers capable of getting into the same kind of serious trouble at once.

In essence, a money market fund is very much like a bank, but not nearly as heavily insured and regulated. The difference for you is that your fund interest is almost invariably higher than that on demand deposits in commercial banks or on conventional savings accounts. It may or may not be higher than the interest on certificates of deposit issued by banks. In a volatile period in which interest rates fluctuate, the money market funds, with money maturing over a period of 120 days, will tend to pay lower interest than banks whose certificates of deposit can immediately reflect higher interest rates. On the other hand, as interest rates level off or decrease, money market funds will pay higher interest than certificates of deposit. (That balance may shift if federal law is changed to allow banks to pay you market rates of interest as high as the funds pay.) At the same time, your funds are not federally insured, making it far more necessary to take considerable care in choosing a fund than in choosing a bank. For many investors, the modest additional risk involved in buying a share in a money market fund is overbalanced by the interest rates and liquidity available in such a fund. For others, directly purchased Treasury bills and other federal obligations seem safer, although usually paying slightly lower rates of interest. For yet others, fully insured bank certificates of deposit, though not as liquid, seem to offer the right mix of safety, liquidity, and rate of return. For those deeply concerned about the safety of the whole banking system, and about the possibility of another Great Depression, money market funds in the main will not do—no debt obligations or ownership shares will. Assuming there will be no second Crash, however, carefully selected debt obligations are a major way of minimizing the impact of inflation and high interest rates.

Many money market funds also have a no-cost checking privilege, usually in a minimum of $500. This is excellent for "float" money, which is being held until it is placed in a more permanent home, or for money to be warehoused as it comes and goes. The money fund investment is not diminished until a check written on it is actually cashed, so it earns daily interest for the period of time between the writing of the check and its tender for payment at the mutual fund bank. Businesses and individuals who write checks for more than $500 can therefore earn daily interest without diverting their funds from their normal business or personal activities.

Yet the very real fear of hard times coupled with inflation—a mixture that can in some ways be worse than the experience of economic depression—has caused many investors to seek out opportunities that were designed to be both inflation-proof and depression-proof. As the pessimistic investment climate and bad economic news of the late 1970s and early 1980s developed, more and more people turned to what were, for them, new investment instruments. It is to these instruments that we now turn.

CHAPTER
6
Hedges and Speculations:

Gold, Silver, and Other Commodities; Stock Options; Collectibles

The future of the American economy has been a subject of great concern in recent years, and for many excellent reasons. Bad economic news and chaotic stock market conditions have caused many people to anticipate a Crash worse than that of 1929, preceded by a runaway inflation more like that of the 1920s in Germany than that of American experience in the same period.

As of this writing, it has not happened—nor do we think it very likely to happen. But even if it does, the very conservative investment strategy and long-term planning approach we think correct should take most people through to the other side of a second Crash.

What will take no one through a second Crash, or for that matter through a deep recession far short of a real Crash, is speculation disguised as hedging against hard times. Nor will anyone be very likely to make a "pile" by becoming an amateur speculator in investment instruments that are extraordinarily risky even in the hands of seasoned professionals who make their livings trading those instruments. Advertisements clutter the pages of the *Wall Street Journal* and other financial periodicals, in which a multitude of soothsayers offer—for a fee—to send advice about how to avoid the impending financial catastrophe. Some of the worst personal financial problems people experience during a period of runaway inflation stem from the panic that such a period engenders. People see their lifetime savings begin to disappear as inflation takes a huge bite out of those savings every year and as the ability to save at all is sharply curtailed by increases in the cost of living that are far from matched by income gains. New prophets, made rich by the sale of their financial advice, not their personal investment records, advise increasingly frightened people to invest their dwindling assets in get-rich-quick investment vehicles. These advisors, often directly contradicting each other, suggest everything from stocking canned food to cornering the gold market. Like many religious sects predicting the end of the world on a given date, these advisors change their predictions as the "doomsday" passes, and they offer a new panacea. Such advisors promise that astute "leveraging" (which means investing with borrowed money) will guarantee wealth— or that astute hoarding of "things" will make it possible to beat inflation and the coming crash.

But leveraging works both ways. When a particular kind of market is rising, working with lots of borrowed money can work fine—for a while. When that market goes down, you can lose your real investment in the twinkling of an eye. And "things," pushed up in value by hundreds of thousands of other frightened people who are also hoarding them, can go down in value as fast as they went up, with those who jumped on a particular fad or bandwagon late buying high and ultimately selling very low, losing much of their painfully acquired savings in the process.

Putting it that way makes speculative investing seem absurd for those trying to do serious, successful, long-term financial planning. And so it is. Yet people panic, often for good reason in bad and uncertain times, and mistake some kinds of speculations for inflation and depression hedges. Under certain circumstances, however, some such "hedges" can be advantageous—as long as they are handled conservatively, not speculatively. Even so, you should explore carefully the particular investment situation, assess soberly the risks involved, and commit only a small percentage of your assets to such ventures.

GOLD AND OTHER COMMODITIES

Gold is a classic example of a hedge against inflation that has far greater risks than most investors anticipate. Because of price swings, gold often becomes a speculative instrument for buyers and sellers, rather than the simple long-term hedge against inflation that many purchasers desire.

Gold is a commodity, and in many ways its market behavior is little different from that of most other commodities. When supply is relatively large, and when world and national economic conditions are relatively stable, it tends to diminish in price. When those conditions are chaotic, and when supply does not increase, or the freely traded supply actually diminishes because of hoarding, it tends to rise in price. Because of hoarding, supply conditions, economic and political sensitivity, and the mystique that surrounds gold, its price in our time tends to rise and fall somewhat more sharply than that of many other commodities. Stated in these terms, gold market behavior is neither full of mystique nor very complicated. What is complicated—and extraordinarily so—are the vagaries of the international gold markets, which depend very heavily on political priorities and the actions of large commodity traders, speculators, hoarders, and users.

In dealing with gold, it is crucial at all times to know that governments, notably those of South Africa, the Soviet Union, and the United States, and such international bodies as the International Monetary Fund can sharply affect the price of gold by either withholding gold from the world's supply or dumping stocks of gold on the world market in pursuit of national and international policy aims. South Africa and the Soviet Union, as major gold producers, can both withhold and dump; the United States and other national and international holders can only dump.

South Africa firmly controls the supply of gold from its mines, determining the annual amount released to the world market in accordance with its own economic needs. The Soviet Union uses its massive gold supplies to soften the impact of its production failures or to help them meet other economic and political objectives. In 1973 and 1974, for example, the Soviet Union put large amounts of its gold on the world market, which drove gold prices down but at the same time allowed the Soviet Union to purchase wheat and other grains at a time when their crops had failed due to drought. Similarly, China's very large gold reserves may very well appear on the world gold market to fund the major industrial and technological modernization programs that China has undertaken since Mao's death. Governmental decisions regarding gold supplies are unpredictable, but the appearance of new gold supplies on the market can only weaken the price of gold.

Traders, speculators, and hoarders can also affect the prices of gold and other precious metals considerably. Hoarders—and they are to be found all over the world, not only in the Middle East and other extremely volatile areas—buy and tend to hold indefinitely, diminishing the amount of gold in trading circulation and tending to drive prices up. Industrial users, such as the jewelry industry, diminish supply by taking gold out of trading circulation. Traders and speculators drive the price of gold up in a rising market as they buy, with a multiplication effect caused by their use of borrowed money.

On the way down, that multiplier can work in reverse, as was most spectacularly demonstrated by the experience of Nelson Bunker Hunt and his associates in early 1980, when their silver purchases turned into very bad speculative investments. They had purchased massive amounts of silver, using both cash and borrowed money, and in the process had driven the price of silver up from about $6 an ounce to about $50 an ounce in a little over a year. As market conditions changed, and as interest rates on borrowed speculative money went up very sharply all over the world—more than tripling in the United States in a short period—other speculators and the Hunts themselves found it increasingly difficult to hold their speculative positions. Ultimately, the bubble burst. Silver went down to a little over $10 an ounce, banks withdrew financing, brokers sold out positions to meet margin requirements and save themselves from bankruptcy, and the speculators lost hundreds of millions of dollars—by some estimates billions of dollars. Many unrelated buyers and sellers of silver were caught up in the downturn, with disastrous results.

Yet the mystique of gold, resulting largely from gold's historic role as the "hardest" store of value and medium of exchange, brings with it an inevitable tendency toward both hoarding and speculation, encouraged by gold's long-term tendency to hold and even increase its real value as compared to all other stores of value. There is one very well defined investment school, that of the "gold bugs," who insist that in the long run gold is the only reliable store of value and that governments inevitably debase their own currencies and repudiate their debts, even to their own people.

That may or may not be true, but does not inevitably lead to the conclusion that gold is the ultimate store of value. The truth is that no major modern government anywhere in the world backs its currency with gold. All major governments, in a closely interconnected set of world economic orders, back their currencies with only their "full faith and credit," which is merely a naked promise to pay, backed by the power of the state. Any government can prohibit—and in this century many have prohibited—ownership of gold and other precious metals by its citizens, and confiscate privately held stocks of precious metals. Without notice, any tomorrow.

Looking at it that way, gold as a refuge against political and economic catastrophe might make sense—for people living on the edge of political disaster all over the Middle East and South America. But for Americans, the saving of gold as such a refuge supposes the ability to store gold in a "safe" foreign country and the ability to go get it and to live on it elsewhere in the world, under conditions of crisis and complete political and economic breakdown in the United States. What is sometimes not so clearly understood is that the kind of breakdown that might destroy the United States' economic system would also destroy that of much of the rest of the world and would probably be accompanied by the kinds of conditions that would make canned goods, pound for pound, quite as valuable as gold. Something you cannot legally hold or trade would not be much of a refuge under such conditions. It might be of some use at a later time, assuming that crises were surmounted and a new political and economic system emerged, but that is a very tenuous reason for burying gold in your backyard.

Putting the classic hoarding reasons aside, then, gold must be considered fundamentally as an investment. As an investment, it has some strengths and some weaknesses. Its outstanding strength is that, in our time, its value does tend to grow at or better than the rate of inflation and should continue to do so over the long run—even if governments do some dumping of gold stocks. Such dumping might have disastrous short-term effects—but on speculators and traders, not on long-term financial planners.

The main thing to bear in mind in this connection is that gold selling in the $400- to $800-per-ounce range is not high. Not high? But it was selling at $35 an ounce as recently as the late 1960s. Yes, but at government-regulated prices. Gold was selling at a government-regulated $20.67 per ounce for most of the nineteenth century and for the first third of the twentieth century. It went up to $35 per ounce in the 1930s and took off to find some kind of real market price when the United States, which had held world prices at that $35 until the late 1960s, eliminated price control. One hundred years ago, gold was selling at $20.67 per ounce at a time when the average weekly wage in the United States was about $8. In the intervening century, supply conditions have changed—more than three-quarters of all the gold in the world has been produced in the twentieth century—but so have demand conditions, in terms of world wealth, population, and usage factors. In a rough and summary comparison, an average weekly wage of about $300 relates to $8 as does a $600 to $800 range to $20.67. Although this comparison may be a gross oversimplification in economic terms, in investment terms it is quite sufficient.

Gold does tend to hold its value in relation to other goods. In a period of inflation and fear, it will probably rise somewhat in relation to other goods. At the same time, it yields no income of any kind until it is sold. That makes it necessary to be able to hold the gold you have purchased for long-term investment purposes until a right time to sell—which may not be when you are ready, but as long as a year or two later.

If you have some money to put into gold—and it should never be more than a small proportion of your investment money—the ideal thing is to buy "against" the market. The only thing you can be sure of in the world of investments is that market prices of all kinds will fluctuate, and gold will fluctuate a great deal, as mystique and panic force its price up in bad times and as a turn to other seemingly more attractive investment opportunities forces its price down in good times. Like many other long-term investments, gold is best bought in good times, when it seems least attractive, and best sold in bad times, when it seems most attractive. The worst possible time to buy it is in a time of panic and fear.

As to speculating in gold and other precious metals—don't. The rationale that there is little "downside" risk, meaning that you will not lose too much of your money if it goes down because of the intrinsic value of the investment, is just that—a rationale. Speculating in gold in a rising market puts you into competition with professional traders and speculators all over the world, who watch gold and other precious metals every hour of every day, as you cannot possibly hope to do. If you buy precious metals high in a rising market and are forced to sell low, you may lose your shirt. If you hold the metals, waiting for long-term factors to reassert themselves, you may sell out your holdings years later at the dollar amounts you paid for them, but lose much of your money anyway, because of the inexorable loss of value of the dollar due to inflation. In the interim, you will also have lost the income that might have been generated by your capital.

There is very little virtue and much danger in speculating "a little," by taking a small percentage of your investment money and putting it into gold or other speculations. Another name for speculation is gambling, especially when it is indulged in by amateurs. Gambling has its own laws of development, being a fever that rises with a little exposure and that can lead to total financial destruction. And gold is particularly seductive to speculators, as it was to alchemists for more than 2000 years.

The development is simple enough. First you take a couple of thousand dollars and put it into gold or some other speculative investment in a rising market for that kind of investment. You make some money and then reinvest it. Sooner or later, and usually with the help of an obliging broker, you discover the delightful possibilities of "leverage" and expand your investments through use of borrowed money in a margin account. Then, as other investments seem less and less attractive in comparison to the one you are riding with, you convince yourself that it is not a speculation at all, but a perfectly sound, sane, and conservative investment vehicle—and further, one that is paying far better than some of your other investments. At that point, entirely seduced by the money you are making, you put yourself wholeheartedly into the speculative investment vehicle, "leveraging" as much as possible, that is, borrowing as much and putting in as little cash as possible. Ultimately, as even such wealthy, professionally advised people as the Hunts found out, the bubble bursts.

Gold, silver, platinum, uranium, diamonds, and other gemstones—all are precious metals and minerals that can be invested in, used, saved, speculated in, and traded. One way of investing in them is to buy and take physical possession of them. Another is to trade in the stocks of companies mining, selling, and trading in precious metals and minerals. These stocks are part of the stock market, but have a special character because of the nature of the goods handled; very often they respond more to the market price movements of the goods these companies produce and sell than to longer-term evaluations of the companies' corporate performances and prospects.

In a sense, that is as it should be; the long-term world price rise in gold in the 1970s and 1980s, for example, changed the profit prospects of gold-mining companies enormously, as it did current valuations of their stocks of gold on hand and their mining properties. Similarly, a sharp drop in silver prices after a speculative price rise may considerably harm the profit anticipations of silver-mining companies for the following year.

However, such market fluctuations are only part of the picture. Normal stock market investment rules apply to precious metals and gemstones stocks. You should not invest in a kind of stock, but rather in a company, no matter how attractive the kind of stock seems at the moment. One company may be better managed than another. One set of mining properties may be nearly exhausted, another carrying decades of proven reserves. One mining company may be located in Canada, whose political situation would be stable enough even if the country split into French- and English-speaking nations; another company, perhaps a leading world producer of gold and diamonds, may be located in South Africa—as so many are—and be a very questionable investment indeed in a period when intense pressure is being exerted upon that white-dominated country by a number of other African nations. Although "Buy American" is not particularly astute investment advice, carrying with it, as it does, a load of emotion that has nothing to do with analysis, "Buy North American" may be a soundly cautious approach to investing in companies in the mining industries. The political questions may be more and more important as this century draws to its close.

For the individual investor, some precious metals and gemstones differ from most other commodities in that they may be purchased and held. An ounce of gold, a pound of silver, a diamond—all may be bought, physically taken, and put away somewhere. Industrial users of these kinds of commodities also buy for use or holding. Kodak, for example, buys hundreds of tons of silver every year for use in its photographic products. For that kind of industrial user, it is imperative that future supplies be assured, and at determinable prices. Therefore, over several centuries of dealing in commodities, a worldwide set of "futures" markets has developed, which deals in both current commodities sales, called "spot" sales, and in contracts to buy commodities up to a year in the future, called "futures" contracts.

Organized commodities exchanges exist all over the world, on which there is trading of a wide variety of spot and future commodities contracts. Some of the commodities traded are corn, wheat, soybeans, pork bellies, cattle, sugar, cocoa, cotton, and precious metals. In addition, in recent years trading has become active in such noncommodities as currency and other financial instruments. What is being traded is a contract specifying future delivery or receipt—stemming from sale or purchase—of stated amounts of the commodity or other item of value at a specific time. Each contract specifies identical quality, quantity, and terms of trade as do all other such contracts; because all are identical, they are tradable on a commodities exchange.

Most commodities trading in which individual investors participate is trading in futures—but that trading is very different from the trading done by industrial users. Such users may sometimes speculate, but basically they buy futures to provide for future use needs; in contrast, individual investors buy futures as pure speculations and do not even contemplate delivery on the contracts they buy, since the quantities involved are appropriate for large industrial users and not for individuals. For example, the standard unit of trade on most exchanges will be several thousand bushels of an agricultural product, scarcely an amount an individual investor is equipped to handle. For the individual investor, the game—and that's what it is, a particularly fast speculative game—involves buying and selling these large contracts on margin, in the hope of making large profits on the "leverage" created by the borrowed money. As always, leverage works both ways, and the possibility of gain must be weighed against the possibility of loss.

Individual investors can speculate in futures themselves or can arrange for others to manage such speculation. Just as in the stock and bond markets, both mutual funds and managed individual accounts are available. Either way, you would need to immerse yourself in this kind of speculative investment to have any chance at all of success in the long term. Oh, you may be able to make a little money—or perhaps quite a lot—as an unknowledgeable gambler in a booming set of futures markets; some have done so, usually losing their gains and their original investments as those markets fluctuated. But in the long run, making this kind of investment requires substantial skill and commitment and thus is not for the amateur.

The rising futures markets in the late 1970s encouraged development of an options market in futures, in which the basic transaction was the purchase of an option to buy or sell a stated quantity of futures at a specified time and price, with the option itself an instrument of value. Such trading had been prohibited in the United States on certain regulated commodities since the mid-1930s, although options trading in several commodities had continued uninterruptedly on London commodities exchanges. However, because of the existence of loopholes in United States regulation of such trading, some commodity options could be traded in the United States, including silver, silver coins, sugar, cocoa, platinum, and copper.

Whenever a market yields quick profits to speculating investors, it becomes a magnet for sharp operators and some outright swindlers. The atmosphere surrounding a currently "hot" kind of speculative investment creates precisely the kind of situation in which it is possible to steal from the gullible. So it was with commodities and commodity options for some years, as it was with Florida real estate in the 1920s and is with Sunbelt real estate today. People bought nonexistent "London commodity options"; they bought "managed accounts," in which commissions of all kinds turned out to be more than 50% of the amounts they had invested; they even bought gemstones worth very little, in packages they agreed not to open until some time in the future in order to ensure the inviolability of the contents and to safeguard the "guarantees" of promoters.

Yet not all commodity options were bad investments. For some speculative investors, they afforded a way to speculate small, with losses limited to the amounts paid for the options and with large gains possible. Commodity options trading is not, in all hands, a bad speculation; it is not, however, a long-term financial planning vehicle.

STOCK OPTIONS

Stock options are another kind of speculative investment, one considerably used in rising stock markets and avoided in falling stock markets. The option itself is the instrument of value, consisting of the right to buy or sell something of value at a specific price and within a certain time, which is the option period. Options to purchase land or commodities work the same way as tradable stock options. Up until the time specified for exercise of the option, that option is a legally enforceable right and may itself be a thing of value. After the period has expired, an unexercised option is worthless.

Such an option is a legally enforceable right; that fact can lead to considerable confusion, as the term "rights" is often incorrectly used as a synonym for "stock options." "Rights" are only one kind of stock option, occurring when current common shareholders of a company are granted the right to buy, in proportion to their current holdings, newly issued company shares set at fixed prices for a specified time. If the price of company stock goes up before expiration, the newly issued rights are valuable and may be exercised or sold by their holders. If the price of company stock does not go up, the rights issued are worthless. Such "rights," when issued to holders of debt obligations and preferred stock, rather than holders of common stock, are called "warrants." They are negotiable if issued alone and nonnegotiable if issued as coupons attached to the debt obligations or preferred stock.

Those who trade in stock options often are described as trading in "puts and calls." A "put" is an option to sell for a set amount before a set time; a "call" is an option to buy for a set amount before a set time. One who buys an option to sell—a put—is speculating that the stock on which the option was purchased will go down more than the difference between its current market value and the price of the put. If so, the speculator will sell at a profit—a large profit, if the stock goes down a good deal. Often, however, the put is bought to hedge against such a sharp drop, with the buyer reasoning that the ability to sell the stock at current market levels is worth the price of the hedging put. If the price of the stock goes up, the price paid for the put is only a small subtraction from profit, and the downside risk is considerably less.

One who buys an option to buy—a call—is speculating that the stock on which the option was purchased will go up more than the difference between its current market value and the price of the call. If so, the speculator will buy at the low price guaranteed by the call and will resell at a profit—sometimes a very large profit. If not, the speculator will lose some or all of the money paid for the call: some, if the stock's price goes up a little, but not as much as the money paid for the call, and all, if the stock's price does not rise.

Taken as part of an overall stock market investment strategy, stock option trading need not be a speculative tactic. For an individual investor who wishes to buy common stock, stock options may be a hedge, using the price of the option as the risk investment toward the purchase of the common stock at a future date. Stock options can effectively limit risk if used in this fashion—but only if the investor is considering the purchase of the common stock as part of long-term financial planning. Risk can also be minimized by the very sophisticated use of "straddles," involving the purchase and sale of options virtually simultaneously, but this method should be avoided by anyone who is not an expert in that investment area.

In short, stock option trading can be used effectively as one of the tools in the professional's kit of tactics, as part of a long-term financial planning approach. Such trading by itself, however, is little more than speculation—modest speculation, but speculation all the same—for the entire amount invested may very easily be lost. All depends on the turn of the short-term stock price wheel—and markets fluctuate.

COLLECTIBLES

The term "collectibles" embraces a wide variety of tangible items which are bought, held, and traded for reasons other than use and for which trading markets have developed. In its investment sense, the term includes antiques, works of art, and tangible items of any age, including some that are brand new, such as newly minted coins and newly printed stamps. It may even include items attached to realty, and legally part of realty, such as ironwork and barbed wire. It may include items collected partly because of their precious metals content, such as silver plates.

The main investment aspect of a collectible is not what it is, but that a market exists—or is thought by many to exist—for it.

People trade in all kinds of things. There are well-defined markets for ancient and modern products of all the visual and decorative arts, such as paintings, furniture, glass, utensils, and sculpture; for everything printed or written, such as books, stamps, periodicals, autographs, theater programs, and photographs; for what were originally industrial products, such as old automobiles; really for everything under the sun, from matchbook covers to comic books to used clothing once worn by celebrities—as long as people collect and trade these items, they are, in an investment sense, collectibles.

In hard and uncertain times, worried individual investors tend to rush into the collectibles market, just as they rush into gold, silver, other precious metals, and gemstones. That rush lends a certain buoyancy to all collectibles markets—a buoyancy that may disappear as better times come and as other investment vehicles regain lost favor. Even worse, the ready market that exists for some kinds of collectibles in hard times may dry up in better times, and investors who bought high may find themselves holding on to items for which there is no market and which therefore may have to be sold at ruinous losses.

There are other possible disadvantages, too. Collectibles yield no dividends and are potentially quite illiquid. They must be sold to realize profit and often must be held for sale at the right time, rather than when you are ready or need to sell. Fads and styles in collecting change, as well, and this decade's fancy for a certain kind of painting, piece of furniture, or kind of printed matter may turn into disinterest in the next decade, when you are ready to sell. In truth, you can lose your shirt in many ways by investing in collectibles.

In light of these facts, can collectibles have a place in your long-term financial planning—even an important place? Yes, indeed—if you know what you are doing. That is the heart of the matter. Collectibles investing can provide you with some extraordinary opportunities, as long as you take the time and trouble to learn everything you can about what you are collecting and trading. Putting it a little differently, the most effective way to lose your shirt in this area is to invest in the "collectibles market," as is true of investing in stock, bond, or commodities markets. The key to successful investment in collectibles is concentration on a single kind of collectible at the start, often on a single small area within a certain kind of collecting. It is quite possible to expand one's set of collecting and trading interests later on, as long as the new interests are mastered as fully as the old.

If this is done, collectibles offer both long-term profit and an opportunity to develop a sideline business to take with you into your later years. If, as we believe, it will be necessary for the overwhelming majority of us to work as long as we can, which may be a very healthy thing to do as well, then developing a collecting hobby that can become a sideline and then a retirement business is one of the few ideal ways to go in terms of long-term financial planning. Collectibles businesses can range all the way from multimillion-dollar international enterprises, such as Sotheby Parke, Bernet, to quite respectable and profitable enterprises run out of a single room at home. A skilled mechanic can collect, maintain, rebuild, and sell antique and classic cars on several acres out in the country; a skilled stamp or coin collector-trader can do what is, in investment and financial planning terms, essentially the same thing out of a small retirement home.

In trying to advise young people on their career choices, it is often fruitful to ask them what kinds of things they most enjoy and to try to build from there to an understanding of what they would like to do with their lives. After all, most people will do best what they *like* to do best; motivation is half the battle. So, too, with collecting. If becoming expert is far more than half the battle of investment success—and it is—and if collecting can be a major opportunity for long-term financial planning and a second career—and it can—then it is important to move into your collecting career as carefully as you would move into any other career. That means seeking out several areas of interest, settling on no more than one or two at the start, reading, subscribing to specialist periodicals, taking courses if possible, and haunting any available shows and sales in your chosen area—in short, finding a second vocation.

It sounds like a lot of work, and it is. It can also be tremendously rewarding, in terms of both money and enjoyment, if done right. To build an investment stake and a second career simultaneously is an opportunity to be grasped, once understood.

Some cautions are necessary in this area, however. One centers on confusing collectability with precious metal or gemstone content. If you buy a silver plate, for example, thinking that the silver content of that plate will always guarantee you resalability and a reasonably good price, you may be sorely disappointed years later when you want to sell it. You may find that you have put investment money into a plate containing silver worth only a small fraction of the money you paid for it, and you may be forced to sell for the value of that silver content alone, receiving no dividends at all on the money you tied up in the plate. The net of such a transaction, after the impact of inflation, is a whopping loss in real dollars. Investors in such "collectibles" have often failed to assess soberly the real value of the precious metals and gemstones in such manufactured goods as silver plates and gemstone figurines. And though the astute promoters of these kinds of items have, in most cases, under government pressure, ingeniously managed to disclaim underlying value as a reason to buy, they have actually stressed resale value and ready marketability.

The truth is that, as long as markets for the kinds of precious metals and gemstones used in such goods are going up, resale value and marketability are generally excellent, buoyed up partly by those rising markets and partly by the expectations of those buying and holding the goods. However, as soon as those markets go down for any period, measured in months or years, expectations disappear, many sellers appear, and marketability at any price much higher than the underlying value of the goods becomes impossible. It suddenly, and far too late, becomes clear that those who promoted these manufactured goods included large promotion costs, substantial manufacturing costs, and a very large profit in their sales price and that they have no intention of making good on their implied, nonbinding promises to make resale markets at high prices for those goods.

Other cautions center on fads and quality. Collectibles sometimes fall out of fashion, which results in a severe impact on prices and sometimes on marketability as well. Yesterday's voguish modern painting by a relative unknown, which sold for $1000 and was sure to triple in value in a few years, may now be worth $200—if you can find a buyer at all. On the other hand, medium- or high-quality stamps, coins, antiques, books, and jewelry seldom lose much of their value, as their markets tend to be well established and worldwide. You can make a collecting specialty of something unusual or relatively new to the collectibles world and make a lot of money at it, but it can be risky, converting what can be long-term income and second-career building into long-term speculation and loss. It would seem far wiser to become expert in a well-established collectibles area before moving into more speculative activities. Of course, there are always exceptions to such a rule. Sometimes interest overcomes prudence. Some people who were fascinated by baseball cards, comic books, or science fiction magazines collected them when they had no great intrinsic value and seemed very unlikely ever to acquire such value. Ultimately, their interest was translated into very valuable collectibles and in some instances into lucrative sidelines and even full careers.

Collecting and trading in collectibles can be very profitable, the genesis of a whole new retirement career, and great fun, too. The trick is to become expert and to keep on sharpening your expert knowledge as long as you live. It will probably also help you to live longer.

Real Estate as a
Planning Tool

For tens of millions of Americans, real estate occupies a unique place in long-term financial planning as the only area in which they have achieved substantial capital accumulation. Oddly enough, that accumulation is very often accomplished accidentally, as a by-product of home or business ownership. For aside from artificially induced land booms and busts, such as those achieved by some large-scale speculators and developers in the Sunbelt, much American real estate has enjoyed a sustained growth in value since World War II.

That growth in value has not been a straight-line matter or without regional and local variations. Blasted areas exist in major cities, such as the South Bronx and Brownsville in New York City, which have, as a practical matter, lost much of their value and resalability for decades. Some smaller towns and cities have become virtual ghost towns because of the loss of major local industries, causing resale value and marketability to have suffered greatly. Generally, however, the trend in real estate value has been up.

Even more significantly, many real estate values have tended, during the late 1970s and early 1980s, to rise faster than the rate of inflation. While the rate of inflation halved the value of the dollar during the 1970s, the rate of appreciation of real estate values more than quadrupled the value of residential real property in many well-established suburban and exurban towns and cities. That appreciation in the value of owner-occupied homes eased the impact of inflation for millions of American families. For many, it meant relatively modest mortgage payments, with interest rates and principal repayment at very low levels by current measures. A home purchased in the late 1960s with a 6%, $25,000 mortgage might, a little over a decade later, have appreciated to $120,000—not at all unusual. The payments on that mortgage are a far cry from the payments on a 12 to 16%, $100,000 mortgage for the same house in the 1980s.

For some homeowners, of course, that appreciation meant the ability to refinance—at progressively higher mortgage rates—in order to be able to meet college costs and to keep their heads above water as inflation hit harder and harder. But for many millions of Americans, that home, cooperative apartment, condominium or even houseboat has meant the difference between something and next to nothing in terms of capital accumulation.

After all was said and done—all the investing, speculating, saving, winning, losing—the land and the structures bought to live in or to run a business in, not as an investment, often turned out to be the best investment of all.

Some businesses found their real estate, purchased as a vehicle for conducting business, more valuable than the businesses themselves. That was a widespread experience in farming, for example. Farmers in areas of growing population often found their land embarrassingly valuable, so valuable that the taxes on their land were more than they could afford to pay, "forcing" them to sell their land at enormous profits—and in the process forcing them out of business. For those who did not mind relocating, such a sale could be a real boon. One nursery owner, a client of one of the authors, looked at a $250,000 check from International Business Machines and chortled, "But I only bought the land to grow my shrubs."

Small, owner-occupied multiple dwellings often became far more valuable than their owners had ever anticipated, especially as more and more small investors found residential housing a fertile and seemingly inexhaustible source of rental and resale profits. In the late 1970s and early 1980s, the residential housing market heated up and overheated as investors "leveraged" their real estate investments, borrowing as much as they possibly could, upgrading the properties purchased, and then reselling to other eager investors, sometimes taking back second mortgages themselves in order to swing the resale.

As interest rates soared, investors moved into real estate lending as direct participants in the second-mortgage market and as buyers of real estate partnerships, or Real Estate Investment Trusts. Others found new interest in real estate syndicates and tax-advantaged ownership participations in real estate purchases.

It was—and is—all part of the huge and intertwined real estate and real estate investment markets. Assessing real estate and real estate investment in terms of long-term financial planning requires identifying and analyzing several underlying factors and facets of those markets.

One such underlying factor in the early 1980s is that the demand for dwellings continues to rise, while the stock of available dwellings continues to diminish, relative to demand. Although birthrates have declined, people are living longer—and the high birthrates of the 1950s and early 1960s have brought many new renters and buyers into the housing market. At the same time, a complex of cost and credit factors has severely limited growth in the nation's housing stock, while existing housing continues to age. The net effect, and it is a long-term one, is that in most areas demand outstrips supply and will continue to do so, building a long-term escalator into dwelling values.

Another underlying factor is that national taxing policy continues to favor real property ownership. The twin concepts of depreciation and depletion continue to be woven into the fabric of the tax law and therefore into the values of real estate and natural resources. These concepts must be understood clearly if the "tax-sheltered" nature of ownership investments in those areas is to be fully appreciated. A tax-sheltered investment literally protects income from taxation, allowing its natural growth in value to compound unimpeded by taxes. The concept of depreciation for non-owner-occupied residential or commercial property builds such protection into real estate ownership investments, while depletion does the same for natural resource ownership investments.

"Depletion" is the concept that natural resources can be and are used up. As reflected in the tax law, the concept results in substantial tax deductions for owners of such resources and is much of the reason for the development of many huge fortunes based on oil and natural gas.

"Depreciation," a concept applied to business assets, is the lessening of an asset's value because of use and age. As reflected in the tax law, it makes possible large and repeated tax deductions for the same property through owner after owner, each new owner beginning the process of depreciation again. Simultaneously, it makes it possible to take those tax deductions very quickly, if any of the several quite legal "accelerated" methods of depreciation are used for tax-deduction purposes. For example, for each $100 of taxable income produced by a multiple dwelling (after all business expenses and other such deductions have been taken), a property might provide $40 in depreciation deductions if the property were depreciated on a "straight-line" basis, which means in equal proportions over the number of years provided for depreciation by law. That in itself is a very substantial tax shelter. However, using any of several "accelerated" depreciation methods, deductions generated might cover the entire $100 of otherwise taxable income, providing an extraordinary tax shelter and one that has long been imbedded in the tax law, with no signs of a change of taxing policy in view.

Even for nonbusiness property, tax policy much favors ownership, as all homeowners know. Tax deductions for property taxes and mortgage interest have long benefited owners of single-family homes and now benefit millions of condominium and cooperative apartment owners as well.

The tax deferrals achieved by the use of depreciation of property are later "recaptured" and must be paid at a future date, but in the interim years the tax savings incurred may be used for additional investments, which is an extremely efficient use of money. Also, the taxes that will eventually have to be paid will be computed at a lower rate as long-term capital gains taxes, not as ordinary income taxes, which is a major benefit to real estate investors.

In the residential housing market in the 1970s and early 1980s, the nature of the mortgage transaction combined with a sustained rise in dwelling values has led—quite by accident—to an extraordinary mass example of "leverage."

When you buy a dwelling, you pay a certain amount down—normally from 10 to 25%, depending mainly on the age of the dwelling and on credit factors—and borrow the rest, in the form of one or more mortgage loans secured by the value of the property. Given the relatively low mortgage rates of the 1960s and 1970s, the fixed nature of those rates, the very favorable tax treatments granted to homeowners with regard to interest and property tax payments, and the steep rise in housing values, millions of homeowners found themselves enjoying truly enormous rates of return on investment during the period. For example, an investment of $10,000 down on a previously owned house in a stable suburban community in the mid-1960s often bought a $50,000 house. In the early 1980s that house might be selling for $250,000, a fairly normal quintupling of market value—but not of investment. For the investment was $10,000, not $50,000. Assuming that payments on the house, taxes, and maintenance costs are offset by owner occupancy, with rental not being paid elsewhere, the true return on investment is *not* 5:1 minus any tax impact on sale, but 25:1. The real net effect was that the owner-occupier of a dwelling achieved a 2500% return on investment, as compared to whatever that $10,000 might have earned elsewhere over roughly the same 15-year period. In the stock market, for example, it might have earned—nothing.

That is "leverage" in a rising market. Of course, as always, leverage can work both ways. Hundreds of thousands of Americans bought homes in the 1920s, but lost those homes and the money invested in them when they could not keep up with mortgage payments and suffered foreclosure during the Great Depression; foreclosing lenders in that deeply depressed housing market resold the houses for less than the outstanding mortgage loans or were forced to hold them unsold. That was leverage, too.

For very high income investors, leverage with interest deductions can work wonders, if the investments they go into are even modestly successful. For homeowners forced to borrow large sums to swing home purchases, leverage can work either way, usually for reasons beyond their control. For the small and medium investor speculating in real estate, leverage can bring wealth—or ruin. However, the decision as to whether or not to refinance is much informed by an understanding of how leverage really works.

Real estate investment can take many forms. Most of those forms range from very safe to highly speculative, depending on how financing is handled. In that respect, real estate is little different from other investment vehicles. Investment in relatively "safe" common stocks can be highly speculative if required margins are very low and if borrowed money is used and pyramided upon, as was precisely the case during the 1920s, when those "safe" stocks began to fall, and margin calls forced them much further down than they would have gone had not leverage worked against them.

Investments in commodity futures, stock options, precious metals, and real estate all become highly speculative when highly leveraged, but may be relatively safe when the leverage is taken out of them—but bear in mind that the leverage has to be taken out of the whole market. It does not do to buy for cash in a market made volatile by highly leveraged speculators, for the market is still volatile, and you still may lose much of your investment, however safe you try to play your gamble. A closely regulated stock market with high margin requirements may be less exciting, but is intrinsically safer than a commodities futures market requiring 10% margins.

Real estate investment uses many vehicles, all variations on a few basic forms—the same forms encountered in other kinds of investments. You can buy, hold, and trade real estate yourself; you can go, with others, into a kind of business based largely on real estate ownership; you can buy an ownership interest in a real estate company; or you can lend money to real estate owners, directly or through funds managed by others.

At its most basic, real estate investment can consist of your purchasing a dwelling in an area unlikely to suffer economic catastrophe, living in that dwelling, and selling it after you reach the age of 55, to take advantage of the very large, one-time tax forgiveness allowed on such a sale. If possible, allowing for such noneconomic factors as the quality of schools and cultural advantage, that house should be located in a relatively low tax area, which speaks strongly for buying in a well-established community, rather than one with large numbers of child-raising families. That community may also be relatively low taxed in direct relation to the amount of industry that has been let in by local zoning policy. Many communities, afraid of industry, have sacrificed economy for exclusivity. A few have found that policy economically beneficial in terms of resale values, but others have found that long-term difficulties are created by the policy, as people find it increasingly difficult to make ends meet.

Dwellings purchased in cities should be carefully examined in terms of neighborhood stability and the possibility of spreading urban decay. Some neighborhoods in some cities offer excellent prospects for long-term living and capital accumulation, and other areas may increase in value dramatically, due to rehabilitation programs, but the long-term trend in residential housing in most major American cities is still downward, as jobs erode, housing stock deteriorates, migration of people and industry to the suburbs and beyond continues, financing grows increasingly difficult, and federal policy continues to look the other way.

If you choose with care, however, and constantly view and evaluate that dwelling as an investment as well as a place to live, it can be a superb investment. Return on investment can scarcely be expected to continue to be 2500%, but there is every reason to believe that the impact of favorable tax laws and long-term upward trends in housing markets will provide returns far better than those possible in almost any other kind of investment and rivaling those available from a successful business of your own.

Some people move from house to house, "upgrading" their holdings as needs and means make necessary and possible, and by so doing develop a considerable real estate holding out of a very modest initial investment. Others work a little more formally, developing the skills needed to rebuild old homes and turning those skills into part- or full-time businesses. They buy somewhat deteriorated old homes in reasonably "good" communities, rebuild them inside and sometimes outside as well, and then resell at considerable profit, moving into more expensive houses—or into more than one house—as they develop capital and skills. Like any real estate investment, such rebuilding can be an excellent source of profits in good housing-market times, but can be difficult in bad times, when credit can become scarce and resale markets can, to some extent, dry up. But the risk in doing it this way is rather small, especially for part-time renovators. Down payments are relatively small, most work performed is done by the renovators themselves—yielding what is called "sweat equity"—and financial risk is thereby minimized. Of course, even this quite conservative approach can be turned into its opposite when too much leverage is sought, with mortgage piled on mortgage, or when part-time work turns into full-time employment and involves the employment of others. Then renovation is turned into a lightly capitalized, high-risk small business, subject to all the risks endemic to any such business.

Moving into a higher-risk venture is the basic problem encountered by those who listen to get-rich-quick advice in this field. It is true that astute property picking and a great deal of hard work can be the keys to a successful real estate renovation and management business, as long as it does not depend on too much borrowed money and consequent debt service to keep afloat. But the kind of speculation urged by some consultants and writers in the late 1970s and early 1980s, consisting of a wild scramble to use and pyramid as much borrowed money as possible in expectation of continually rising real estate values, easy sales, and ready refinancing arrangements, is a ticket to the poorhouse. Real estate markets go up and go down. Credit can be easy, and credit can be tight. Occupancy rates can be high, but can also fall low, resulting in much less income and cash flow available to meet obligations. In such circumstances people can lose their total investment and may be forced into personal bankruptcy—all because a get-rich-quick approach has spoiled an otherwise sound business.

Expansion from part-time real estate investment in a personal residence to what is virtually a small business involves other potential hazards as well. Absentee ownership, for example, usually means less profits because of the additional costs involved, which can be magnified by the irresponsibility, incompetence, or pure chicanery of the on-the-scene management. In addition, real estate must continually be reevaluated in the context of changing conditions. The building of a nuclear plant within hailing distance, the move of an industrial plant that provides jobs and a stable tax base to the community, or the construction of a highway in the middle of one's property, for example, may adversely affect the value of property. Ultimately, real estate, like any business, must be judged using the same criteria you would use in judging any investment in order to buy and sell appropriately.

Sole or substantial ownership and management of your own property, whether personal residence or business property, is not the only way to invest in a real estate ownership interest. Another, and very widely adopted, mode of real estate ownership is that of the "limited partnership." The essence of such an ownership interest is that the limited partner is part owner of the property invested in, but shares in profit and loss possibilities only to a specified extent, in contrast to the general partner, who carries unlimited personal liability and possibility of gain, as in any regular partnership. The corporate form would provide limited liability to common stockholders, rather than the unlimited liability to which general partners may be subjected. However, tax laws, as currently written, usually dictate that many real estate transactions use the partnership rather than the corporate form.

A properly constructed limited partnership provides limited liability to the limited partners, while allowing the losses and gains of the partnership to be passed through to the limited partners. This is especially important in those real estate transactions which, by their nature, will show losses in the early life of the partnership, because these losses can be passed through as desirable tax deductions to the limited partners. The partnership form also has value later, when income or profits are earned, because it avoids the effects of the double taxation that exists under the corporate form, where first the corporation is taxed on its profits and then the shareholders are taxed on the earnings they receive from the corporation.

The essence of the matter is that profits and losses in partnerships pass through directly to the partners, making it possible for the losses generated by accelerated depreciation and high interest payments in the early years of ownership to pass through to the partners; these losses are used as personal income-tax deductions. That leaves general partners able to minimize tax payments, although their personal positions are more vulnerable because of the absence of the limited liability shield carried by corporate stockholders. But for limited partners, both limited liability and tax deductions are available—a classic case of having your cake and eating it too.

That is the basic tax and investment situation that has made participation in limited real estate partnership so attractive to many high-income taxpayers. For the affluent, it has for decades been possible, using the device of the limited partnership, to finance real estate investments at little risk of liability and wholly with government money in the form of taxes which otherwise would have had to be paid on income. For many years it was actually possible to make a good deal of money in unpaid taxes, even if the real estate investment yielded no profits at all at any time—sometimes even if it was a total loss; in recent years, however, some limits have been placed on this basic transaction.

Such an arrangement sounds like a fine way to take a good deal of risk out of investment and to maximize return on investments actually made—and so it is. A few words of caution are in order, however. A poor investment is still a poor investment, no matter how tax advantaged. An office building occupied by a single tenant in a small town or city may look wonderful on initial investment, but the same building a few years later may be a white elephant, its tenant gone and no other tenant in sight, its mortgagor foreclosing and all investment lost. Commercial property on a well travelled highway may lose its value overnight if a new highway is built nearby that bypasses that property. An inventive and unscrupulous set of general partners may find ways to milk a property, leaving the limited partners high and dry, somewhat tax advantaged, and wholly shorn of invested capital. Here, as with all other investment forms, one should invest in a property, not in a market; in a specific real estate investment, not in "real estate."

Other possibilities also exist for tax "write-offs" in real estate investment. Real estate investment firms constantly seek to develop new ways of enhancing the tax advantages available in real estate financing and management. The Internal Revenue Service constantly seeks to limit those tax advantages. The result is a constant small "war" and a good deal of contention and litigation between private investors and federal regulators in this area, as in so many other areas of government–business interface. That makes it absolutely necessary for anyone wishing to invest in limited partnerships in real estate—and in any other tax-sheltered transactions, for that matter—to seek professional counsel before investing. That means counsel beyond that provided by sellers of tax-advantaged investments. The best of such sellers routinely and properly advise prospective purchasers to seek tax and legal advice from their accountants and attorneys before investing. Real estate consultants may also be called in to evaluate the property. Whatever your real estate investment plans, you would be wise to seek professional advice.

CHAPTER

8

Insurance Planning

We are surrounded by a dozen different kinds of insurance. We participate in some kinds voluntarily, as through purchase of life, health, accident, fire, and casualty insurance. Some are forced upon us, usually, but not always, with our willing acquiescence, such as Social Security, unemployment insurance, workers' compensation, and automobile liability insurance. We pay for all of them, voluntarily or not, by personal check or business check and through direct and indirect taxes. In this book we focus primarily on insurance that we pay for voluntarily, for it is here that choices can be made, but we also look at "involuntary insurances," since they are a very real part of our total financial pictures and plans.

Insurance is often sold to us rather hard, so much so that most Americans have become wary of the overaggressive insurance agent, as of most salespersons. That may be a proper caution, but it has impeded many people from taking a proper, all-around consideration of their insurance needs and desires. That consideration is critical in assessing insurance for financial planning purposes, for it poses the proper first question first, which is not "How much insurance should I buy?" but "What am I buying insurance for?"

That is really the basic question for all insurance; it goes to the question of risk, which is the heart of any insurance transaction,

126

while at the same time making it necessary to consider an insurance-buying decision within the context of your whole financial picture. The question arises around such modest matters as the size of the deductible provision in an auto insurance policy and around such major matters as how much life insurance to purchase, if any, when you already have considerable company-paid group life insurance. The answer usually depends on how well you understand that the most important thing to insure against is the occurrence of personal catastrophe, such as death, major illness, or disability; of total destruction of insured property; or of bankrupting liability claims. If you think of insurance first of all as catastrophe insurance—rather than as life, health, accident, fire, and casualty insurance—you have the key to making the right insurance decisions.

LIFE INSURANCE

The term "life insurance" is a triumphant euphemism. The catastrophe that is contemplated by the basic insurance transaction is death, and others are being protected from the impact resulting from the death of the insured. The insurer takes payments, or premiums, from those it insures and pays death benefits to those designated on the insurance policy as beneficiaries, basing its premium rates mainly on average life expectancies. The company's cost of doing business, interest rates, and profit motivation are among the factors that affect the premium rates. Under a legal reserve system, a portion of the premiums paid by the owner of the policy are invested by the insurance company to provide for benefit payments. The amount of the reserve and the nature of the investments vary, being determined by state law and the insurance department of each state.

Many kinds of life insurance arrangements also include investment or savings features, which we discuss later, but the basic life insurance transaction does not. That basic transaction is encountered under several names, but is most generally called "term insurance." Term insurance involves purchase of an amount of insurance on the life of the insured, guaranteed to be paid by the insurance company upon the death of the insured; it is subject to premium payments payable for a specific term of years at rates varying with the age of the insured and usually rising as the insured ages. The policyholder may cancel the policy at any time, but the insurance company may not cancel the policy during the period specified in the contract except for failure to pay premiums. In the long run term insurance is by far the least expensive kind of life insurance to purchase, because it is life insurance with no savings or investment component. Millions of individual term policies have been sold directly to consumers by insurance agents, with very low premium payments during those years in which relatively young families with relatively low incomes found those low premiums very attractive.

Several kinds of term insurance policies can be purchased, such as yearly renewable term, in which the premium goes up while the face amount of the insurance remains level every year, therefore being as low as possible for each year of the term; five-year term, in which the premium payments change at stated five-year intervals, level term, in which premiums may remain constant until age 65 or 70; and decreasing term, in which premiums stay level, while the amount of insurance carried diminishes as the insured grows older. Which one you choose and from whom you purchase will depend on your current cash flow and your anticipated long-term needs. Costs, contractual provisions, and the potential value of the agent or other seller to your overall financial planning are all factors to consider in choosing a policy. All are purely term insurance policies, with no savings component, reflecting only a transaction between insurer and insured covering the catastrophe of death.

Group life insurance, used by employers to insure the lives of groups of employees, is usually term insurance. As a "fringe" employment benefit, the employer purchases insurance on employees, with death benefits payable to beneficiaries designated by the insured employees, and keeps that insurance in force as long as employment lasts and the insurance contract allows. This insurance coverage is not guaranteed, since the insurer may cancel the policy or increase premiums at its option; also, the employer may at any time terminate the group contract or the coverage available to employees.

On termination of employment, employees are usually able to carry their life insurance with them, converting from a group to an individual, permanent, noncancelable life insurance policy with the same insurer, without medical examinations. Below a certain level of insurance, $50,000 at the time of this writing, the premiums paid by the employer to the insurance company are a business expense to the employer and are not taxable as income to the employee. Beyond that level, employees must add the cost of the additional premiums to their personal income as taxable compensation, at a rate determined by the Internal Revenue Service. A relatively new group nonterm arrangement, called "Retired Lives Reserve," allows an employer to continue death benefit coverage after the employee's retirement, as a special, somewhat expensive fringe, with no premiums paid by the employee.

Group life insurance is a fine and widespread fringe benefit. It is also a very substantial personal financial planning trap into which many can—and do—fall. The problem is that, though group term contracts held by employers are convertible, they are seldom, if ever, convertible into individual term insurance policies. Instead, insurers insist on conversion into "whole life policies," which are policies with a savings component. When converting from a group term policy into an individual whole life policy, insurers gauge premium charges on the basis of the current age of the insured, as they would with anyone buying a new insurance policy. The net effect is that the cost of the new whole life policy is very high, usually much more than the former employee is able to pay in order to carry the same amount of life insurance formerly carried by the employer on the employee's life. Some group plans funded by individual term policies are available; these are portable, and may be kept by terminated employees, but are usually offered only to highly paid employees in large face amount insurance policies.

Then why not forget about converting the insurance and just purchase term insurance as an individual? At that point, many do. That is not the trap, although the insurance purchased may be more expensive to the individual than it was to the employer. This is so because the employer gets a premium discount as a result of the volume of insurance purchased for all employees and the "mortality spread" for the group, calculated by the insurance company actuaries, which means that the insurer has less risk for a group than for an individual. The trap is that the former employee may no longer be able to pass a medical examination for life insurance and is therefore insurable only at higher substandard rates or totally uninsurable. The only choice that former employee has then is to exercise the conversion option on the group term insurance policy, whereby he or she winds up with far more expensive insurance than is either needed or affordable. If, to save money, the insured converts the policy to a lower amount of coverage, he or she ends up with less insurance than is needed at a far higher cost than need have been paid.

The only way to avoid this trap is to carry a basic individual life insurance policy of your own, no matter what group life insurance you carry. It may be a term policy, or it may be a whole life policy with a savings component and a level premium payment, but either way it can be purchased when the person is insurable, usually at a relatively early age and therefore with relatively low premium payments. No matter which you choose, some independently owned policy is necessary as a basic protection.

How large should a basic life insurance policy be? There are almost as many ways of looking at that question as there are individual needs and inventive life insurance sellers. After all is said, done, and estimated, however, the answers will vary with the resources, commitments, time of life, and long-term inflation estimates of the person to be insured. Only one thing is sure—that "basic individual life insurance policy" does not mean a "small individual life insurance policy." Quite the contrary. A 40-year-old man or woman looking forward to sending three teenage children through college and to fulfilling other family commitments in the next 25 to 30 years, having a currently modest net worth, and anticipating as little as an 8 to 10% yearly rate of inflation may well do some calculating and realize that a basic $200,000 term insurance policy, costing about $330 that year and increasing periodically, might barely cover felt need if death were to occur tomorrow. Someone else, 20 years older, with children and other commitments accounted for, having by then accumulated some substantial assets, and wanting only enough life insurance to achieve some modest estate tax planning goals, might carry a quarter of that much insurance, or $50,000. That $50,000, at age 60, would cost $360, because of the greater insurance risk that comes with greater age.

Before attempting to determine the size of a life insurance policy, it is necessary to review one's total assets. Life insurance companies and agents tend to view life insurance as one's sole resource upon death. This is hardly the case. An individual who has financial assets in the form of savings, stocks, bonds, and pension benefits, for example, will have these assets, valued upon date of death, available for passing on to his or her beneficiary, in addition to the proceeds of a life insurance policy. Of course, caution dictates that, in evaluating such a financial estate, one consider the stability and liquidity of the assets and the net proceeds after probate costs and taxes. A financial estate that includes a $1 million piece of real estate with no potential buyers for many years cannot totally substitute for life insurance proceeds, which are defined and liquid. Also, a stock portfolio in volatile over-the-counter stocks cannot be valued at today's prices in determining one's financial resources in anticipation of death 10 or 20 years in the future.

In evaluating the size of a life insurance contract, one must judiciously consider *all* present and potential assets as part of the estate as well as all liabilities, such as support of one's beneficiaries. A seemingly contradictory phenomenon occurs in evaluating life insurance needs over one's lifetime.

For example, a 32-year-old business person or corporate employee may have a family living on a gross income of $35,000 per year, with a $40,000 mortgage; two children who will have educational needs of $100,000 over the next 15 years; a spouse with modest job skills; and few assets beyond a small equity in the home or the business. Such a person would probably need at least a $250,000 life insurance policy, because if death came immediately, all plans for the family would be frustrated. The same individual 15 years hence may not need more than $50,000 of life insurance, since the children have now completed their education, the home is now all but paid off and has increased many times in value, and he or she has accrued $100,000 of value in the business or pension plan or both. The contradiction may arise 10 years later, at age 57. By then, the person has a home worth $250,000, an investment portfolio worth $150,000, a pension plan worth $125,000, and a small business, which may have little sale value, but which is evaluated by the IRS as being worth $250,000 because of past profits and income derived by the owner. With an estate valued at $775,000, the beneficiaries will face the problem of paying estate taxes, which may force the sale of the house, business, or investment portfolio under distressed circumstances. Thus, at this stage of life, a $100,000 insurance policy, or even more, may be necessary to protect the assets for the beneficiaries when death occurs.

The amount of life insurance, then, is not a decision to be made once and forgotten. Rather, it must be reevaluated periodically as individual circumstances and economic conditions change.

How much insurance should you carry? As always, it is a question of how much you need to protect those you wish to protect from the potential catastrophe of your death. How much can you afford? That is a personal matter, having to do with your own priorities. Strip the insurance coverage decision down to catastrophe insurance, and you can make a sound decision.

Mortgage insurance is another kind of term insurance; it is decreasing term insurance, which diminishes as the principal of the mortgage diminishes over the years. It is required by lending institutions and is a classic example of involuntary but invaluable protection by insurance that is forced upon individuals. The survivors of the insured are protected against foreclosure of the mortgage for nonpayment after the death of the mortgage holder, but the additional beneficiary is the lending institution, which is thereby protected against default on the mortgage. Similar insurance is also available on many personal installment loans.

Term insurance can be purchased in a wide variety of ways. In addition to a direct purchase from a life insurance company agent, for example, term insurance may be purchased from a savings bank, through a professional or fraternal association, from a direct mail solicitation, through a credit card organization, or through a mutual fund.

People involved in business relationships often have life insurance needs beyond those relating to family. Small business owners who have partners or other stockholders may need business insurance to protect their assets upon death. A key employee who has no equity in the business may wish to obtain insurance on the life of the business owner, to provide funds to buy that business in the event of the owner's death. Bank loans, tax obligations, and a wide variety of normal business transactions may call for life insurance to protect the owner's family, estate, and business associates, with the amounts and forms of insurance depending on business needs, evaluations of the worth of the business, and the cost of the insurance.

Life insurance, in at least its term insurance form, is a must, one of the basic components of any kind of coherent long-term financial planning. Life insurance that combines insurance and savings in one insurance policy is another matter, for then you must separate insurance aspects as much as possible from the savings aspects, for evaluative purposes. You must subject the investment aspects to the same searching, comparative scrutiny you would give any other investment vehicles, in terms of yield, liquidity, safety, tax advantage, and all the other factors one must consider when considering a debt or equity investment.

The savings component found in life insurance policies is the cash value found in and paid for by those insured under whole life insurance policies. These are also often called "straight life" or "permanent life" insurance policies. These policies are usually characterized by level premiums throughout the life of the policy for level death benefit payments to beneficiaries; endowment—that is, payment to the insured—usually at ages 95 to 100; and the creation of a savings fund in each policy by application of a portion of premium proceeds to that fund. The fund may be borrowed against by the insured (an 8% interest factor is used by many insurance companies today), may be used to pay unpaid premiums automatically or as desired by the insured, or may be turned into cash on cancellation of the policy by the insured. The fund accretes on a tax-deferred basis, which is a real plus. Taxation is incurred only if the policyholder accretes and removes more in cash amounts than the premiums paid.

The problem is, however, that as an investment, even a tax-deferred one, the cash surrender value in life insurance is pathetically inadequate when compared with almost any other kind of available investment. Its tenacity as a major life insurance instrument for savings and investment purposes is a tribute to the selling prowess of several generations of life insurance sellers and to the fact that insurance policies bought decades ago carry level premiums that cannot be replaced now except by policies carrying much higher premium levels, because those who bought them then are older now or unable to buy new term insurance because of medical problems. For, in fact, life insurance companies, which in most states are heavily regulated, invest these funds prudently and conservatively, secure far higher yields than those passed on to the insured's cash surrender value investment funds, and accumulate the rest as company business income. Very often, the yields of investment portfolios of life insurance companies are estimated conservatively in the 7 to 10% range, while the growth rate plugged into the cash surrender value investment components of their whole life insurance policies is approximately 3¾%. For people who feel they need some kind of modest forced savings plan, because they are unable to do coherent financial planning or in some instances any saving at all, that kind of life insurance policy may make some sense—maybe, unless a Christmas club or United States savings bond yields better, which in many instances both do. But for people who are ready and willing to do some serious, long-term financial planning, and who are not locked into such life insurance policies because of life insurance buying decisions made decades ago, such policies make no sense at all.

A classic debate in the insurance industry is whether the insured is making a wiser economic choice in purchasing a whole life form of insurance (x) or in purchasing a term policy (y) and investing the difference $(x - y)$ in some form of savings or investment. In assessing what kind of policy you should buy, compare the two approaches and weigh the validity for your own situation. Among the factors that should always be considered are the amount of death benefit available (in the case of "purchasing term and investing the difference," that means the insurance death benefit plus the savings or investment account); taxation, liquidity; and, ultimately, the amounts of monies available at all times to you if you live or to your beneficiary if you die. It is obvious from our remarks that we opt for purchasing term and investing the difference, since the major beneficiary of this approach is not the insurance company or agent, but rather the policyholder and those he or she wishes to protect. It is far better to buy term life insurance as catastrophe insurance and to build a body of assets in several of the dozen or more different and better ways available. The sales commissions on whole life policies are far higher than those generated on term life policies, which partially explains the continuing popularity of the former among some life insurance sellers, but that is no reason to buy them.

There are always exceptions to this general thesis. Tax and ownership considerations in the more sophisticated and complex estates of the very wealthy and in corporation situations can minimize the value of purchasing term insurance and investing the difference. The nature of the deferral, the person to be taxed, the use of pension trusts, the timing of the taxation, or the type of taxes to be paid will, on occasion, recommend the use of whole life, or permanent, insurance, rather than term insurance and the usually more efficient use of monies involved therein. If your situation is this complex, you should have financial planning advisors to help you clarify and weigh these alternatives.

Some annuity policies may be different, though. Although certain annuity policies share the problem of low accretion rate with the whole life insurance policies, some others provide far higher rates of accretion and considerable tax advantage as well, including the single-premium deferred annuity, which we discuss shortly.

Annuities have traditionally been retirement insurance vehicles. The individual buys an insurance policy, making periodic premium payments, a single lump-sum payment, or some combination of both. When the policy matures, the insured receives payments in one of many possible payment modes, including lump-sum and periodic payments. The annuity is the only kind of life insurance in which the basic transaction actually involves paying the insured during life and which therefore really is primarily "life," rather than "death," insurance.

The problem intrinsic to annuities, as it is to whole, or straight, life insurance policies, has been the very low rate of accretion. Insurance agents and companies have done extraordinarily well selling them, but people buying them have, in most instances, actually made some of the worst investments possible. The traditional annuity policy offered by most life insurance companies provides for so small an investment buildup over the years that its payments many years later turn out to be pathetically inadequate when calculated in terms of the impact of inflation on the value of the dollar. On the overwhelming number of annuity policies sold from 1960 to 1980, the net loss in real dollars has been enormous. Although such annuities are very profitable policies for life insurance companies, they should be carefully avoided, except for people in very special personal situations. For example, for some high-income people, annuities can be useful in providing for incompetents, where no trustworthy money managers are available. If you are in one of those special situations, you can be sure that your accountant, attorney, or insurance advisor will be quick to tell you so. But for people trying to accomplish effective financial planning, the standard annuity policy is, to put it very gently, strikingly inappropriate.

However, some modern annuity insurance policies do accrete investment values rapidly. One such policy is the "single-premium deferred annuity." The basic transaction, as of this writing, consists of the purchase of an annuity policy from a company on a deferred basis, with the purchaser having the right to turn the purchase into an immediate annuity at any time, but also having the right to withdraw all or part of the lump sum paid at the start of the transaction at any time. The insurance company therefore does not have irrevocable control over the lump-sum premium paid and the accumulated interest, as it does over the values in a standard annuity contract.

The money so held by the insurance company is, in essence, used as an investment fund. The insurance company declares a specified rate of interest usually on an annual basis, to policyholders, and usually related to rates currently paid by money funds, and waives any charges for premature fund withdrawal if that guaranteed interest rate is not paid. Interest accruing on money held in the fund is tax deferred until withdrawal and then is taxed as ordinary income; but that tax deferral allows far faster buildup of values than if interest were taxable to its recipients in the year accrued, as is true of savings account interest.

Many companies charge no front-load commissions to buyers of single-premium deferred annuities, but usually do apply "back-load" charges when those insured withdraw their money before specified times, unless interest payments have dropped below declared levels for the year.

A variation on the single-premium deferred annuity is the "flexible-premium deferred annuity." This plan allows periodic premium deposits, rather than requiring a single lump-sum deposit, but is similar to the single-premium plan in all other major respects. Insurance company charges do tend to be somewhat higher on flexible-premium than on single-premium policies.

Another modern annuity plan that has achieved some popularity is the "variable annuity." Here the basic transaction in terms of tax deferral is the same as that of the single-premium and flexible-premium annuities, but the value of the annuity interest purchased depends directly upon the value of the investment portfolio developed by the insurance company. The premium is a fixed amount or group of amounts; the annuity purchased varies in value as the portfolio fluctuates.

In all of these modern annuity plans, net yields to insured individuals may be substantial, and their attractiveness is enhanced by their tax deferral aspects.

When considering the purchase of such an annuity, you should carefully review all the terms of the policy as to cost and conditions. Many variations are offered, and you should look for the contract that suits your needs. The stability of the insurance company, guaranteed and current interest rates, sales and other charges on purchase and liquidation, settlement options, and terms offered for conversion into an immediate annuity should all be examined closely. Care should be taken to purchase such an annuity either from a company headquartered in a state with rigid insurance company reserve and regulatory requirements, such as New York, or from a very large national insurance company. You should be extremely wary about purchasing from a small company in an ill-regulated state.

As new financial techniques and instruments develop during the latter part of the century, and as the American banking, insurance, and securities industries tend more and more to merge into a single financial industry, we can expect the annuity arrangements available to grow in number and complexity, offering new financial planning opportunities. Under the pressure of new and intense competition, the low-yielding whole life insurance funds of the recent past can reasonably be expected to become archaic forms, replaced by higher-yielding and more attractive investment forms, including insurance, investments, and as much tax advantage as can be gained and held in the ever-changing areas of contention between taxpayers and taxing authorities.

Whatever the type of policy, the beneficiary of a life insurance policy is determined by the owner of the policy. The life insurance company requires that the beneficiary have an "insurable interest" in the life of the insured, meaning that the beneficiary would demonstrably suffer a loss by the death of the insured. Other than for that demand, however, the owner can name any beneficiary desired for any of a variety of personal, business, or philanthropic reasons. The owner may change beneficiaries at will or on purchase of the policy may establish an irrevocable beneficiary, which is often done when the insurance policy is taken to fund a legal obligation.

The owner of the policy may also establish the mode and method of payment to the beneficiary upon the death of the insured. Benefits can be paid to beneficiaries in a wide range of ways. There are "lump-sum payments," meaning payment of the value of the policy in a single payment on the death of the insured, and there are "settlement options," meaning a series of alternative installment modes of payment.

Where the insured is concerned about whether beneficiaries are competent enough or can be relied upon to spend benefits wisely, alternative installment modes of payment are available. In that situation, it is wise to consult your insurance agent as to which alternatives are available and, with the help of your accountant and lawyer, decide which option best establishes your intent. In certain circumstances, it may be wise to leave the death proceeds in the hands of the insurance company. Business obligations, tax considerations, irresponsibility or incompetence on the part of the beneficiary, or divorce settlement terms, for example, may dictate that option.

The key thing to bear in mind here, however, is that whenever a life insurance company holds money benefits, your proper working assumption is that it has figured out a way to make money on the money it is holding—and that your beneficiaries may be able to make more, if they take what is due them and invest it advantageously. Life insurance benefits can start a substantial investment fund, which can accrete rapidly and yield far more in total proceeds than the amount paid by a life insurance company after its profits and expenses have been discounted.

Some "prior" options are worth considering upon purchase of a policy. One, which is routinely offered by most insurance sellers, is a "waiver of premium." With this option, in the event that the insured is totally disabled for a period of time during the premium-paying life of the policy, the insurance company will keep the policy in force, waiving all premium payments during the term of disability, even though it may be for the life of the insurance contract. This is a form of disability insurance that costs relatively little and is much worth having.

Another prior option is a guarantee on the part of the insurance company, available at a modest additional premium, that states that additional amounts of insurance will be sold to you at your option for a stated time into the future beyond your original insurance purchase and without the need for further medical or other qualification on your part. This is not so routinely offered, nor is it carried by all life insurance companies, but it is worth asking about and pursuing during your earlier years.

A third prior option is that of purchasing other kinds of insurance in a package with your life insurance policy, such as accident insurance—usually in the form of a "double indemnity," meaning payment of twice the face amount of the policy if death occurs in stated accidental ways—or disability insurance, other than the waiver of premium. These kinds of insurance should be considered on their own and taken if you want them, but should not be considered necessarily as part of the life insurance decision. There is a tendency, which all experienced and skillful sellers know about and exploit whether they are selling shoes or life insurance, to keep on buying once you have bought. That is why you may walk out of a shoe store with two pairs of shoes and a dozen pairs of socks, when you went in looking for one pair of shoes—and why you may buy life insurance, accident insurance, disability insurance, and perhaps a share in an investment fund, when you had originally intended only to inquire about life insurance. That is a tendency to be staunchly resisted. The life insurance decision is best handled as a decision to buy catastrophe insurance, not as part of a series of other insurance and investment decisions.

The inability to buy any life insurance at all can be a vexing problem. Although some companies are more strict than others regarding insurability, and "shopping around" can sometimes solve the problem, many people still have great difficulty in purchasing individual life insurance—especially in purchasing such insurance from a "safe" company. Surely some company can almost always be found to insure you, even though you may have substantial medical problems, but the insurance may not be worth very much if the insurer is questionable—and that defeats the main purpose of life insurance, which is to provide an unassailable keystone in your total financial planning. It would seem pointless to consider buying questionable life insurance.

Another way to proceed is to buy life insurance on a "substandard" risk basis from a reputable company. You will pay higher rates on that basis and may encounter company limitations on the amounts and kinds of life insurance that you will be issued, but in some instances that is still better than no life insurance at all.

A relatively new type of contract offered by a limited number of companies in some states is a "guaranteed issue policy," offered regardless of medical conditions. An individual who suffered a coronary attack yesterday would purchase such a policy today without any medical examination. Such a contract has various limitations, of course. For example, in some, if the insured dies from sickness within three years of the issue of the policy, the beneficiary receives only a return of premium paid plus interest; if death results from accident at any time, the policy would pay the beneficiary the full face amount of the policy and a return of premium plus interest. At the end of three years, the full face amount of the policy will be paid, regardless of the cause of death. The premium for such a policy is higher than that for a conventional policy, but for many uninsurables it is worth considering, although the limitations of each individual policy should be carefully examined.

Another, often quite fruitful way to proceed is to be a participant in a nonmedical, guaranteed group insurance policy, as so many millions of employees are, and to convert some or all of that insurance over to individual insurance on termination of employment. We previously discussed this as a trap, because term insurance so converted can be relatively very expensive. But for someone who is otherwise virtually uninsurable, nonmedical group insurance provides a superb way to secure individual insurance in those instances in which no medical examination is required for the issuance of the conversion policy. That is, in a sense, "the luck of the draw," as employees cannot pick and choose among employers with the nature of life insurance conversion arrangements in mind—but it is by far the best way to go, if available.

Life insurance may also be obtained through membership in a fraternal or professional organization that has a group or association life insurance policy available for purchase by its members on a guaranteed issue basis. These policies are usually limited in the amount of insurance available to be purchased and perhaps in convertibility rights, but are often an excellent, inexpensive way of obtaining the necessary catastrophe protection.

Bank credit insurance and a variety of organizations such as credit card companies and travel associations may also provide guaranteed insurance. These options usually will not fulfill one's fundamental life insurance needs, but may serve to narrow the gap between one's needs and the availability of other policies. Since these policies are not sold by life insurance agents, it may take searching and ingenuity to find them, but they are often available. Life insurance accompanying mortgage and other loans also can serve a stopgap function, if necessary.

A life insurance purchase presumes a very long relationship between insurer and insured. When you buy life insurance, you assume that the company you have purchased from will stay in business and be able to make good on its legal obligations for as long as, or longer than, three-quarters of a century after the date of purchase. If that company should be unable to do so when its obligation to you comes due, then much of your lifetime financial planning may go for naught. Children may be robbed of education and career prospects; your spouse may be forced to live out life in poverty; and your own retirement plans may be destroyed. Even if a life insurance company should fail long before your death or the maturity of an annuity, you may lose a great deal more than money, if you are, by then, no longer insurable. The reliability of the insurance company you do business with is of central importance to you. That is why so many insurance companies of all kinds take great pains to advertise themselves as huge and totally reliable, using such confidence-building images as the Rock of Gibraltar, frontier cavalry, and huge cupped hands in which the insured sits sheltered from the vicissitudes of life.

Insurance companies are regulated by the states rather than federally, and state statutes and regulations regarding both the reserves that life insurance companies must keep in order to pay policyholders and the restrictions on company investments and operations vary widely. Some very large companies, like Prudential or Metropolitan, would probably be considered "safe" in any state in which they were doing business. Others should be considered "safe" only because they are doing business in states such as New York, Ohio, and Massachusetts, which are careful regulators and require that high reserves be held. Some states, such as Texas, have for decades been much less rigorous in their approach to reserves and regulation, and small insurance companies, often selling by mail into other states, have flocked to them.

The net result is that a life insurance policy written by a major company or any company headquartered in such a state as New

York can reasonably be relied on for bedrock financial planning—
barring nationwide economic or political catastrophe, of course.
The life insurance policy written by a small Texas or perhaps Ar-
izona company, across state lines, may prove to be little more
than a cruel delusion a generation or two later, when you or your
survivors try to collect benefits due. Life insurance companies
headquartered in states that regulate poorly and that require inadequate reserves may not be in business at all in later years, as
poor management and investment policies force them out of
business. Poor choice of insurer is one of the major traps in lifetime financial planning, and every attempt should be made to
avoid it by careful selection, with company size and location of its
headquarters very much in mind.

HEALTH INSURANCE

Health insurance really can help ensure that you have the best
possible chance of staying in good health. The best health insurance arrangements make it relatively easy for those insured to
practice preventive health care, with periodic and thorough
checkups aimed at early diagnosis of potential problems. Sound
health insurance can also help you resolve health problems earlier, by allowing you to seek treatment in a timely fashion when
you do have a problem, without worrying about where the money will come from to pay the inevitably high bills associated with
treatment. It helps guard against going back to work too soon
after illness and against the kinds of money worries that can impede recuperation when you should be concentrating on getting
well.

In financial planning terms, the many kinds of insurance generally classified as health insurance are, taken together, just as
much catastrophe insurance as is life insurance, since failure to
properly assess and plan for meeting health insurance needs can
bring about economic catastrophe. That possibility is great because of the steeply rising cost of medical care, which has, for
decades, far outpaced both inflation and incomes. In the 1980s,

even a short hospital stay, if uninsured or inadequately insured, can prove a substantial drain on the finances of most families, while a long illness can be a financial disaster, wiping out all assets. It is not at all unusual for hospital costs of all kinds to exceed $300 per day, to which must be added all necessary surgical and aftercare costs plus those amounts of income that are foregone because of illness. In truth, catastrophic illness can have a much greater financial impact on families than death, even when substantial health insurance is carried.

For people who have very little in the way of assets and very low incomes, there is government-supplied Medicaid, which will cover most health care expenses. For people over 65—at this writing—there is Medicare, which will do the same, although supplementary health care insurance is also very important. However, for people under 65 who have assets, sound health insurance planning is as much a cornerstone of financial planning as is sound life insurance planning. And as with life insurance, there are public, business, and personal insurance arrangements to consider and substantial hazards to avoid.

Several tax-funded, publicly administered kinds of health insurance cover individuals. In addition to Medicaid and Medicare, these include disability insurance under the federal Social Security law, as well as some state disability insurance coverages and workers' compensation, which provide varying amounts of coverage as provided by state law.

The amounts provided by these additional kinds of public insurance are often rather small in terms of the needs of those who are sick or disabled, but in some instances they can be substantial. For example, disability insurance may be payable not only to those who are totally unable to pursue any kind of gainful employment, but also to those who are unable to pursue the kind of work they are trained and able to do, enabling them to pursue some kinds of alternate employment. In those circumstances, a combination of long-term, tax-free disability benefits and modest income from other kinds of less demanding work can mean the ability to live a fruitful, productive life, even if severely impaired by work-connected disability.

For long-term planning, though, those with earning power and assets should regard public insurance with great caution. Greatly lengthened lifespans and the continuing impact of inflation place considerable strain on public insurance systems now; there will be much more strain later. In our time, we will see a protracted battle between pensioners and younger taxpayers. Pensioners have every reason to expect public insurance to rise to meet rising costs; younger taxpayers have every reason to seek relief from increasingly oppressive tax burdens. There will be more and more pensioners as lifespans lengthen; that means more potential political strength, if it can be channeled. There will be fewer younger taxpayers, but still a majority, with greater grievances; that means far more pressure from the majority to scale down social insurance expenditures. The outcome is not properly predictable. Americans may ultimately opt for a comprehensive national social insurance system, as many other industrial countries have done, or they may choose to develop social insurance systems that leave pensioners with no personal resources living at poverty levels, with social insurance that barely covers minimal needs, as is increasingly true now. However it goes, sound planning demands preparation for the latter situation; to assume that social insurance will cover you now or later in the event of serious illness or disability is to run the risk of destroying all financial plans.

Most Americans are covered by basic hospital–surgical medical care plans that require no physical examinations to qualify for coverage, whether they are employed by others, are self-employed, or are family members of those so employed. Blue Cross–Blue Shield is the largest single insurer, although many large companies, governments, and other institutions contract with other substantial insurance companies for employee health coverage that often yields far better benefits than the Blue Cross–Blue Shield plans. Some plans provide dental care and substantial outpatient and posthospital care and also pay for doctors' visits, drugs, and psychiatric care. Some of the best plans provide for substantial payment of all health care costs after a modest yearly deductible amount has been paid by the covered employee. Some plans, especially in small, family-run companies, pay all health care costs of any kind, providing a means of paying such costs out of pretax, rather than aftertax, income, which is a considerable advantage.

The question of preexisting conditions is the main potential trap in the area of hospital-surgical insurance. Almost all such insurance contracts specify that insurance benefits will not be payable to the insured should illness or disability result from conditions existing before commencement of coverage. For example, someone hospitalized because of a heart attack may not be covered by an employer's insurance plan if employment, and therefore coverage, started six months before and if the heart condition can be shown to have existed prior to employment. Many plans ease the pain of this provision by specifying that, after a stated period—often one year—all conditions will be considered to be current, in essence waiving the preexisting conditions provision after that time. However, the occurrence of a serious illness during that first year can be a personal catastrophe if uncovered by any insurance.

People who are moving from one Blue Cross–Blue Shield plan to another have a real advantage. In recent years, Blue Cross–Blue Shield plans have begun to provide for transfer of contracts from group to personal coverage, or from one group to another, on termination of employment, without the need for the clock to start running again on preexisting conditions—a very important safeguard for the insured. The coverage available will be as good or nearly as good as before, although you will be paying for it yourself, when before it may have been wholly or partly employer supplied. If your new employer carries insurance with a different company, you may well need to carry your Blue Cross–Blue Shield policy at the same time your new employer is carrying your insurance, if that insurance has a waiting period on preexisting conditions. That can be expensive for a year-long waiting period, but the protection is worth the cost. If you know in advance that you will be terminating employment—for example, if you are going into business for yourself—you would be wise to obtain an individual policy a year ahead of time, to be sure you will have passed through any waiting period before terminating your employment and, with it, your other insurance.

When the coverage with your present employer is provided by a company other than Blue Cross–Blue Shield, you will probably be able to convert to an individual policy, but at very high cost and with very limited benefits. That can be a problem, because in order to fill the current potential gap in coverage, and especially if you do indeed have a health condition dating from before your change of insurers, you may have to pay for both the converted individual policy and a new Blue Cross–Blue Shield policy—and that set of costs can become prohibitive. We think the best solution to that problem lies in the purchase of a personal major medical plan policy, which we discuss in the context of such major medical coverage.

Major medical expense coverage is catastrophe insurance, which takes over and pays all or a large portion of costs when short-term insurance has been used up. Like other forms of health insurance, it can be written on an individual or a family basis, with younger family members losing coverage or being required to convert to individual policies as they leave school or reach specified ages. It is a widely provided "fringe benefit" in American industry; it is also, like life insurance, more and more an insurance that is purchased by individuals as a basic coverage and cornerstone of financial planning, whether or not provided by employers.

When the purchaser of major medical insurance is a large group, such as a substantial employer or an association, physical examinations to qualify for coverage are not usually required of those to be covered. When individuals or small groups are the purchasers, physical examinations are usually required.

Major medical, whether held personally or as part of a group coverage, usually pays 80 to 100% of all specified costs incurred after other hospital-surgical plans have stopped paying or in the absence of any payment from basic hospital-surgical plans. For example, major medical may take over 90% of hospital costs incurred during a long hospital stay after Blue Cross–Blue Shield has run out, may pay 90% of certain in-hospital costs not covered by Blue Cross–Blue Shield from the start of the hospital stay, and may pay 90% of certain posthospital costs.

Often there is a "deductible" involved, meaning that major medical will take over its stated share of costs only after a certain sum has been paid wholly by the insured. For example, the 90% paid in the instance just cited might begin to be payable only after the first $500 of uncovered expenses had been paid by the patient.

"Coordination of benefits" usually, but not always, applies to all basic and major medical policies, meaning that when an insured has been reimbursed for an insured cost by one insurer, another insurer will not duplicate that payment. When that rule does not apply, insurance companies stress that fact very clearly to policyholders, as it is a prime selling point.

Major medical insurance policies often reimburse policyholders up into the $50,000 range, though some have, in recent years, begun to feature higher maximums—at higher premium levels, of course. However, because the cost of medical care has skyrocketed during the last two decades, the $50,000 maximum that seemed entirely adequate in the 1960s and early 1970s may prove to be entirely inadequate in the 1980s. A two-year combined hospital and nursing home stay, including expensive surgical and emergency procedures, may easily result in a total bill of $100,000 to $150,000 for a single illness. Therefore, many companies and institutions supplying group coverage for their employees have raised maximums to a range of $500,000 to $1 million, and many individuals, purchasing as individuals or as association members, have purchased "excess" major medical policies with similar maximums.

These policies, also called "piggyback" major medical policies, are designed to supplement basic hospitalization and major medical coverage. They are geared to fill the void created when one's benefits are completed under the basic contract, but when the nature of the accident or illness keeps additional medical bills coming. An excess major medical policy with a $15,000 deductible and a $1 million maximum benefit, for example, would come into play only after $15,000 of bills were incurred, but would continue to pay bills up to $1 million. Premiums on such policies are relatively low, since the insurer assumes a risk only when the insured or the basic contract has taken responsibility for the first $15,000 of bills. Such a policy is worth serious consideration by everyone.

In the area of major medical catastrophe insurance, you should be very sure to have uninterrupted coverage, for in this area hundreds of thousands of people have found that an enormous planning trap exists. It is all too common for a perfectly healthy, insurable person to go to work for a company or institution, enjoy company-paid major medical coverage for many years, incur serious illness at some time during those years of employment, become unemployed or change jobs, and suffer catastrophic illness before the preexisting conditions period has run through under a new insurance contract, with resulting financial disaster. Group major medical coverage is very often either not convertible to personal major medical or convertible at very low levels of coverage and at prohibitively high premium costs.

Even if someone is "uninsurable"—that is, quite unable to pass a medical examination for personal major medical coverage at any premium price—such coverage can often be obtained on a non-medical-examination basis by affiliation with a voluntary association, such as an alumni, social, or religious group, that makes group insurance available to its members. Many plans are written with sound, large, well-funded national insurance companies and carry excellent catastrophe insurance benefits.

But, again, the trap that can be created by a preexisting conditions period must be avoided, since it can destroy all financial plans. The only sure way to avoid it is to carry major medical catastrophe insurance from the time you realize you need it to when government insurance takes over. Carry the largest deductible you think reasonable—perhaps $500 to $1000 beyond surgical-medical insurance—on the theory that you can afford to pay that amount of medical bills out of your pocket to keep your premiums low or that you will probably be covered by some kind of company insurance at almost all times. But hedge your bet by carrying a personal major medical insurance policy that is issued on a guaranteed renewable basis by a substantial and well-funded national insurance company. "Guaranteed renewable" means that the company cannot cancel the policy as long as premium payments are paid and cannot raise premium rates unless they are raised on the whole class of policies of which the individual policy is part. Policies may be issued on a "noncancelable and guaranteed renewable" basis as well, which means that, as long as premiums are paid, the policy cannot be canceled and premium rates must be those specified in the individual policy itself. That is the firmest possible protection, but it also carries the highest premium rates and is rarely offered for major medical policies.

The potential financial catastrophe of long-term, high-cost illness or injury can be partly averted by well-planned, adequate health insurance coverage. However, that kind of illness or injury often also brings with it another kind of financial disaster, as income is foregone during the illness and sometimes for many years afterward. A totally disabled middle-management executive with a family of four and earning $40,000 a year may receive as much as $10,000 a year tax free in combined federal disability payments until his or her children reach their early 20s—age 22, as of this writing—and $6000 a year or more tax free thereafter. However, that is a long way from the $30,000 or more a year that the executive takes home today, and it does not take into account either inflation or increased earning expectations cut off by that disability. Companies may partially fill the gap with company-paid disability plans; some do and some do not. Individuals may partly prepare for the possibility of disabling accident or illness by the purchase of individual disability income plans.

Some company-paid disability income plans coordinate federal and company benefits, providing a combined guarantee that diminishes the company's share of total payments as federal payments go up over the years. Most individually purchased disability income plans do not coordinate benefits, providing that fixed payments be made regardless of whatever other plans and payments may be in existence. Individual plans paying meaningful benefit amounts are rather expensive, though, and thought should be given as to how much one is willing to spend on this kind of protection and how much protection is needed. A sole provider in his or her early forties, with several children to support and send through school and with many years of life ahead, may feel the need for a higher disability payout level than a married person who is 55 years old and has no children to support. Since the premium is determined not only by the age of the insured and the amount of disability income to be paid, but also by the waiting period before the payments start and the benefit period during which the company is committed to pay benefits, all of these factors should be examined carefully in evaluating policies for purchase.

As with life insurance, some disability insurance contracts provide the ability to purchase more insurance without medical examination in later years; that is a real plus to be looked for. Other standard provisions include waiver of further premium payments in the event of total disability and the availability of additional benefits—for additional premium payments—for hospital-surgical and accident coverages. When considering such other options, bear in mind that disability insurance is rather expensive—though necessary—catastrophe insurance; try not to add unnecessary additional costs for elements of coverage you already carry, and will continue to carry, through other kinds of insurance.

PROPERTY AND LIABILITY INSURANCE

Because insurers and insurance policies often lump together two basic, but quite different, kinds of insurance—property and liability—it is best to discuss them together. However, to understand the roles these kinds of insurance play in personal financial planning, the basic insuring transactions must first be understood.

Property insurance pays you for losses you incur as a result of the partial or total loss of value of property, such as in fire loss, automobile damage, or theft. Liability insurance pays others for costs for which you may be held legally responsible, as when the property and person of another are damaged because of collision with your car, or when someone is injured because of a fall on an icy walk outside your home.

Property insurance insures determinable values. A house or car is insured up to a set value or a determinable upper range of value, with premium and payouts generally foreseeable far in advance. Liability insurance is a far more open-ended matter. For example, if your provable negligence causes the total disability of a 40-year-old, highly paid corporate executive, with at least 25 years of earnings therefore cut off, a jury may award that executive several hundred thousand dollars. Should liability insurance prove grossly inadequate to meet that judgment, it will be levied against your assets—and what of financial planning then? A huge uninsured liability claim can wipe you out.

Property and liability insurance are, like other kinds of insurance, best assessed, for financial planning purposes, as catastrophe insurance. Seen that way, it is possible to distinguish between what it pays to insure and what it is uneconomical to insure, between which risks you essentially "self-insure" and which risks you pay to have insured by others.

The "deductible" is the most common means of self-insurance. For example, an automobile collision insurance policy with a $250 deductible reflects an insuring transaction in which the insured self-insures for the first $250 of damage to the vehicle and pays an insurance company for insurance on more than $250 worth of damage, up to the total value of the vehicle. As a practical matter, many automobile owners do not even bother to put in minor claims, quite correctly reasoning that it usually costs considerably more in the long run to pay the increased insurance premiums resulting from those claims than to self-insure them. Some large companies find it economical to self-insure major risks, such as plant and equipment damage, but that is not a course that can be taken by most individuals. Individuals must insure themselves through insurers against major property losses and substantial potential liabilities, but should carefully consider self-insuring through use of deductibles for lesser amounts.

Insurers wrap up such major coverages in two kinds of standard policies: the homeowner's or renter's policy and the automobile policy.

The homeowner's policy insures a residence and its contents, in stated ways and up to stated limits, against losses due to the most common kinds of catastrophes, starting with fire and fire-related damages. Simultaneously, it insures against personal liability up to stated amounts. Although coverages and terms tend to be quite standard—so standard that the specifics are best discussed with your property and liability agent—there are, as in all kinds of insurance, some hazards to guard against.

One notable hazard lies in the area of the upper limit of liability insurance coverage. A homeowner's policy that is quite satisfactory in all other respects may carry a personal liability maximum of $100,000, creating a very substantial gap in insurance coverage in these days of debased currency and the ever-increasing claims of the litigation-conscious and their lawyers. We tend to be very conscious of this risk when securing automobile insurance coverage, but to overlook it when purchasing homeowner's coverage. It is worthwhile to examine additional coverage in this area; many companies, for example, offer "umbrella" coverage for a wide range of liabilities up to high maximums, such as $1 million, for very little premium cost.

Another substantial hazard lies in the amount for which your dwelling is insured. In some jurisdictions, coverage that is less than a fixed percentage of replacement cost—for example, 80% in parts of New York State—may result in a far smaller insurance settlement than that necessary to replace a totally destroyed dwelling. Especially during periods of rapid inflation, you should reevaluate your coverage annually—and raise your protection to meet current needs.

A smaller, but sometimes rather substantial, hazard lies in the area of limits placed by the insurer on some kinds of claims—sometimes called "internal limits" within your homeowner's policy. You may, for example, be limited to the collection of $1000 for a certain kind of collectible, but have a collection valued at far more. Your house may be insured for $75,000, and its contents for $50,000, $10,000 of which is your collection. Even if your contents loss is $30,000, not $50,000, but $10,000 of the loss is your whole collection, you may get only $1000 in insurance payments because of this internal limitation. That hazard is best guarded against by purchase of additional insurance, which specially insures your collection, and usually other valuables as well, by description and specific valuation, for insurable losses occurring anywhere in the country and often anywhere in the world. Such coverage is called a "floater," so named because it moves with the items insured, rather than insuring them in a specified location.

Privately purchased catastrophe insurance becomes a legal necessity in many jurisdictions when we turn to the automobile, that very dangerous and most prolific source of insurance claims. Collision and theft insurance are useful tools for diminishing risk when dealing with late-model vehicles, and you can substantially cut the cost by taking high deductibles, self-insuring for the initial amounts. For older vehicles collision insurance is questionable, usually being too expensive for the value provided. But liability insurance—as much as is reasonably possible—is a must for all vehicles. Even where the law specifies minimum amounts of liability insurance that must be in force, liability insurance far above the legal limits is a vitally important feature of personal financial planning, to cover you against catastrophe.

That is true even in the presence of some form of state-mandated no-fault insurance. No-fault mandates payments and tends to diminish the number of claims that go into litigation, but most emphatically does not eliminate the possibility of a ruinous judgment against you following an automobile accident. Moving the upper limits of your automobile liability coverage into the $500,000 plus range per accident may cost surprisingly little if your driving record is good, and it may bar financial disaster.

Another way to handle the question of personal liability catastrophe insurance is to purchase excess liability coverage, which functions to cover you against major claims after your other kinds of insurance have run to their upper limits, much as an "excess" major medical policy functions. Such coverage can be quite inexpensive.

On balance, your total property and liability insurance bills may go up little, or not at all, if you exchange deductibles for excess coverage, saving unnecessary premium costs by the adoption of high deductibles and putting the money saved into catastrophe insurance.

CHAPTER 9

Accumulating for Your
Later Years

In a very real sense, much of this book, so far, has had to do with funding your later years. We have previously discussed such central matters as the impact of inflation and currency debasement, the hazards involved in too much reliance on government and employers, the need to guard against financial catastrophe through astute insurance planning, and the myth of retirement; in addition, we have examined ways to build financial health carefully and creatively during your high-earning years to meet current needs and desires—and to help make the later years good ones as well. It is important to think through early how to continue productive economic activity during your later years— for most of us that will probably be essential to the maintenance of any kind of real economic health, as we discuss in Chapter 10. But to have the best possible chance of effectively funding one's later years, it is important to plan and assess well in advance what can be expected in real dollars from government, institutional, and private sector retirement plans; from other tax-advantaged retirement plan possibilities; and from savings and investments.

SOCIAL SECURITY

For financial planning purposes, you can reasonably project a combination of federal Social Security and federal health insurance to provide most of your bare-bones needs during your later years, barring the kinds of national economic and political storms that destroy all personal plans

However, it is imprudent to suppose that government retirement benefits will be any larger in real dollars than they are today and quite prudent to suppose that they will be somewhat smaller. Given the rapidly lengthening lifespans and economic problems that characterize our period, it is prudent to suppose that the "retirement age" will, within this century, be raised beyond 65 years; that the effectively bankrupt Social Security funding system will be replaced by one whose funding is based on general tax revenues in addition to employer-employee contributions; and that there will be constant pressure to diminish real benefits.

Social Security retirement benefits are now effectively "indexed," meaning that they rise as the cost of living rises. But what can be done by Congress can be undone by Congress, and it seems quite probable that multiple pressures will produce changes in the indexing formulas in coming years, forcing the real level of benefits down even further, even though older Americans who rely on Social Security today often live at or below minimum needs levels.

However, most basic subsistence and health care needs will be covered, and that is not to be underestimated in investment terms, for that is worth a good deal. For example, as little as $4000 a year in combined Social Security and health care payments is approximately equivalent to $50,000 in savings put into fixed-income investments with a net aftertax return of 8%. But investment capital does not grow if you are using its earnings to live on, while Social Security payments do, to some extent reflecting the impact of inflation. Over a 20-year period beyond age 65—and many of us will live until we are 85 or older—and assuming annual inflation in the 10% range, that $50,000 would have to grow to \$336,375 in order to yield the equivalent of \$4000 in today's dollars at the same 8%. That is what inflation does to us and to our financial planning. In light of this, it is one of the extraordinary ironies of our time that some people, who will need benefits and health care desperately in their later years, are today fighting hard to reduce the Social Security benefits available to those over 65, with some even campaigning for abolition of the Social Security and health care systems.

Given the impact of inflation and the indexing of Social Security payments, it is not very meaningful to calculate the specific amounts of payments you are likely to receive until you are very close to retirement. What you can assume, if you have been regularly employed for the minimum number of years in your working life, is that you will receive a basic contribution of your minimum living expenses in your retirement. It is wise to confirm with the Social Security offices that your records are in order—a call to the local office will get you a form for doing so—but otherwise to focus your attention on making your own provision for your later years.

TAX-ADVANTAGED PLANS

Beyond Social Security are many types of tax-advantaged pension and profit-sharing plans. Funds may legally be accumulated in these plans in a manner that allows contributions to the plan to be tax deductible, that allows the assets of the plan to compound on a tax-free basis, and that allows tax-advantaged income upon retirement. Individuals generally have three choices with such plans: to take the income in a lump sum and pay the taxes due at postretirement tax levels, take the income over a number of years, or to defer receipt of income entirely until a future date, thereby advantageously spreading and modifying the taxes to be paid in a way that suits individual economic needs and tax planning.

Corporate pension and profit-sharing plans that are organized and administered so as to meet federal statutory requirements are enormously tax advantaged. Owner-employees in smaller businesses who use the corporate form to develop such qualified pension plans are, in essence, able to grow tax-advantaged personal pension funds. People employed by corporations providing such plans can and often do share to some extent in such growth, receiving considerably larger pension payments than would be possible if the tax advantages were not built into the private pension system by statute.

Businesses are not taxed on the amounts they contribute to these tax-advantaged, qualified corporate pension plans. Corporate contributions are treated as business expenses. Individual voluntary contributions, if any, are made with aftertax income. One major thing to consider about payout is that pension funds, whatever the source of contributions, accrete earnings tax free; they are thus able to grow much faster than personal investment funds, which, except for various tax-shelter arrangements, must pay taxes on current earnings. If you are in a set of federal, state, and municipal tax brackets that add up to a 50% levy on incremental income, past a certain point you pay $1 for every $2 earned. In 20 years, $1 at 8% becomes $6.72, assuming you reinvest all net earnings. But $2, the pretax amount, would become $38.92 in 20 years, almost six times as much. That is how the mechanics of compound interest and deferred taxation can work to your advantage.

In order for pension and profit-sharing plans to qualify for favorable tax treatment under the Employee Retirement Income Security Act of 1974 (ERISA), thus becoming "qualified" plans, they must, by law, adhere to legally mandated reporting requirements and meet several other statutory necessities.

Most people employed by others have little or no control over their work-connected pension plans. Whether the plans are entirely a matter of company discretion within statutory requirements or a matter of negotiation between company and employee organization, such funds are quite outside the control of individual pensioners; they cannot be handled and moved about from investment to investment, as can personal investment assets. If you are a nonowner of the firm by which you are employed, and if you are paid wages or commissions by this employer, only the employer has the legal right to establish and administer such a plan. You may find that the plan established by the employer allows you to add "voluntary contributions"; you will also have certain rights available, such as in naming your own beneficiary under the plan and perhaps in determining the time and method for you to obtain the proceeds due you. In the main, however, the plan is controlled by the employer, under government regulations, and you are solely a participant. In financial planning terms, work-connected pensions are much like Social Security benefits—not really controllable, but very much a cornerstone element in assessing what funds will be available in your later years.

For many people, Social Security and work-connected pensions are substantially all there is—and that can be dangerous. Although some safeguards are forced on the private pension system by law, those who rely solely or largely on pensions for their income in later years still face substantial hazards.

Corporation pension and profit-sharing plans must conform to the requirements of the Employee Retirement Income Security Act; they are monitored by the Internal Revenue Service, the Department of Labor, and, for certain types of plans, the Pension Benefit Guarantee Corporation. From the time they are instituted until they are terminated, the trust and plan are under the jurisdiction of these agencies and must conform in order to maintain their tax-advantaged status.

This law and the monitoring process have remedied many of the poor management problems and plain chicanery involving corporate plans in the past. A dramatic example occurred when the Studebaker Corporation went out of business; employees who anticipated benefits after decades of employment and participation in the company pension plan found that there were no assets available in the plan. Corporations can, even under the new law, still mismanage or even deliberately and illegally deprive their employees of pension benefits due them; as long as someone else, other than you, is in control, that is always a possibility.

However, the greater danger to anticipated benefits from a private pension plan may lie elsewhere. For example, a corporation simply may not earn enough money to be able to afford and contribute to a plan. Even the best-intentioned corporate executives who have set up a plan beneficial to their employees may, if their business ceases to be successful, be forced to terminate the plan or amend it drastically so its benefits will be insignificant.

Also, in small corporations a plan may be legally written so that only the owner-employees, supervisors, or highly paid workers receive significant benefits. This may very well suit your purpose if you are in control of the plan, but if you are not, you may participate in a plan for 40 years and end up with insignificant benefits.

In addition, your benefits from a pension or profit-sharing plan depend largely on the investment intelligence of the trustees of the plan or their advisors. Although the Employee Retirement Income Security Act specifies that the trustees follow the "prudent man" rule, which means that the trustee should act for the plan—in the nature and diversification of the investment—as a "prudent man" would act for himself, it is quite possible to stay within the boundaries of this definition and suffer great losses in the assets of a plan. The record is replete with examples of badly managed plans, which consistently lost monies in their investment of plan funds or obtained returns far lower than those they could have obtained if they had done no more than put the plan monies in bank savings accounts. Such mismanagement has happened and is happening today—and it can be disastrous for an employee depending upon certain benefits at retirement.

"Defined" or "fixed" benefit plans can have another pitfall. In this type of plan the participant will receive a fixed sum of money at retirement based upon the plan formula, his or her own wage scale, and perhaps the number of years of employment. That money should be available to the plan participant upon retirement, regardless of the investment decisions of the trustees, for in these plans the investment results are usually predicated upon a modest interest assumption, from 5 to 6%; even more important, the results of the investments are reviewed annually, and if the corporation earns less than the interest assumption, it is supposed to remedy that problem by making a greater contribution that year. But there is no guarantee that the plan will be there at full strength on retirement.

The Pension Benefit Guarantee Corporation is, as of this writing, operating rather effectively to remedy any failure of corporations with fixed or defined benefit plans to meet their obligations to participants for past benefits to which they are legally entitled. However, no law or regulation requires a corporation to continue a plan or to maintain a benefit for the future if poor investment experience, lack of ability to contribute adequate funds, or a management decision for whatever reason causes a termination or reduction of benefits under a plan. Even if the plan is not reduced and receives all required funds, a plan established 30 years before retirement and not adjusted periodically to account for inflation may very well provide the dollars that were anticipated, but these will be so eroded in value that they will be insignificant in helping fund one's retirement adequately.

In addition, many pension plans pay fixed pension amounts, while at the same time coordinating payments with Social Security. Therein can lie another pensioner's delusion, created by the inexorable process of inflation. That fixed payment from a corporate pension plan, no matter how high it seems when you retire, may become relatively minuscule 20 years later. In truth, it may not even exist; Social Security payments, indexed to inflation, may by then have increased to the point where your pension fund is relieved of all or most of its obligation to contribute to your support. It is not so simple as to urge that government legislate the "indexing" of private pension fund payments—though in the future it may come to that—for the drain then on company profits may make that course of action prohibitively expensive. The federal government can legislate increases or indexing of Social Security payments; it has the taxing power to do so. Private companies may not be able to do the same.

For all these reasons, full reliance for retirement income on a company pension or profit-sharing plan may prove for many to be a cruel delusion, as some of the pension and profit-sharing funds that now seem huge prove inadequate to meet pensioners' claims in later years.

The answer, if there is one, lies in regarding private pension and profit-sharing funds with pleasurable anticipation but also in evaluating their true worth periodically. When pension time comes, and for many years beyond, you may find yourself receiving handsome benefits from an amply funded pension or profit-sharing plan. Or you may find yourself receiving the most modest of payments, with their value further decreased by the continuing erosion of the dollar's purchasing power. You would be best advised to hope for the former and to plan for the latter, doing your best to develop assets and skills of your own to take you through your later years.

For some people employed by others, the corporate deferred compensation plan offers a real and controllable way to develop assets for later years. The basic transaction consists of a promise by the employer to the employee to defer some part of compensation until later years, usually until retirement. That transaction is embodied in an employment contract, which sometimes specifies that the sums so deferred will include an interest factor or an agreed-upon funding vehicle, so that the employee will not be penalized by the passage of time, the mechanics of inflation, and foregone potential investment earnings on the deferred compensation. The deferred amounts, finally paid, are ordinary income to the employee, since these arrangements are tax advantaged only by deferral and not upon receipt. They are, however, taxable at postretirement income levels, which are often far lower than those faced by key employees in their highest earning years. On the other hand, such deferred compensation arrangements are long-term contracts payable entirely in the sometimes rather distant future and depend very much on the employer's continuing good economic health.

People employed by others, but not covered by company or government employee pension plans, are able to set up modest, but meaningful, tax-advantaged individual private pension plans under statutory limits set by the Employee Retirement Income Security Act, as later amended and regulated. Such a plan is called an "Individual Retirement Account" (IRA). An individual may place up to $1500 a year or 15% of yearly compensation, whichever is less, into an IRA and may treat that amount as a deduction from taxable income that year. A couple, with one of the two not working, can divide up to $1750 in two separate accounts yearly. Money in the account accretes tax free until withdrawal at retirement, then to be taxed at presumably lower postretirement rates. To avoid tax penalties, the money in an IRA must be withdrawn between the ages of 59½ and 70½.

Individuals who have an IRA or Keogh plan, and who are now age 70½, have another interesting tax-advantaged option. They can continue to contribute the maximum allowed under the law and can simultaneously withdraw a portion of those funds on a "life expectancy basis." Since the funds contributed are totally tax deductible and only a portion of the funds being withdrawn each year are treated as taxable income, tax payments are minimized and such individuals continue to have the remaining funds in the plan compounding on a tax-deferred basis.

An IRA may be set up with any institution that has properly filed a Master IRA Custodial or Trust Agreement, which has been approved or qualified by the IRS. Many banks and other financial institutions are qualified to hold IRA accounts as custodians; in addition, many insurance companies and mutual fund management companies have qualified plans available for people who wish to fund their IRA plans with their products. Such products may include annuities, but, by law, cannot include insurance company policies whose major purpose is to provide a death benefit.

More recently, plans have been filed by and approved for other types of institutions, including stock exchange firms, associations, and an institution called a "trust company," whose only function is to act as an administrative shell for the various types of plans available under ERISA. Depending upon how the plan is written, the planholder may buy stocks or bonds, participate in owning oil wells, or purchase gold, silver, collectibles, and a variety of other products (still excluding death benefit life insurance). Those custodians or trustees that sell products to fund such plans usually charge little or no fee for administration of the account, while banks and trust companies, which usually do not sell products, invariably charge a fee for their services.

A plan may also be set up by the purchase of federal retirement bonds, but interest rates are currently so low that they are an unattractive investment, even though no administration fees are involved. As with Series E and HH savings bonds, the federal government is relying on patriotic fervor and a desire for close-to-absolute safety to make these bonds acceptable at the lower interest rates.

Whatever the type of IRA, you gain tax advantage, but relinquish access to your funds until age 59½, unless you are prepared to pay a tax penalty. Investment discretion and physical control are in other hands; however, by your choice of plan, you can determine to a large extent how the funds will be invested. You can also have more than one IRA plan or can change the custodian or trustee, although no more than once annually. Procedures for making such changes are simple, and, as long as you do not take the fund assets back into your name (unless you are disabled) prior to age 59½, the changes will not trigger any taxes prematurely.

Another plan available under the ERISA statute is called the "Individual Retirement Account Rollover." Such plans are designed to accept only assets that are being transferred from other tax-qualified plans; no fresh monies can be added to them from the planholder's pocket. The tax-free rollover transaction is provided by statute so that circumstances beyond the planholder's control, or a planholder's desire to end contributions to another tax-qualified plan, do not force him or her to take the funds prematurely. The planholder is also bound to remove assets, as in an IRA, between the ages of 59½ and 70½.

Users of the rollover plan may be employees whose employer has terminated a corporation pension plan, a profit-sharing plan, or a Keogh plan and who do not wish the use of their monies vested in the plan at that time, or employees who have terminated their employment with a company providing such a plan. The aim of this tax-free rollover statute is to see that circumstances will not frustrate legislative intent regarding these plans, which is to provide a pension plan alternative to such employees or former employees.

The same legislative intent will probably result in a raising of contribution limits for IRA plans in the years ahead. It is quite possible that the limit of 15% of yearly compensation will remain the same, but the $1500 or $1750 top contribution will clearly be less and less realistic as inflation proceeds. A $1500 top contribution limit in 1974 might properly be a $3000 limit in the early 1980s, when the dollar is worth half of its 1974 value.

Most individuals who work for public or nonprofit organizations, such as schools, hospitals, and foundations, are covered by organization pension plans that are often very good, that being one of the substantial attractions of the work for many such employees. In addition they can make voluntary contributions in the form of the "Tax Deferred Annuity" (TDA), which enables such employees to put 16 to 20% of annual income into an annuity or mutual fund, deduct that amount from taxable income, accrete earnings on that income tax free until retirement, and then pay income taxes on the resulting sums.

Owner-employees of a sole proprietorship or partnership have several tax-advantaged plans available. Such self-employed people can develop IRAs, as previously discussed. However, the maximum annual contribution to an IRA is $1500, or $1750 if one's spouse is not working, although future changes in the law may allow an increase in these sums. If these modest amounts are the most a planholder can afford to put away in an IRA, then this simple tax-advantaged plan is very useful.

Owner-employees who are sole proprietors or partners and who can afford to put aside annually a larger sum of tax-advantaged money have another option: the Keogh, or HR-10, plan. Congressman Charles Keogh was the sponsor of HR-10, the number of the Congressional bill which created this plan. Since the original bill was passed, additional legislation has doubled the tax advantages of the contribution, and more recently the Internal Revenue Service has issued regulations allowing a "defined benefit" Keogh plan, with larger contributions available to appropriate planholders than the original law allowed.

As of this writing, the Keogh plan, which was originally similar to a corporation profit-sharing plan, allows the owners of unincorporated businesses to put 15%, or up to $7500, of yearly net income into a tax-advantaged pension plan, deferring taxes on it until retirement, much as in an IRA. (Even higher amounts are allowed to be put into a defined benefit plan.) Basically, the total expenses of the business, including wages, are deducted from the total income of the business to arrive at "net income before taxes," and then the 15% or $7500 formula is applied. All eligible employees, which means all those working 1000 hours for a year or more, and having 3 years of employment, *must* be included, with contributions made on the same percentage basis as for the owner-employees. The employees, once participants in the plan, become fully vested in their shares of the plan.

Investment and administration of such plans are handled either through a financial institution, an insurance company annuity purchase, trust companies or a combination of these. The main advantages, and they are substantial ones, are that the sum contributed is not considered income for tax purposes in the year contributed and that the earnings compound tax-free. In addition, a Simplified Employee Pension Plan may be established, which was introduced to eliminate most of the trust and reporting requirements. Contributions and benefits under such a plan are limited to the maximums permitted under the Keogh plan criteria.

Another difference between the IRA and the Keogh plan should be mentioned. Under a Keogh plan, as opposed to an IRA, life insurance policies with a death benefit can be purchased with up to 50% of the dollars contributed to the plan. In evaluating the true benefits of Keogh plans, owner-employees will have to consider the contributions they are required to make for eligible employees, if any. For a one-person business the benefits of a Keogh plan are dramatically clear; however, if you have a large number of employees, you will have to weigh carefully the contributions you make on their behalf against the individual benefits you will receive. If your contributions for employees would be more than you could afford, you can always use an IRA plan, which does not require inclusion of your employees.

Whether you choose an IRA or a Keogh plan, if you are an owner-employee of an unincorporated business, a tax-advantaged plan may be as important to your economic welfare as any other business decision you will make. Even in cases where, after years of hard, creative work and of earning an adequate income, an owner ends business activities with a firm worth little or nothing, such a plan may be of enough value to guarantee the owner's future economic security.

Internal Revenue Service regulations allow a "defined benefit Keogh plan" which should be carefully examined by all self-employed people with high incomes, since its one main advantage is that one can contribute more than $7500 annually to the plan, while maintaining a noncorporate status. The defined-benefit Keogh plan, which is similar to the corporate defined-benefit plan, is geared to pay the participant a fixed amount of dollars upon retirement, based upon earnings, age, and number of years to retirement. The monies contributed each year to the plan, predicated on a given interest assumption, should provide precisely that amount of dollars upon retirement. In this fashion, the dollars necessary to fund the plan may be greater than the $7500 maximum used in the standard profit-sharing Keogh plan. Such plans can be especially appropriate for one-person businesses or for businesses with few employees in which the owner has a high income; doctors or attorneys, for example, are prime candidates.

A word of warning is necessary: Although annual contributions of as much as $18,000 are theoretically possible under certain interpretations of the defined-benefit Keogh plan, the limits of these IRS regulations have not, as of this writing, been tested, and at present the IRS frowns upon use of factors that will generate this degree of contribution. Viewed conservatively, IRS rulings may keep the maximum annual contribution nearer to $10,000 to $11,000 and, in many cases, depending upon the age and earnings of the participant, may make the contribution no greater than the original $7500 allowed. Contributions of sums greater than those noted here can place the planholder at risk, since it will be some years before the courts rule on these regulations, giving interpretive guidelines. Stretching the law could result not only in the loss of tax advantage on excess amounts, but, more important, in the disqualification of the whole plan, with resulting loss of *all* tax advantage. If you are considering such a plan, examine it carefully and very conservatively with your accountant and other financial advisors.

With any of the pension plans discussed, favorable tax treatment is available. For the IRA and Keogh plan, installment payments that are to be paid to beneficiaries under annuity funding arrangements are, for tax purposes, excluded from the estate of the deceased, although lump-sum distributions are included and are therefore taxable.

Owner-employees of unincorporated businesses have another option as well: They can incorporate solely in order to set up tax-advantaged corporate pension plans. (Incorporation in the so-called Sub-chapter S form, however, allows annual contributions only up to the maximums placed upon the Keogh plan.) It is possible to develop an IRS-approved tax-advantaged plan that will allow you to accumulate as much as $1 million over a 10-year period.

Another advantage of a corporate plan is that, if death occurs prior to your taking the proceeds, the funds go to your named beneficiary without estate tax or probate costs. You may have your insurance premium paid on a tax-deductible basis, and upon reaching the retirement age or terminating the plan at your option, you may continue to take advantage of the tax law and spread tax payments over your lifetime. That is, you can defer taking the proceeds until a much later date without any current tax liability, allowing the monies to continue compounding on a tax-deferred basis; you can remove only that portion of the monies you currently need, pay taxes solely on that amount, and defer the remainder; or you can take the full sum of the proceeds in a lump sum and pay taxes on a special 10-year averaging basis. People who have had plans for many years may also receive capital gains treatment for part of the proceeds.

For all these reasons, if you own an unincorporated business, it will be worth your while to explore the tax-advantaged possibility of the corporation. Many people are deterred from incorporation because they believe that establishing these tax-advantaged plans involves high costs, complex reporting and administration, and inflexibility in creating changes. These criticisms may be valid for plans handled by people who are inexpert, but they need not be true for plans handled by professionals in the field. Even where these problems do exist to some extent, the benefits of the plan often far outweigh the negative considerations.

Corporate profit-sharing and pension plans come in a variety of shapes, with a range of objectives. In all of these plans, if established properly under ERISA, the contributions are tax deductible, the assets compound tax free, and tax benefits are available at the time of distribution of proceeds. The plans differ in what triggers the contribution, the amount and method of determining the amount of contribution and the benefits, and relatively minor miscellaneous regulations and administrative and reporting procedures.

A profit-sharing plan has three fundamental restrictions: a corporation may make a contribution to the plan only if it earns profits; the maximum contribution for any participant is no greater than 15% of his or her wages; and the benefits available for the participants are not defined at the outset, but will be based upon the amount of money contributed to the plan for the participant and upon the results of investing that money.

Profit-sharing plans provide great flexibility from the outset, since contributions are allowed only if profits are earned and since the corporate owners can, through a simple corporate resolution, vary the percentage of wages they will be contributing each year up to the 15% maximum. If in any given year they contribute less than 15% of wages, they can make up this lost contribution by additional future contributions. A participant also has the right to make a voluntary contribution of up to 10% of annual wages. Profit-sharing plans may also, under certain conditions, be used together with pension plans; the use of both plans for small, closely held corporations can trigger very substantial tax-deferred contributions for the participants.

Corporations that are volatile businesses, with their profits or losses varying drastically and unpredictably each year, often use profit-sharing plans rather than pension plans. Since they do not have fixed commitments, they can treat their plans comfortably, contributing during the profit years and ignoring contributions during the years of losses.

Another reason for a corporation to choose the profit-sharing route is that it can motivate nonowner employees in both large and small corporations to earn profits. As with all plans established by owner-employees of small corporations, the profit-sharing plan may be designed legally so that a higher-paid employee receives a greater percentage of contribution on his or her behalf than a lower-paid employee. Although the IRS requires that the plan be "nondiscriminatory," the type of plan, wages, ages, years of service, and full-time employment all are factors that can be used to provide greater benefits for some employees than for others.

If you are an independent business owner considering a profit-sharing or pension plan, you should not allow yourself to be confused by the many options available to you. Pursue the same course of action that you use in running your business—learn about all the facts and opportunities, assess which plans are appropriate for you and your business, determine your costs and obligations, and make your decision. Use your present financial advisors to the extent of their knowledge of this specialty, and then, as necessary, hire an expert pension consultant.

If all this seems too complicated and costly for the size of your plan, you can always adopt one of the many "prototype" plans offered by banks, insurance companies, and mutual fund organizations which have been approved by the Internal Revenue Service. If you are wise, you will consider these tax-advantaged plans as dynamic, not static, investments, to be reviewed annually as if you were entering into the transaction for the first time. Monitor the plan and amend, terminate, or change it whenever it is to your advantage to do so, just as you review your business constantly with an eye to changing personal, economic, tax, and legal factors.

ESTATE PLANNING

Finally, we come to the twin questions of estate planning and minimization of potential estate taxes, both of which can be and often are overemphasized by many individuals. All too often, careful people of less than very substantial means focus far too much on avoiding death taxes, to their own detriment while alive and to the detriment of their heirs as well. Too many people very carefully plan a series of life insurance, gift, and trust vehicles from which the net results are funds that are smaller than necessary for living and smaller than would have resulted from wise control of assets during life.

For planning purposes, the key things to keep in mind are that you are likely to live longer than you had really expected and that the dollar is likely to shrink in value faster than you had expected. Those two assumptions, taken together, place a very high premium on growing your living funds as rapidly, but as safely, as possible and on your keeping complete control over those funds. Except for the very affluent, the assets you give away today—or whose control you give away—may be sorely missed when you are 85 going on 100.

Bearing this in mind, planning to minimize estate taxes can be put in its proper perspective. The main concern should be to-minimize the impact of death taxes, for that impact can, in some circumstances, have graver consequences than the amount of tax levied. Should your estate be composed almost entirely of real property or of an ownership share in a business, your heirs could face a ruinous distress sale in order to meet federal and state taxes. That is a legitimate cause for concern and a situation that can be avoided with a minimum of planning, involving the provision of liquid funds to pay possible taxes.

Under present law, each married couple can, on the death of one spouse, claim a marital deduction of $250,000 or half of the value of the taxable estate, whichever is larger. For example, an estate consisting of a home, a wholly owned business, the proceeds of a life insurance policy, some cash, and miscellaneous investments, and totaling $600,000 in value, will have a marital deduction of $300,000, with $300,000 in taxables remaining. If the total value of the taxable estate had been $400,000, the deduction would have been $250,000, with $150,000 in taxables remaining.

In addition to the marital deduction, federal law at this time provides a "unified estate and gift tax deduction" of up to $47,000. That is a direct deduction from any federal death taxes that may be due, rather than a deduction of taxables, and is equivalent to a little more than $175,000 in deductions, on top of the $250,000 marital deduction. The result is a total deductible of a little over $425,000 for married people and $175,000 for single people. Gifts made during life must be subtracted from the "unified deduction," so that the deduction may be somewhat smaller than the top allowable $47,000. State death taxes, existing debts, and costs associated with death and estate administration are all deductible from the taxable estate. In estate planning, you should consider assigning life insurance proceeds to a named beneficiary to avoid estate taxes.

Death tax avoidance and estate planning are very much matters to be handled with your accountant, lawyer, and financial consultant. Each instance is different, state death taxes differ considerably, individual aims must be taken into account, and there are documents to be drawn up that must be precise and that must allow for several contingencies. Your specific and general intents must be translated into wills, insurance, and trust documents that will cause your beneficiaries no expensive difficulties later on in possible confrontation with taxing authorities and even with other beneficiaries. In addition, although the marital deduction and unified tax credit will take care of most potential death tax problems, it is wise to make some formal preparation for death tax avoidance and passage of assets to intended beneficiaries long before the anticipated event.

The first necessity is, of course, a will; it is astonishing how many otherwise careful, thinking people die without one, causing sometimes grievous difficulties for their survivors. If you have no will right now, as you are reading this book, then without delay call your attorney and make an appointment to discuss the matter. Make a will and be prepared to remake it as circumstances and intentions change—but make a will now, if you have not yet done so.

The second necessity is to give some thought to taking taxables out of your potential estate, but without relinquishing lifetime control of your assets and the ability to grow those assets for lifetime needs. Joint ownership of assets, such as a home, may not accomplish that—quite the contrary. Jointly owned assets will very often be included in the taxable estate of the first spouse to die and then in the taxable estate of the other spouse upon death, thus being taxed twice. It is far better, for death tax purposes, to attempt to achieve rough justice and equality of ownership by sharing assets between spouses—one owning the home, the other having a larger share of a business or investments, for example—than to try to achieve such equality through joint ownership. On the other hand, death taxes are, for many people, far less important than equality of ownership during life; if the objective of equality outweighs minimization of potential death taxes, and other "balancing" moves are not available, then joint ownership it must be. That is a matter of attitudes and goals and well illustrates the need to see each situation as unique, within the context of a general understanding of how the death tax system works.

In states with community property laws, joint ownership of assets is a matter of law, and the law provides for the application of the marital deduction to those assets in this way: Only half of community property is included in the taxable estate of a deceased. If that provides a deduction of $250,000 or more, it substitutes for the marital deduction; if it provides a deduction of less than $250,000, the balance becomes an additional deduction. For example, a taxable estate of $400,000 in a community property state will have $200,000 excluded from the estate and an additional $50,000 of marital deduction available.

Insurance can be excluded from taxable estates, however, if treated properly. Trust devices can be used to skip generations, for example, with specific forms and techniques to be worked out with your lawyer, accountant, and insurance agent, if the size of your potential estate warrants the use of the devices available. It is also possible to give your interest in a personally owned life insurance policy to others, as well as any interest you may hold in a group life policy, as long as the gift is irrevocable and meets current tax statutes and regulations in form. You can arrange insurance so that it is owned from the first by your spouse—an excellent tax device, but one that depends rather heavily on your estimate of the future stability of your marriage.

One of the classic uses of life insurance has been to provide "estate liquidity"—that is, to provide survivors with cash to pay costs and taxes so that they will not have to sell such assets as homes and businesses at distress prices. That is still a very legitimate function, but if you live a normal lifespan and your survivors ultimately really need life insurance proceeds to perform that function, it may also reflect inadequate planning on your part during life. Surely, those who die young must be adequately insured, and estate liquidity will be one of the functions provided by life insurance. However, those who live longer should find their need for life insurance diminishing as they grow older, meet lifetime obligations, and accrete funds for their later years. It makes a great deal more sense, in terms of both lifetime needs and eventual estate size, to buy term life insurance over the years—treating it as catastrophe insurance—than to buy large and increasing amounts of "permanent" insurance in which the investment portion of the premiums you pay is bound to accrete very slowly, as we discussed in Chapter 8.

One significant exception to that general rule should be mentioned; it applies when an overwhelming portion of an estate is clearly going to be the value of an existing business. Failure to provide liquidity in such a situation well in advance has forced many a distress sale and has ruined the financial prospects of many a surviving family. In that situation, life insurance may play a very desirable role. A buy-sell agreement, in which the surviving stockholders in a business—they can be members of the same family—agree to purchase the stock of a deceased stockholder at a stated price, funding that purchase with the proceeds of life insurance policies, can effectively avert a potential disaster. The life insurance premiums will not be tax deductible, but that is a small price to pay for saving a business for one's heirs and partners.

A buy-sell agreement, if it realistically reflects the value of a business, can also serve to place a value on the business for tax purposes. It is often very difficult to evaluate the worth of a business, and one of the most difficult questions in estate taxation is establishing the value of business interests for estate tax purposes. The existence of a realistic set of buy-sell agreements can help establish that value and thus avoid expensive confrontation and possible litigation with taxing authorities. In the past, buy-sell agreements have often been regarded mainly as devices to protect survivors in the event of the untimely death of a business owner. The question does not come up in the same way if an owner has sold a business, or an ownership share in a business, and retired. But in a period in which more and more owners are quite likely to recognize that "retirement" is imprudent in the face of longer life expectancy and protracted inflation, the need is clear for buy-sell agreements and other moves that guarantee liquidity.

What is becoming even more apparent is that, for the overwhelming majority of us, death tax and estate questions are little more than peripheral to the central and increasingly vexing question of how to get through life with enough income to let us live in a modestly acceptable way. Savings, investments, pension plans, and insurance all can help a great deal to meet the needs of our later years—but for most of us that will not be enough. That is increasingly evident. What is necessary is to be able to turn the skills and experiences of our lifetimes into gainful economic activity in our later years. It is to that question that we now turn.

Continuing to Earn in Your Later Years

This chapter could have been titled "How to Make a Few Dollars to Help Make Ends Meet in Your Later Years"—except that we are not really discussing the question of a "part-time job in your golden years," that staple of books and articles on retirement.

In fact, we very much doubt that the concept of "retirement" is any longer valid. Lengthened lifespans and plain economic necessity have conspired to rob that always doubtful concept of any real meaning. Pensions and savings do not add up to reasonably good living standards for most of us now and will amount to even less in coming years. Increasingly, as people live longer, they will see their productive lives as longer and will work longer. There is no choice; it must be so. The law already precludes most involuntary retirement up to the age of 70 and will, in coming years, raise that retirement age even further. Permissible earnings levels for those receiving Social Security payments at age 65 or older are now in the $5000 range—double that for a wage earner with a dependent spouse—between the ages of 65 and 72, meaning that there is no penalty deduction from Social Security payments up to those levels. Beyond age 72, there is no penalty at all, and in 1981 there is no penalty at age 70. Public policy as expressed in statutes may face these realities in coming years and peg the age at which retirement payments begin far beyond age 65.

The main question is not whether to pursue gainful economic activity in your later years, but *how*. Some can continue along the lines of their current activity, but for most it is not that simple.

For people working as independent professionals, continuing to work can be an easy matter, health permitting. Hundreds of thousands of 65- to 90-year-old lawyers, doctors, accountants, architects, and independent business owners are practicing and doing business "in place," in the business and personal environments in which they have long since set their roots. Under those circumstances, it can be very easy indeed to maintain gainful, relatively high-income employment that uses your established experience, skills, and web of associations. You know and are often very highly valued by the people with whom you do business, who are able to evaluate your contributions properly. Gainful employment in the later years is often little more than "slowing down a little." An accountant, lawyer, doctor, or other practicing professional often brings in younger people, works a few days a week or less, is on call for consultation, and can put together a lifelong pattern of gainful, entirely satisfying, life-enhancing employment. A business owner can bring in a partner, hire a manager, or even sell out and go into a related, less demanding business in the same locality. By doing so, you can enjoy a sound, growing income and the kind of interesting work that can keep you feeling a lot younger than you are.

For such people, the key can be as simple as deciding to stay at home and not cut off roots. Study after study indicates that life enhancement and longevity are much aided by continuing to work, if possible in a familiar, satisfying environment in which you enjoy high esteem. Increasingly, it is clear that living in the sun is worth a lot less than living in a sound, familiar working and living environment, no matter how bad the weather might be.

In economic terms, the differences can be extraordinary. A practicing professional, late in his or her career, may continue to gross from $20,000 to $50,000 a year for very little actual work, for experience and skills usually grow, rather than diminish, as the years pass. For example, it is not at all unusual for a 75-year-old lawyer, heading a firm that it has taken decades to build, to earn more than anyone else in the firm, while putting in fewer hours than anyone else. That lawyer, trapped in a "retirement community," cut off from friends and community ties, and reduced to the most modest kind of beginner's practice—if it is even worthwhile to take the trouble to qualify for practice in a different state—may have trouble making ends meet. Such a person may quite properly feel used up and wasted and may live far less happily and for fewer years than would have been possible at home.

There is no very good economic reason to leave a business that has "been your life" because of advancing years. You may get what seems to be a good price for your business, but it is important to bear in mind that, after you pay capital gains taxes, you will need to find ways to make as much money on your new capital as you did on the capital you had tied up in the business— and that is often very, very hard. A successful, growing business yields a real rate of return on investment far higher than that yielded by most other forms of investment and can often continue to do so even when you have taken on additional employees to make up for your lesser physical involvement in the business. If you decide to get out because of ill health, competition, or an overwhelming desire to try a different lifestyle, by all means do so, but only after considerable soul-searching. The prudent presumption is that you will not "retire" in the conventional sense, but rather that you will find new ways to conduct gainful economic activity within existing contexts. If you do leave a business, carefully consider the possibility of going into another kind of gainful activity that uses your established skills and experience. People who have run businesses of their own usually have organizing, people-handling, and numbers skills usable in many areas outside the kinds of businesses they have been running.

Many professionals work for others, but they, too, can move into independent professional activity in their later years. For example, the accountant or attorney who has been working for a company and commuting into a city for 40 years can take on a few local clients in the years before retirement from the company, build a small part-time practice, and then move into a limited practice in his or her later years. The editor or commercial artist can move into a free-lance stance, often working with the same people and firms as before, but on a much more flexible schedule and from home or a small office near home.

Such options are relatively easily available to millions of professionals and entrepreneurs. They are not so easily available to tens of millions of employees, surviving spouses, older people with health problems, and those who change their lifestyles. Winning through to gainful economic activity in our later years is not so easy for most of us—but it is not necessarily so hard, either. Except for those who are physically or emotionally disabled, it is almost always possible to develop gainful activities for the later years—if you plan well, start preparing for the activities of those years early enough, and see yourself as someone becoming ready to embark on a whole new career. For that is what you are doing; sometimes it is even the career you always dreamed of pursuing.

If you start planning early enough, you may be able to start with the right career-planning questions: What are my resources, aptitudes, and skills? What in this world would I most like to do? What other attractive alternatives exist? Within the whole range of choices opened up by these questions, what are my realistic possibilities? What, then, will I explore, prepare for, try, move into as time goes by, and pursue as fully as I wish in my later years?

What you want to do may take formal preparation, apprenticeship, or ability to invest. The corporate executive who is passionately interested in racquet sports may, while still in his or her forties or fifties, invest in the first of what may one day be a group of tennis clubs, looking forward to active management of a club in the later years. The police officer who left college to join the force may go to school nights and weekends to get a degree, planning to "retire" after 25 years and become the history teacher he or she originally intended to be. The woman who has raised a family and who now feels that she has the time to take on a part-time job may decide to try becoming the writer she always wanted to be, rather than taking an ill-paid job at a local boutique. More satisfying, surely—but it also makes much more economic sense, for a competent free-lance writer can earn a great deal more money in the long run than a store clerk, and continue to earn in the later years.

Collectors can turn their activities into vocations in their later years, receiving far higher rates of return than they would working as security guards and baby-sitters, two of the occupations seemingly most favored by those who, with good will and bad judgment, urge older people to shelve the skills and experience built up over long productive lives and become unskilled entry-level workers.

There are enormous differences between dull, unrewarding, unskilled work and the kind of work you have become attuned to over a lifetime of career achievement. Some of the matter is emotional—you are very likely to feel better and live longer if you do satisfying work. And some of the matter is economic—work that is in line with your proven skills and the new skills you develop in preparation for the later years will always prove to pay far better than the kind of unskilled work you will be "lucky" enough to find if you do not think through your later-years' work early enough to prepare for it properly.

Consider the difference between what you would make at a part-time job as a store clerk, security guard, home worker, or child sitter—if you can find such work—and what you now make, assuming the same relative rates of pay when you reach your later years. (We will leave out fringe benefits, which are not properly comparable.) Fifteen hours per week at $4 per hour, is $60 per week, or $3120 per year. How does that compare with your current rate of pay if you are an employee or with your real rate of income if you are a business owner? If your salary or real business income is $30,000 to $60,000 a year, that is a real hourly rate of $19 to $38 an hour. Can't your skills and experience be turned into something closer to $19 to $38 an hour than $4 an hour? And given the tax breaks intrinsically available through business ownership, can't the money you earn through some kind of small business ownership—low on investment, high on labor, the classic labor-intensive small business—add up to something very close to the kind of pay rate you enjoyed during your high-earning years? Looking at it that way, isn't one of the best investments of a lifetime the time and money needed to prepare for a later-years' career? After all, the difference between even $19 an hour and $4 an hour is $15 an hour. Fifteen dollars an hour more, for 15 hours a week, adds up to $225 more a week, or $11,700 more a year. That is quite a difference—perhaps the difference between poverty and comfort in your later years.

Let us look at it a little differently. If you assume you can net 8% on your money yearly, earning $11,700 more a year is like going into your later years with $145,200 more than you actually have—and it is like having it grow despite inflation and taxes, yielding the equivalent of that same $11,700 as the years go by. That is quite a return for your having had the good sense and self-discipline to prepare adequately for your later years. In fact, there is nothing else remotely like it. It is made possible by your investment in that asset which has been your prime asset all your life: yourself, including your own skills and experience.

By far the best way to prepare for the later years is to plan to be an independent business owner or professional. If you go out to get a job, full- or part-time, you are very likely to encounter age discrimination, no matter how strong the anti-age-discrimination laws that are on the books. Yet the same firm that will not hire you as an outside salesperson for all kinds of insurance and operations reasons, as well as because of age discrimination, will cheerfully take you on as an independent manufacturer's representative, valuing greatly your 40 years of experience in the industry and understanding that working part-time and almost exclusively over the phone you can produce far more than most younger full-time people. The same firm that will prefer to hire a younger bookkeeper will bring you in to do the books if you are running a bookkeeping service or have gone back to school in your sixties to learn accounting and have developed a modest later-years' practice. The school or institution that would not hire you in your later years as a teacher or social worker may be delighted to refer students to you for several kinds of remediation and counseling.

It is an old, old story. Independence breeds respect. Old, dependent, and cut off from roots, contacts, and experience, you are a liability, a charity case, someone who American society—and alas, all too often your own loved ones—will sweep under the rug as soon as possible. Free, equal, independent, at home, and fully functioning, you are a respected member of the community, whose skills and experience will be widely sought and paid for. That is the key to the future for all of us.

PART

III

PERSONAL FINANCIAL PLANNING SITUATIONS:

Twenty Practical Plans

To make all that has gone before in this book even more tangible—and even more helpful—here is a series of practical financial planning examples, drawn from the joint experience of the authors. All situations discussed are drawn from real life, though the people and specifics are largely constructed for purposes of illustration. The names used are in all instances fictitious, and any resemblance to living persons is entirely accidental.

Most of the stories are to some extent "success stories," for effective financial planning is just that. Not all are, though. For many of the younger people discussed, how all the planning, saving, and investment works out will remain an open question for many years—and a question that will always depend considerably upon factors quite outside their control. All you can ever do is to give yourself the best possible chance of reaching some of your goals; there can be no guarantees. For some of the older people discussed, it is clear that their resources will not meet their desires, and possibly not even their needs, if they live long. For them, effective financial planning must inevitably mean continuing to work even when that is not desired or sharply lessening their expectations, expressed in much more modest retirement plans than had been anticipated.

You can be sure of one thing, though. As the following examples indicate, people who involve themselves in effective lifelong financial planning have a very substantial advantage over those who do not.

We have tried to present a wide range of examples, including people in their early, middle, and late financial planning years and people whose incomes, assets, pension expectations, and personal situations vary. They are included in roughly reverse chronological order, from older to younger, so that, if you wish, you may find people of about your age and in a similar situation by scanning until you reach a corresponding example. Of course there are as many specific personal situations as there are people, and nothing substitutes for long-term, careful exploration of your own situation with your own financial advisors. Yet many basic situations have striking similarities, and there are not so very many alternative basic solutions—which is why we think what follows may prove helpful.

We have, wherever relevant, taken tax considerations into account, both in the earlier planning years and later in life. Those considerations change as tax laws, earnings, and personal circumstances change, and the tax impact of financial planning moves must be reevaluated often.

That, indeed, is one of the keys to effective long-term financial planning; it must be reevaluated often. Every total financial plan should be reevaluated at least yearly—no plan that is allowed to run without that kind of careful periodic evaluation will long remain sound. It is within that context that we present the following sample situations.

1

George and Maureen Craft

Here are two people who seem to have done rather well. George is 61 and a highly regarded guidance professional who works for a major school system. Maureen is 59 and a nurse supervisor in a major suburban hospital. Both have job security until they retire. They have raised three children, all now self-supporting, although they have been paying off the educational loans of the one who went into a theater career—an obligation that is now ending, much to everyone's relief. Their home is fully paid for, and they have no debts other than a few credit card charges now and then. Their other assets amount to $175,000, mostly in common stock, mutual funds, and municipal bonds.

Both plan to retire on reaching 65 and can look forward to a combined pension income, including Social Security payments, of $35,000 per year. George thinks he may do "a little consulting," while Maureen can think of nothing she would like better than to retire completely and devote her time to her grandchildren, though she is not entirely sure that she really will be able to stay home indefinitely.

Both agree that they want to stay in the suburban Chicago area in which they have lived for the past 40 years. Their children and grandchildren are there, as well as a whole web of other ties they are unwilling to break. Their plan is to essentially swap the house they own, which is far too big for them now—and far too expensive to run—for a smaller cooperative or condominium apartment in the area; live modestly, but well, on their pensions and investment income; and continue to live the life they have lived since they were young marrieds.

On the face of it, it's a good plan, and it may very well work out exactly as they think it will. But they may come up a little short—and if they live long, they may come up very short. The potential problem is that they may have underestimated the impact of inflation on their fixed pension income—and they may not have fully thought through the possibility that one or both of them may live a very long time by the standards of their youth.

If the inflation rates of the 1970s and early 1980s continue, their yearly $35,000 pension income will be worth half of its present value eight years after retirement, even allowing for increases in pension amounts to reflect somewhat inflation and small wage increases during those years. And the possibility exists that inflation will accelerate, rather than decrease or stay relatively level. A 15% yearly inflation rate, such as that experienced in England for some years during the 1970s and early 1980s, will halve that pension's value in a little less than five years.

It may not be quite that bad, because the Social Security portion of the pension may be partly or wholly indexed to the inflation rate—but it may *not* be so indexed in the future or may lag seriously behind. Even if it is indexed, the main portion of their combined pensions is the fixed income portion, which is very likely to erode drastically in a very short time after retirement. It is quite possible that, 10 years after retirement, their $35,000-per-year pension will be worth little more than Social Security alone.

That may not be—but it could pose a tremendous financial problem, and one that should be addressed now, in the highest-earning years. It could have been addressed 10 to 20 years ago, in the course of making lifestyle and college choices—and their $175,000 in other assets might now have been $600,000 to $800,000. But that is ancient history for George and Maureen. Their problem exists now.

They would be well advised to do several things. First, they should most emphatically plan to do some relatively painless belt tightening between now and planned retirement. Their current high combined income will let them save $12,000 per year, with which they can, as nonprofit institution employees, buy tax sheltered annuities. They may be able, in the next 4 to 6 years, to turn their $175,000 into something much more like $350-400,000, allowing for investment growth and reinvestment of dividends and interest. What they invest in will depend largely on which investment opportunities provide the most growth with relative safety in the years ahead—a matter for them to take up with their investment advisor eagerly and often.

George and Maureen should also give a great deal of thought to the possibility of pursuing their current occupations in the years after "retirement." They are both well-established professionals and quite capable of continuing to work at their professions part-time, and at very respectable rates of pay. They can very easily do so because they have no plans to cut their ties by moving away from their home area. Maureen could easily teach nursing at a local proprietary school or college and do rather well at it financially as well as finding this new kind of work within her profession satisfying and challenging. George might very well do more than "a little" consulting; he could open his own small, personal consulting firm and secure some long-term, open-ended contracts with the very people he has worked with and trained in his field for decades.

With these amendments—and they are not small amendments, but neither are they far from the plans George and Maureen now have in mind—they can continue to live, work, and play together as they have all their lives, rather than facing what otherwise might be a very uncertain economic future in what can and should indeed be golden years.

Abraham and Tamara Rosen

Abe and Tamara came from the same small town in Russia as children, he, with his family, as a child of 4, she as a 3-year-old orphan, traveling with a family that took a chance on deportation and that got her past the American immigration authorities by saying she was their own child. Both of them came out of the Old World in the 1920s, with families fleeing the storms of war and revolution, and grew up in the United States as children of the Great Depression and yet another world war. They knew each other as children on New York's Lower East Side, married after World War II, and moved to Minneapolis, because Tamara's cousin there had a sales job for Abe. There they raised two children, and there Abe went into business for himself, ultimately as an independent manufacturer's representative, while Tamara stayed home, raised four children, and kept the books of the family business.

They did rather well—well enough to buy a home and to put two children through college and two others through vocational schools. Later, well enough to save almost $50,000. Sam had a stroke of luck in his choice of financial advisors, too. His accountant insisted that he set up a corporate pension plan 10 years ago, when the children were all out on their own, and he had a little extra cash in the business. The mechanics of tax deferral being what they are, that plan is now worth $140,000, a sum Abe and

Tamara had never dreamed of amassing. When asked in his later years—really without being asked, and at every opportunity— Abe was fond of calling himself "an immigrant boy who grabbed a piece of the American dream."

Abe is 64 now; Tamara is 63—and the American dream is threatening to come apart a little at the seams. Abe has just lost his largest client, a firm he has represented for almost 30 years, because the firm decided to hire its own house salespeople rather than use manufacturer's representatives. No reflection on Abe; the firm offered to hire him, in spite of his age—at $10,000 a year less than he was making, of course, and he would have had to give up his own business.

The trouble was that it turned out he had to give up his business anyway. At 64, he decided he simply did not have the drive to "start all over again." He and Tamara had, for years, been looking forward to selling the business and retiring to Florida as soon as he turned 65. They had vacationed in the Miami area often, had friends there, and after lifetimes spent in the cold northern winter wanted to "live in the sunny South."

They abandoned their now worthless business, sold their house, bought a very nice, smallish condominium in the Miami area, and plan to make it on Social Security, interest, and dividends, without impairing capital too much.

Their action is entirely understandable. After a lifetime of work and the experience of success in personal and economic terms, it is logical to look forward to retirement. Since World War II, Social Security, other private and public pension plans, and lengthening lifespans have combined to produce mass retirement at 65 and a mass migration from the North to warmer southern climates.

But, though understandable, their move may cause them grievous difficulty. If they live even 10 years more, they may very well find themselves on the edge of poverty. Even if they do not severely impair capital in the early years of retirement, they will find that capital shrinking fast because of the impact of inflation, and the interest and dividends produced by that shrinking capital will shrink proportionately. Soon it will be necessary to go into capital to maintain living standards, which means that even less interest and fewer dividends will be yielded by the remaining capital. In those circumstances capital disappears fast, and what remains is Social Security alone, and that means living at little better than a poverty level, as virtual wards of the state.

Abe and Tamara have not come this far without the ability to size it all up, however. Rather quickly, they will begin to see that their capital is inadequate to meet their needs. Then it is likely that one or both will try to find work, she without skills and he with his old selling skills intact. They may find work—but they will also find a great many other people their own age looking for work in the Miami area, and for the same reasons.

How will they solve it? We don't know. Abe is an experienced and resourceful person, good at business and good at selling. He may be able to find work as a salesperson, or even open his own part-time manufacturer's representation operation. He still has contacts with some manufacturers he used to represent in Minnesota, and some of them distribute nationally, including the Miami area. The chances are better than even that he will find a way to make it all over again. But it will be hard, very hard. He is swimming now in an alien sea; what would have come very easily at home in Minneapolis will be very hard to accomplish in Miami.

Abe and Tamara would be very well advised to live carefully and to resist the temptation to "take a flyer" with their retirement money in investments promising very high yield, but being commensurately risky. They might very well put some of their limited investment funds into money market funds, which combine liquidity and relative safety; though not federally insured, these are invested in such short-term obligations so as to make them resistant to all but an economic collapse resulting in the simultaneous and sudden bankruptcy of many major companies. Some of their funds might go into intermediate-term, top-rated corporate bonds. A small portion—perhaps from 15 to 20% of their assets—might go into an equity investment, a sound income-oriented real estate limited partnership, a "blue-chip" common stock mutual fund, perhaps the purchase of already producing oil and gas wells as a limited partner in programs sponsored by established oil companies. Although some of these moves may be a little riskier than the other investments, they may be worth while if seen as an attempt to keep up with inflation to some degree. With these moves, Abe and Tamara may be able to retain the independence that is so precious to them.

Joseph Napolitano

Joe Napolitano was a poor kid on the Hoboken docks during the Great Depression. His father was a longshoreman who couldn't find work for literally months on end; his mother stayed home with their seven children and took in piecework from garment shops to help make ends meet. Joe hit the road in the late 1930s, went through the war in the infantry, and eventually wound up in San Francisco. There, in the late 1940s, he took advantage of the GI Bill to get two years of college under his belt and then found a job as a field representative for a national company, building a little college, some selling skill, and a lot of drive into a career in marketing.

Joe is a widower now, with three grown children. His son has embarked on a marketing career, like his father. His two daughters have married, settled down in southern California, and have so far had one child each, with more probably to come. Both are happy, but neither has a great deal of money coming in; one married a teacher, the other runs a small family farm with her husband.

Joe is 65 and able to retire now from a sales management job, having lived and based his work in San Diego for many years. His family is nearby, San Diego is itself a prime "retirement" community, and he has no intention at all of going elsewhere. The only change he really plans to make in lifestyle is to swap his house for a condominium apartment, not so much for savings as for convenience—though savings are a factor in making the decision. With the federal once-in-a-lifetime tax exemption he will take on the capital gains from sale of his house, it will make sense for him to take a mortage on the condominium, because the net of his aftertax investment yield minus his aftertax mortage interest payments will come out better than would the use of his money to buy a condominium for cash.

Joe is in good health, quite enjoys life, and will have, after his house swap, approximately $275,000 in assets and a condominium. On retirement, he will—correctly—choose the option of receiving a little more than $100,000 in a lump-sum pension settlement. With Social Security and investment returns, and assuming the modest lifestyle that he will unquestionably adopt— that lifestyle being merely an extension of his current one—he really has nothing at all to worry about financially, except perhaps a little erosion of principal late in life, and even that may not occur.

He recognizes only two problems—neither directly financial— one that is quite real and the other, something that he thinks is probably quite irrational, but nonetheless very real to him. The first is that he is not at all sure he will be as happy in retirement as he is working. He likes a certain amount of action and says that he has seen "too many old guys out there on the golf course making believe they're having fun when they're really dying of boredom."

The second is that all his life he has been haunted by the insecurity he experienced as a child. It scarred him, as it did so many other children of the Great Depression. He sees his daughters beginning to have children—his grandchildren—and worries about their future in what he sees as an increasingly uncertain world. He is extremely anxious to use as little capital as possible in coming years, so that he "can leave something for my grandchildren. I want to see to it they get a better break than I did."

He is taking steps. His company, which thinks a great deal of his work, has accepted with applause his decision to stay on the job. Corporate management understands very well that, should the job begin to prove physically difficult, Joe will be the first to recognize it, and believes that he would then retire or move to a less demanding job in the company. For both Joe and his company there is hazard in staying on—even experienced people sometimes refuse to recognize growing physical incapacity in their later years and can hurt themselves and their work when that happens. But that is a hazard all concerned recognize, or at least say they do, and claim to be ready to handle if necessary.

Since Joe is no longer qualified to participate in his corporate pension plan, he can establish a tax-deductible and tax-deferred Individual Retirement Account, even while he is working for his old company. He can continue this plan even if he leaves the company and becomes self-employed. Although he must, by law, start taking out a portion of the IRA proceeds beginning at age 70½, he can still contribute to the plan regardless of his age, as long as he continues to earn income. Joe can make his grandchildren the beneficiaries of his IRA so that the tax-sheltered dollars he is accumulating will go directly to them, if he dies before obtaining the proceeds.

Later, after retirement from his company at 70, or, if necessary, earlier, Joe plans to keep on working at some kind of selling job. He has done it all his life and is very, very good at his work. He figures that there has to be some way to work part-time, as a sales agent or manufacturer's representative handling one or more small company lines in the San Diego area. He would then be able to travel only a little, do most of his work by telephone, and work well on into his later years. What he really hopes to do is keep himself interested and active, while actually increasing his grandchildren's inheritance. A realist, he knows that his chances are small of growing their nest egg in real terms, given the impact of inflation, but he thinks he has an excellent chance of at least conserving much of what he now has for his heirs.

Recognizing that there can be appreciable taxes levied on what he leaves to his grandchildren—while also being concerned about the possibilities of needing all or most of his resources for his own old age, if he lives long and inflation accelerates—he has decided to set up modest, irrevocable trusts for his grandchildren now and to reevaluate them periodically. Once his assets

are so pledged, he has given them up entirely, and they are re-
moved from his taxable estate. He has thought about setting up
some custodian accounts, to be turned over to their recipients as
specified by state law when they reach a stated age, usually 18,
but has decided against that course of action for the time being,
as he thinks that at 18 his grandchildren may be too young to
handle properly what will, by then, be substantial sums of money. He may set up some revocable trusts a little later, in which
he keeps control of the funds and the trust principal remains in
his estate for tax purposes, but yield earned on that principal
flows to his named beneficiaries and is not taxable to him, and
probate costs on that principal will be bypassed on his death. For
now, he will set up the irrevocable trusts, stay at work, move to
a condominium, and continue to live his own life, leaving himself
flexible, with other options for the future.

Susan Hawkins

Susan went out on her own a long time ago, before it was at all fashionable for a woman to do so. She grew up in rural Georgia in the 1930s and went up to Detroit with her family during the War, where her father found a war job; after the War, the family moved on to New York, where her father found a job on the subways. It was a union job, and one that paid well enough that she did not have to go to work immediately after high school, but instead was able to go to City College, which was free, and then on scholarship to Columbia's School of Social Work. Armed with her master's degree, she went to work for a charitable organization in Manhattan, starting a career in social work that has lasted over 40 years.

She married once, in her early twenties, took time off to have one child and then another, divorced her husband when she was in her early thirties, and went on alone. It was her choice; she said later that she had given up early on finding a man who could accept her total dedication to her chosen career and to the principle of absolute equality between the sexes. It was not an easy choice; there was never very much money, and raising two children and putting them through college took whatever there was—and then some. At the age of 57, she finished paying off college debts.

Now 65, Susan is about to retire. She will have Social Security and private pension payments amounting to a total of about $20,000 per year on retirement, with pension payments fixed and tied to Social Security payments, so that as Social Security payments go up, pension payments will go down. That means that in relatively few years the pension payments will largely evaporate, as Social Security payments go up in some relation-ship to the pace of inflation. All she will ever have is that $20,000 per year.

In the past eight years, since she finished paying off college debts, she has managed to amass assets of about $100,000 through a combination of frugality and rather lucky, quite spec-ulative investments. Knowing nothing at all about investments, but not trusting the American economy at all, given the experi-ence of her own lifetime, she bought gold when it was low and sold it when it was high. She even bought gambling stocks on a "tip" from someone just as uninformed as she was and made a good deal of money on them.

But that was just play—and plain luck. She is a strong, intelli-gent, and far-from-naive person. Facing retirement, she has no intention of stopping work to live alone on what she knows would soon be very modest circumstances and later on a poverty level. Aside from that, she likes to work; her work has been most of her life. Her basic question is how best to grow her $100,000 rather safely, while continuing to support herself in her chosen work. She intends to take her pension and continue to work in her field as a teacher and consultant, while living partly on her continually eroding pension. She would like to be able to leave some money to her children and grandchildren, but recognizes that long life and inflation may preclude her doing so. What she wants to pre-serve at all costs is her independence; she has always felt free and entirely her own woman and has no intention of either turn-ing to her children for support or becoming a ward of the state in her old age. Yet she recognizes that there may come a time when consulting and teaching are no longer possible, when her pension is down to Social Security payments, and when what can make the difference between freedom and dependence is that $100,000 kernel of capital. Until then, she wants to grow it, rather than live on it or its proceeds, and feels that she cannot afford to take chances on losing it.

When Susan retires, she will have a good deal of taxable income from a combination of taxable private pension income, yield from current investments, and postretirement earnings. She will attempt to grow her assets during the early years of retirement, using anything coming in over living costs for additional investment. That means taking tax aspects into consideration in investing her current $100,000 and anything further during those years; avoiding investments on which returns may be heavily taxed, sharply limiting their growth; and focusing on investments with tax-advantaged yields, which may grow far more quickly. She will immediately establish an Individual Retirement Account as part of this thinking.

Still, she must be careful not to tie down her limited assets in long-term investments that may make those assets unavailable if needed. She would probably be best advised to consider a combination of investments aimed at safety, liquidity, partial tax deferral, and growth, bearing in mind that, whatever her plan, it must be reevaluated at least yearly in light of her goals, the pace of inflation, her health, her income, and all other relevant factors.

In this period, just after retirement, when her earning powers are still relatively high, Susan should probably put her funds into money market funds, for liquidity and yield, even though the proceeds are taxable; a tax-deferred, single-premium deferred annuity; some top-rated intermediate-term corporate bonds, for safety and yield; perhaps a tax-deferred variable annuity; perhaps a small participation in an oil and gas extraction limited partnership, but only one involved in already producing oil and gas properties, not in highly speculative new drilling activities; and perhaps an equity fund or common stocks, in a small amount. As the years go by, needs and means will change, and so will the nature of her investments.

Rose West

Forty-two years ago, Rose West, then 18-year-old Rose Terraro, worked as a sewing machine operator in a small garment factory in Newark. There she met and eventually married Sam West, then 30 and the owner of the factory. Soon after they married, she quit work and started having children—five of them, now all grown and self-supporting.

She never worked again. Sam stayed in business and did fairly, but not exceptionally, well. Seven years ago, when Sam was 65, they sold their business, bought a condominium apartment in the Miami area, and settled down to "live the good life." Rose was 53 then.

It *was* a good life—but Sam died last year, after a long and rather expensive illness. He left a little life insurance, some stocks and bonds, some short-term Treasury securities, and a small amount of money in a savings account for current expenses. It all added up to about $50,000. Rose has that, the apartment, a small federal survivorship income, some wonderful memories, and a lot of children and grandchildren back in New Jersey.

And she will soon be in very deep economic trouble, like so many other people in retirement communities all over the country. She is 60 and in excellent health and will probably live a long time. Her income is small; Sam had planned it otherwise, but everything cost more than he had thought it would, with in-

flation compounding at between two and three times its anticipated rate, and his final illness was expensive. Her skills are nil;
except for doing semiskilled work on a sewing machine for a couple of years four decades ago, she has never worked. If she stays
in Florida, she will find it almost impossible to find a job, and
her money will soon run out. If she goes back to Newark, she
faces the unwelcome prospect of living alone in a small apartment or with one of her children, while her money erodes more
slowly. She is lonely, frightened, and uprooted and feels that her
world has come to an end.

There are no easy solutions for Rose West, or for millions of
other older Americans sliding into poverty in a society that
seems to prefer pushing them aside and trying to forget them,
rather than providing retraining and meaningful work. Many already live in poverty; many more seem likely to join them in the
years ahead.

In this instance, Rose took the advice of her accountant daughter and, with her help, sold the condominium, which had substantially appreciated in value in seven years. She put the
proceeds of that sale and Sam's life insurance into the safest,
highest-yielding investments her daughter could find, including
a money market fund and "Ginnie Maes" (Government National
Mortgage Association), a pool of mortgages guaranteed by the
full faith and credit of the United States government; rented a
little apartment in New Jersey, near one of her other daughters;
and found a job in a department store. She will never have much
income and will probably have to rely on her children more than
she would like in her later years, but at least in these years she
will maximize her income. She will also be working where there
are people of all ages to talk with and living near her children
and grandchildren. She misses the warm Florida sun, but somehow feels better back home—at least she is self-supporting there.
Mostly she misses Sam, but knows that life must go on.

6

Henry Kraus

Henry Kraus has been worried about the state of the American economy ever since 1929. He is almost 70 now, but has never been able to eradicate the memory of how his father's face looked the day the bank foreclosed on the family's southern Illinois farm. Of course, it did turn out to be one of the justly famous $1 foreclosure sales of the Great Depression days. The day of the sale, every farmer came from miles around, plus a large delegation of unemployed miners, and everybody was armed. The banker who came out from Springfield looked angry and frustrated; the sheriff and his deputies looked scared. There was just one bid—$1—from one of the neighbors. And that was that. After a while, everybody went home, and Henry's family stayed on the farm.

Henry still worries about the economy, though. About five years ago, just before he sold his successful farm implements business in Springfield, he began to be aware that he had a great deal of worrying company. He began to read books about the coming crisis, which, if you were to believe what you read, was going to come sometime about the middle of next week.

He *did* believe what he was reading. He bought a good deal of canned food, some bottled water, and even some extra guns and ammunition and put it all in the old fallout shelter he had built back in the late 1950s. It had been well built, and in a way it was nice to see it had not entirely gone to waste. He pulled whatever money he could out of his property, closed up his brokerage account, and did whatever he could to turn his assets into hard goods capable of withstanding the worst economic, social, and political collapse this country would ever see.

But Henry Kraus is a far-from-stupid man. After some years of this, he began to form the distinct impression that the world was not quite coming to the sudden end that had been predicted. Those who had predicted collapse were still predicting collapse, but he began to think, as he put it to his best friend, "that the day of judgment has been postponed."

He hadn't done so badly, really, Most of his hard goods had yielded nothing in the way of dividends, but some of the commodities and collectibles, such as gold, stamps, and silver, which he had bought before they became popular, had done very well. On balance, even after paying some fairly substantial capital gains taxes, he feels that he came out of those years in as good a condition, relative to inflation, as he would have had he maintained the investment stance he had held before he pulled out of equities and debt instruments.

Henry might even have stayed in canned goods, buried currency, gold, and guns if he had not been concerned about his grandchildren. His wife died back in the 1970s, but not before living to see two of her grandchildren, the son and daughter of her only child. Now there are three grandchildren, and Henry wants to leave his very considerable pile of the world's goods to them, with as little tax bite on their inheritances as possible. He wants to do this legally, so that no government snoops will bother them in later years. As his lawyer and accountant informed him, there are no very good ways to do that without getting into some instruments that presume that the United States, in its present form, will be around for a fair while longer.

Henry is a worrier, though. He is concerned about the twin impacts of inflation and long life and is not willing to run the risk of giving away control of his assets irrevocably during his life, only to find himself living to 100 and needing those assets to live on. That's the problem he put to the financial advisor his accountant took him to in Chicago.

Given Henry's goals and concerns, the financial advisor could do little more than assess with Henry and his accountant the probable course of inflation, help develop an estimate of how much principal Henry might need if he lived until he was 100, and strongly urge Henry to place the balance of his assets into irrevocable trusts, thereby taking those funds out of his taxable estate, while leaving him the income from the underlying trust investments. He also suggested a diversified program of liquid, high-yielding fixed-dollar investments.

Henry went home and thought about it. Still a worrier, he finally decided to put half of the indicated amount into irrevocable trusts, review his entire financial situation with his new advisor in Chicago once a year, and at that time decide whether or not to set up additional trusts for his grandchildren. He recognizes that additional legal costs will result, but emotionally it is worth it to him to do it that way.

Margaret and Walter Olson

Margaret and Walter Olson have done it all together. They both grew up in the same small town in Maine, fell in love in high school, and married in their early twenties. Neither of them could afford much education after college. Margaret's family staked her to a course that included both secretarial skills and bookkeeping; Walter, who had thought about engineering school, went instead to work in his uncle's garage, soon becoming a crackerjack auto and truck mechanic.

Margaret worked as a one-woman office staff for a local lawyer before her marriage and for a little while afterward. She quit to have her first child and stayed at home for a good while after that, until her third and last child had started first grade. At that point, she convinced Walter that they could do a lot better in their own business, with Walter handling the mechanical side and Margaret handling the business side. Like so many others, they tried it and it worked.

After 35 successful years in business—actually a succession of businesses, the last being a substantial auto parts company—and both 63 years old, they face the question of retirement. Their children are by now self-supporting, their son an aerospace engineer in California, one daughter a computer systems analyst in Boston, and the other a teacher in Augusta. They have done fairly well—their home is worth about $80,000, the business about

$250,000, their savings and investments about $75,000. As Margaret puts it, "We look like very solid citizens here, but somewhere else we'd be very small fry indeed." Unfortunately, their accountant, while hardworking and dedicated, had not suggested any tax-qualified pension plans or their assets would have been greater.

They are both in good health, but Walter is slowing down a little. The Maine winter, which he used to enjoy enormously, now chills him a bit. He hunts in the fall, but is thinking about selling his snowmobile for lack of use and looks forward more and more to the Florida vacations he and Margaret have been taking every winter for the past few years. Margaret is still going strong, but knows that the day will come when she has to slow down, too.

Yet—their town is home. When they walk down the street or go into a local store, they know everybody but a few of the new young people who have to come to Maine to go back to the land. They are getting to know some of them, too, and rather like most of them. Although their children have grown up and moved away, the people in town are more like an extended family than anything else, and it is hard to think of moving away.

On the financial side, it is clear that their assets, with Social Security payments, could support them modestly if they decided to retire in two years, when they become 65. But only modestly, and with the pace of inflation, they believe that one or both of them might have to work at least part-time, whether they sold out and stayed home or sold out and moved to Florida. Actually, if they moved to Florida, things might be considerably tighter than if they sold out and stayed at home.

One option is to sell the business and take a partially deferred payout, also working part-time in the business for some years. Their accountant tells them that that could have some favorable tax consequences, if structured properly.

Another option is to sell out, go to Florida, and develop a part-time business, probably repairing autos or other machines—or to do the same at home.

A third option is to keep the business, hire a manager, and take life a little easier. They would remain active in the business, take salaries small enough to ensure that they would receive full

Social Security benefits when eligible, and take the rest of their business income as dividends. There would be a somewhat adverse tax impact, since the sums they take in dividends would have been taxed as corporate profits before being passed on to them, and they would have to pay some income taxes on them as well, but those tax consequences would be much more than offset by their Social Security benefits and deductions.

On balance, they have tentatively decided to go with the third option, assuming, of course, that they both keep their health and ability to work. In essence, they have decided to lengthen their working lives, to continue doing what they have done so successfully all these years: to work together in a wholly familiar and warmly loved environment.

8

Sam and Alice Louison

Sam and Alice are classic examples of how people in extraordinarily difficult circumstances can make things work. He is an unusually tough and resilient man; she, a woman with the will to move ahead despite extreme adversity. They would have to be so, for Sam became a paraplegic as a result of combat injuries sustained during World War II. He and Alice had no money when he entered the Army as a youth and none when he came out. Sam spent years in veteran's hospitals; Alice went to work to support their two children, aided by Sam's disabled veteran's pension.

When Sam came out of hospital, they received Army disability payments, and their home was partially paid for by the government because of his special disability. It was enough to prevent starvation and to provide shelter, but Sam had no economic future, as well as having to cope with a wheelchair and all of the problems of a paraplegic. However, he and Alice managed to finish paying for their home, to help send their children through college and graduate school, and to live a satisfying and by no means economically impoverished life of their own.

How? Sam became an expert investor. Although he spent a great deal of his time as a volunteer working in disabled veterans' causes, he also concentrated hard on taking the very small amounts of savings he and Alice were able to generate over the years and making every penny saved work effectively for them. He constantly moved the few dollars they had to the highest available yields consonant with relative safety. Oh, he took a few risks in common stocks along the way, but never with more than a small portion of their assets.

In a modest, but for them crucially important way, it worked. Now, in their late fifties, their assets amount to $400,000, including home, savings, and investments. With their children grown and self-supporting, with Alice's work, and with Sam's continuing pension, they can make it the rest of the way.

Jim and Mary Raeburn

Sometimes Jim Raeburn feels as if he's a long way from home. He grew up in western Tennessee, married a girl he met while he was stationed in Texas, and moved with her out to Portland, Oregon, after the war. Neither he nor Mary ever had much formal education, although he became a pretty good jack-of-all-trades while working at a series of industrial jobs for the next 35 years. Mary raised their four children, watched them all grow up and leave home, and then went to work as a salesclerk in a local store.

Now they are both approaching 65 and are facing the question of how to handle the later years of their lives. Social Security payments will be there for both of them, and they have saved about $20,000 since the last of their children left home, but that's it, except for the modest income they get for the rental of a small apartment in their basement. All together, that will be far from enough to live on, and the very real specter of poverty lies before them, unless they are able to reach a sounder economic footing. Neither of them has any illusions about continuing to be employable as the years go by—they are very familiar with the plight of relatively unskilled people like themselves when they grow old. Mary says, "They shove you under the rug, and try their best to forget all about you." As far as they are concerned, they have been on their own ever since Tennessee and Texas and will be on their own for the rest of their lives.

Their plan is to try to provide for their later years by going further into the rental housing business. They have explored the local zoning laws and have found that there is no bar to their converting their house—the big old house in which they raised a family—into a multiple dwelling. Using Jim's modest, but adequate, skills and the skills and volunteer labor of two of their sons, who live nearby, they will convert the upper floor of their home into two apartments, occupying one of them; put a small apartment in the attic about the same size as the one in the basement; and use the ground floor for a single large apartment. Even with the "sweat equity" they are themselves contributing, it will take about half of their savings, and they recognize that it may take a bank loan besides, since they are unwilling to use all their savings for the project. But they calculate that the three new rental apartments they are creating will go a long way toward solving their long-term support problems and that, by living on the premises and managing the place themselves, they will maximize their income.

If it works—and they have every reason to believe it will, given the housing shortage in their booming city and the fact that their neighborhood is a stable one—Jim and Mary may be able to go a step further. With the experience of one such conversion under their belts, they think they may be able to buy another big old house in the neighborhood later on and convert it the same way, thereby providing an even sounder basis for their later years.

John Harrison

John didn't exactly start out to be a "rich doctor"; all he had really wanted to do was to heal people. In fact, many times during college and medical school, with debts piling up, he wondered whether or not he had done the right thing. It would have been easy enough to go into the family's small hardware business and really make something of it. He had worked in the business every summer during school and often on school holidays and knew he had a good business head, at least for the hardware business. But he persevered and went through an internship and the early years of practice, paying off debts every step of the way. Ultimately, in his early thirties, he took the big step, going much further into debt in order to open his own practice and to survive the early lean period.

It wasn't a very long lean period, though. He survived, then prospered, developed a specialty, and then his practice and income took off. His net earnings soon reached the $250,000-per-year level and stayed there, growing with inflation. Now almost 50, he's a millionaire—and he still has a good business head. What he has done is to pay attention to financial planning, hire expert advisors, structure the financial side of his life carefully, and continually watch his investments.

Recognizing very early that taxes would take a great deal of his income unless he took some legal tax-avoidance measures, John sought out tax-advantaged investments, especially in real estate and oil and gas drilling, reasoning that these special interests were very powerful and that their tax protection was part of the fabric of American financial life. At the same time, he sheltered a little of his income by starting a Keogh plan.

A few years after his flood of income started, he bought a very substantial and expensive dwelling for his family—then consisting of himself, his wife, two children, and one more on the way—reasoning that, at his level of income, such a dwelling was not foolish conspicuous consumption, but instead an excellent investment, accompanied by the tax advantages inherent in home ownership.

A little later, he incorporated, which allowed him to make a variety of tax-related financial moves and, most of all, to start a large corporate pension plan.

The net of it all is that he is indeed a rich doctor, who before long will be a very rich doctor. His personal investment portfolio has grown to be worth much more than $1 million. His home has grown in value even faster and is now worth almost $500,000. His corporate pension plan, a 10-year plan aiming at "retirement" at 55, will be worth $750,000 by then. And the money keeps coming in.

Harrison's personal circumstances are unusual; very few of us can expect his kind of current income. But what is equally unusual is his business head; thousands of other professionals in basically similar circumstances plan far less well or not at all, pay large taxes, and reap only a small fraction of the gain that he experiences. The difference lies wholly in the way they plan the financial sides of their lives.

Five years ago, Tom Regan was a quite competent middle-level engineer working for a medium-sized division of a major high-technology company. He was reasonably well paid, making then $37,500 per year, and lived comfortably in a considerably mortgaged house located in one of the more affluent suburbs of St. Louis. He was 41, had a good career ahead of him, was happily married, and was watching four children begin to grow up. His wife, Lucille, was seriously thinking of going back to school to finish the program in psychology that she had left when she went to work to support Tom through engineering school. They had managed to save about $15,000 in all, had a little life insurance beyond Tom's company-supplied group insurance, and were beginning to realize that in four years their oldest daughter would be starting college, to be followed at almost regular two-year intervals by their three other children.

Several things have happened in the last five years. First, Tom surveyed his personal and family situation on the morning of his 42nd birthday and decided to succumb to the entrepreneurial bug. He had always wanted to try a business of his own and later said he had looked in the mirror that morning and had had that "now or never" feeling. To summarize a fairly complex train of events, six months later he had remortgaged the house, cashed in most of their savings, borrowed a good deal more, and gone into partnership in a small electronics firm with a man from the marketing side of his company, who had had the itch to do the same for years. His partner handled the selling and most of the administrative chores; Tom handled the technical side of the business. The business worked almost from the start, given the impetus of a healthy, long-term contract from the very company they had just left.

It was very lucky that it did, for three years later something else happened. If it had happened first, Tom would probably never have gone into business at all. Lucille had gone back to school at about the time Tom went into business. There, her dissatisfactions with her marriage surfaced—to hear Tom tell it, she met a man. Alas, for whatever reason, they split—and that meant a property settlement, alimony, child support, two habitations, and all the other substantial financial drains accompanying such a split.

However, a profitable business can be a far more lucrative and flexible instrument than a salaried job. Tom's business absorbed all of his costs. As soon as he had started to make money, at the rate of well over $100,000 a year, he had set up pension and profit-sharing plans and had started a personal investment portfolio, placing strong emphasis on tax deferrals and tax shelters, while relying on current income to meet current needs.

And that's the way it's working. Tom will not have a great deal to put into personal investments for the next few years, but his pension and profit-sharing plans are accreting at a great rate. His oldest daughter is in college—a state college, luckily. His oldest son will soon follow. Tom's business continues to do well. Lucille has remarried, and he is thinking of remarrying, too. His intended has four children of her own. Tom has not thought about providing for his grandchildren yet, but he will.

Stanley and Paula Wykowski

In 1879, at the age of 18, Casimir Wykowski, 12th of 14 children, emigrated from Poland to America. Years before, his second oldest brother had gone out to Wisconsin, worked on a farm, bought a little land, and become a farmer, as he had been in Poland. In time, six of the other Wykowski children joined him there, four of them brothers, who lived and worked with him until they could buy their own farms, and two of them sisters, who married farmers in the area.

Casimir was Stanley's great-grandfather, Stanley is the fourth generation to work the land, some of it land that was part of Casimir's first American farm. Now 45, he is a superb farmer, who works the farm with his wife, Paula, who is 43 and also a fourth-generation farmer—in fact, her great-grandmother's people were from "two towns over" in Poland. They have six children, ranging in age from 5 to 14, and have every intention of seeing to it that all who want to will go to college, that those who want to will be able to continue to work the land after they are gone, and that they will be a burden to no one in their old age.

When you are a family farmer with six children, that takes some planning, especially when whatever cash you have had to spend so far has gone right back into the farm or for current family needs and when your oldest child has expressed a very strong desire to go to college in four years—and agricultural school, at that, reinforcing your determination to help finance college costs.

It is unrealistic for Stanley and Paula to think seriously about investment portfolios and tax-sheltered personal investments. The farm has done well enough, with the land accreting in value a good deal every year and with very little taxable income shown—but very little cash is available. At the same time, as their accountant advised them a few years ago, it was clearly wise for them to incorporate, set up a corporate pension plan, and put whatever was possible into it over the years. In that pension plan they have started accreting tax-deferred sums far faster than in the savings accounts that, without advice, they would have relied on.

That accretion of land value may be more of a threat than a blessing, as their accountant pointed out at the same time. When land values rise, taxes tend to rise, though not necessarily on a one-to-one basis. Even worse, land-rich, but cash-poor heirs may be forced to sell farms to meet estate taxes in later years, as has occurred in recent decades all over North America. Recognizing the problem, Stanley and Paula have purchased substantial amounts of life insurance aimed at helping survivors pay estate taxes without losing their ability to continue to farm the land. They think this is likely to be as important to some or all of their children as it has been to them. In addition, they have made wills and certain other arrangements calculated to minimize estate taxes.

Having started a modest tax-advantaged fund for their later years and having taken defensive steps regarding estate taxes, they turned to the looming question of college costs. In this area they plan two kinds of moves. First, they have begun the process of making it clear to their children that Wisconsin has an excellent state university system, which provides an education second to none. They will not even come near having the money to send their children to expensive colleges, but quite correctly see that it is important for the children to realize that, even if there were enough money, it would be wasteful to spend it on expensive colleges when equally good or better education is available at a small fraction of the cost. This kind of early discussion also helps guarantee that the children will not foolishly go into truly enormous debt to put themselves through expensive colleges and spend years paying back debts that need not have been incurred. This approach also means that any of their children who want to go to graduate school, which may be expensive, can get some help from home when it is needed and go into debt themselves only when there is good reason.

The other move Stanley and Paula plan is to employ their children during summers all through college, thereby supplying college financial help through pretax business expense dollars rather than out of aftertax personal income—a difference that can be very substantial.

Stanley and Paula feel that these moves, taken together, will guard against loss of their farm now or later, will begin a later-years' fund for themselves, and will help guarantee their children's ability to go through college without any of them incurring a crushing burden of debt. None of it promises to be particularly easy; three or four bad years in a row can wash away all their plans and the farm itself—but that is always possible. They continue to work, hope, and plan—like their great-grandparents, who came to work the Wisconsin land more than 100 years ago.

13

Ed Baker

Ed calls himself "what's left of a good, old show business family." His grandparents were a vaudeville act until his grandmother started having babies; then his grandfather did a single act. His father, now retired, was a musician. Ed himself is an actor.

"With me," he says, "the show stops." For Ed is 44, has never married, doesn't intend to marry, and plans no children. He has, for the last eight years, had a satisfying, stable relationship with another man, a relationship they both feel is likely to continue for many years, but they are both independent professionals and highly unlikely to become economically dependent on one another. Ed's father and mother are alive, however, and though they are now well able to take care of themselves, they may need a little help later on in life.

Ed is a relative rarity among actors: he finds work most of the time. Not extraordinarily well paid work—he is not a leading player—but he has been and will continue to be in demand for a wide range of minor roles for years. When people see him on the street, they often feel that they "have seen him somewhere before." They have, playing a hundred different roles in a hundred different plays, films, and television shows. It all adds up to a good living, though not without some ups and downs. Ed earned $65,000 last year and has averaged about that for the last five years.

He hasn't saved a nickel. If he broke a leg tomorrow and could not work for six months, he would be dependent on the charity of friends within two months. As it is, he often has to borrow from friends to make it through infrequent nonworking periods. The closest he has ever come to investing has been in making three loans to friends for business ventures in the theater, all of which were lost when the ventures proved—to put it gently—unrealistic.

The passage of time and an adverse experience or two can, however, raise questions in the minds of even the most improvident. Last year, one of Ed's best friends was in a serious autommobile accident; he may not be able to work on stage again, has no resources, and came to Ed, among others, for help. Ed lent him a little money, helped him get another kind of job in the theater, and then wondered a little about himself. Last month, Ed had one of his rare bouts of illness—only a touch of influenza, but enough to put him in bed for a week and debilitating enough to put him out of action for almost a month.

It all ultimately led him to call his accountant, who said, "That's what I've been trying to tell you for years." His accountant gave him the telephone number of the financial advisor he had worked with for two decades. A week later, Ed, his accountant, and his new financial advisor met.

At that meeting, they talked about a lot of insurance, savings, and investment vehicles. Mostly, though, Ed's accountant and financial advisor tried to make it clear to Ed that nobody could really help him but himself. No matter how soundly laid his financial plans may be, they cannot be accomplished without saving. Ed needs no life insurance and is covered by an excellent union major medical plan; all that remains is to save and invest. They urged him to build a small reserve fund; to build enough assets to be able to put a down payment on the kind of cooperative apartment he wants, which might be both an excellent investment and, in a sense, a means of forcing savings and investment; and, then to move into such other investment vehicles as seem indicated during his yearly financial review.

Ed left the meeting clear on the necessity to engage in organized saving and investment and resolved to do so. How it will all work out is very much an open question, but anything he does along these lines will be more rewarding than his previous pattern.

14

Anne and Walter Kovacs

For the last several years, Anne and Walter have had the growing feeling that they are "playing the game of life against a stacked deck," as Walter rather colorfully puts it. He is a high school English teacher who writes a little on the side and who should be forgiven such excesses after a weekend spent reading student essays. Anne, who teaches history and economics in a neighboring school, calls it "the pauperization of the American middle class in a period of economic stagnation."

They both entered teaching right out of college in the early 1960s, and neither has the slightest regret as to choice of profession. They are both dedicated teachers and love working with young minds and ideas. They both have master's degrees, and Anne has a doctorate; they are in fine, relatively high-paying school systems; and they live with their two children decently, but not at all extravagantly. The problem is that they are always broke. After taxes—which are high because you cannot do much about tax shelters and deferrals when you spend almost everything you make for current needs and prior debts—they have enough to make the first mortgage, second mortgage, personal loan, home improvement loan, credit card, and automobile payments; buy necessities; go to a movie or eat out once in a while; and put what little is left, which isn't much, into the college fund.

For many years, they have also both taught summer school for the extra income the work provided. All the while, inflation has exceeded the pace of pay raises. In fact, last year Anne's teacher's union signed a two-year contract carrying an increase of 6% a year, even though it was clear that inflation would come to at least 12% a year, resulting in a net real loss to the teachers of 6% each year, or 12% in two years. It was, as they knew, that or strike. As it was, the school board nearly lost the next school budget vote because of that wage settlement, no matter that it was inadequate, given the fear and rage over rising education costs its opponents were able to promote in the district.

Anne and Walter are both intelligent people. They know that one or both of them will have to leave teaching to try something else that pays better, unless they can figure out a way to make more money. They know there are no short-term solutions to inflation, but they are determined to send their children to college—state colleges, certainly, but that will still cost some thousands of dollars a year they don't have. They have no intention of living on the edge of poverty for decades and then slipping into poverty soon after retirement. Their love of teaching will not, in the long run, overcome their common sense, and if the community is willing to lose its finest teachers, then so be it.

But not without a struggle; these are people who love what they are doing. They have decided to try developing, in a neighboring town, a part-time business that requires very little capital, one that they can work in themselves on weekends, evenings, and holidays as well as all summer and that they can hire others to handle during their working hours. They are quite willing to go back to school to learn whatever skills may be necessary to run their business and to borrow money from family and friends if necessary, recognizing that they will have difficulty in securing financing from conventional sources in the early stages. They also plan to work in similar businesses as "apprentices," if necessary, to prepare for opening their own business. The only way they can see staying in their chosen profession while meeting their financial needs is to develop an entirely different source of income, and they plan to substitute their own labor for some of the

capital that otherwise might be required. He calls it a 'bootstrap"
operation; she calls it "sweat equity."

How will it work out? Nobody can really say at this early
point—but when two intelligent, healthy, highly motivated people set out to develop a second income in a thoroughly planned
way, there is always a chance of success. In this instance, it is
probably a very good chance.

Joyce Raymond

Up until a little while ago, Joyce had, for 22 years, been Mrs. Gary Jones. Now, for the first time since she was 23, she is Joyce Raymond again.

Therein certainly lies far more than a financial planning problem. Yet sound financial planning can considerably minimize the problem of transition to a life alone; lack of it can enormously magnify the difficulties encountered in that transition.

The split itself had been an enormous shock. There they were—Joyce, Gary, Ann, and Erica—living in a fair-sized house in a rather expensive suburb of Atlanta. Gary had, and still has, a good job with a local company; Ann and Erica are both in college; Joyce had gone back to school to finish her graduate degree in social work, the one she had started and then stopped when she married. Quite suddenly, Gary announced that he had fallen in love with his secretary and was leaving Joyce, and then he did. How banal. How final. There was never a chance of reconciliation. Joyce now owns half a house, a car, $20,000 in stocks and bonds of varying quality and yield, and the right to receive alimony forever or until she remarries and to receive child support until the children are out of college. Gary will pay for their education and keep up payments on the house until it is sold, if ever.

But Joyce faces a set of lifestyle costs she cannot possibly maintain on alimony and child support. She has some choices to make. One of them is whether or not to sell the family home. If she does, her daughters will not have a place to live when school is not in session, which, with long summer closings, intersessions, and holidays, is about one-third of each year. They could, on the other hand, stay with her or their father in smaller quarters or live on or off campus at their colleges all year round. If she does not sell the house, she will undoubtedly have to stop going to school herself and go right to work at the best-paying job she can find—but she has no real skills, even office skills, and cannot expect to earn much.

It wasn't really a hard choice, once the alternatives were laid out on a sheet of paper, with living costs, investment returns, and pay rates compared. Joyce has one more year of graduate school to go. After that, she will be able to look forward to finding satisfying professional work and to earning a salary $5000 to $8000 a year higher than she would be able to command as an unskilled person. Later, as she gathers experience, the differential will be even more. Aside from the question of doing satisfying or stultifying work—a question that is in itself crucial—it is clear that no investment she could possibly make would be even nearly as economically productive as payment for another full-time year in school, including her own living costs for that year. She might do it by selling her stocks and bonds, but then would find herself barely able to make ends meet on a social worker's salary in an expensive environment, rather than being a self-supporting professional in an affordable environment. The house is now listed for sale.

She also has to buy life insurance and major medical coverage, open bank accounts, apply for credit cards, and thereby begin to develop her own credit rating—all the things someone going on his or her own must do to develop an independent life.

She also needs to examine that $20,000 stock and bond portfolio. A portfolio developed as part of her former husband's financial plan—or without a coherent financial plan, as is true of most modest portfolios—is probably not entirely right for her. Her investment goals as a single woman must inevitably differ from those of a family of four with children in college. Her investment goals as someone with no assets other than the stocks and bonds and her half of the net proceeds of the house sale must differ from those of someone with much larger assets, which include several kinds of investments. For example, after finishing school and getting a job, she may want to use a good deal of her assets to buy her own home, both as a living place and as an investment, reasoning that she will do far better economically as a homeowner than as a renter; at that point she will be able to support a much less expensive home than the family home she now plans to vacate. That would argue strongly for evaluating her investments in terms of her ability to turn some of them into cash soon for both her coming school year and a possible down payment on a home a little later.

It is hard, after many years spent otherwise, but Joyce is now getting into the habit of thinking of herself as an economically independent person and is beginning to develop the skills that must accompany that independence. In the short run, the decisions she has just made will carry her through the difficult period of transition. In the long run, it is her developing financial planning skills that will determine the state of her economic health.

Gary says, "It could have been worse. We could have had five small children and a mountain of debts when we split. Then I would have had to live poverty for 20 years, instead of just the next three or four." Joyce Raymond's ex-husband isn't particularly bitter about it; after all, he fell in love with another woman, and he recognizes his obligations to his former wife and his children as entirely legitimate. At least he says he does, although he has been heard urging friends to introduce his former wife to "someone nice," who might bring an end to his otherwise perpetual alimony obligation.

Right now, he and Elizabeth Leggett, his second wife, are having considerable financial difficulty. She brought to her second marriage her two young children and some debts from the years she spent trying to raise those children on a secretary's salary. They all needed a place to live, so Gary put most of his remaining assets into a modest house. They both work, he at a reasonably well-paid middle-management job, she as a secretary, but their combined take-home pay must stretch to cover the cost of two houses, alimony, two children in college, and her debt repayments, as well as normal living costs.

As for so many other divorced people, and especially those with children, financial planning under those circumstances is extraordinarily difficult. Mostly you try to hold your own, adopting a defensive stance that cuts out everything but the barest necessities. Among those necessities Gary and Elizabeth include some basic life and major medical insurance, to protect themselves and their various dependents in the event of a catastrophe occurring at a time when work-connected insurance coverages are not available.

Long-term financial planning does not end in periods of adversity. Gary and Elizabeth have kept some basic insurance coverage. They also both have company pension plans in force, which are accreting tax-deferred assets every day they are employed. They have become homeowners again, and the modest house they bought is growing in value faster than the pace of inflation.

When Gary's old house is sold, he will get some cash out of it, although that will use up his one-time federal house-sale tax exemption. They will use some of that cash to meet current expenses, some to build a small emergency fund, and the rest to begin a college fund for Elizabeth's children. Their current thinking is that it will be wise for the first few years to keep that fund in short-term federal securities or money market funds, depending on then-current estimates of relative safety and yield. Later, as their financial situation begins to clear up a little—especially if Joyce remarries—they may consider moving into common stocks and real estate, but right now they are afraid that financial problems might force them to tap the college funds at a time when common stocks might have to be sold at a loss or when real estate might not be salable quickly enough to meet short-term needs.

They may be in trouble, but they are still thinking and planning. There is no way of telling now how their plans will work out—like so many other divorced people, needs may ultimately overwhelm resources. If, however, no extraordinary expenses occur for the next couple of years, they stand a good chance of coming out of their present difficulties in a debt-free, asset-developing position.

Carrie Woodson

One day last month, Carrie Woodson put her sales reports aside, leaned back in her office chair, looked out the window at the New York skyline, and said aloud, "This is it. Here I am. That's the way it's going to be." She studied the picture of her 12-year-old daughter that sat on her desk and traveled with her all over the country, rose, moved to the window, thought briefly about both of her ex-husbands, went back to her desk, picked up the telephone, and called her accountant. Her accountant was, of course, out, in some other client's office. So much for drama. But within a month, she had some long-term financial plans.

Carrie Woodson is 36 and has a good job as regional sales manager of a major office products firm. It pays $40,000 a year and carries stock options along with a wide and satisfying range of fringe benefits. She has been with the same firm for the last eight years, right through the breakup of her second marriage five years ago, and plans to stay as long as the firm will have her—which will probably be forever. She is legally due alimony and child support from her first husband, but that dried up years ago, when he moved on to parts unknown. She has one daughter, Angelica, and absolutely no plans to marry again or have any other children. She thinks it might be interesting to live with another man some day, but without strings and with completely independent financial arrangements, feeling that two of the best things that ever happened to her were financial independence and her daughter—and two of the worst, her two husbands.

Although she has not been able to save very much, she has managed to put aside $10,000—$2,000 of it in a savings account for emergencies and $8,000 in United States savings bonds. She has become increasingly concerned about her decision to hold those bonds as the pace of inflation has quickened and as she has learned more about such matters as interest rates and return on investment in the course of her work. She is also increasingly concerned about what might happen if she lost her job, even though it is as safe as a job can be, because she has no insurance arrangements other than those provided as fringe benefits by her employer. And although she intends to send Angelica, starting in six years, to "the best college money can buy," she is beginning to worry now about how to pay for that college education, knowing that an expensive college is likely to cost far more than she will be able to pay when the time comes.

Carrie conferred with her accountant, who then sent her to several other professonals. She thought about the advice they all gave her and made several decisions. First, she bought some term life insurance as a basic protection for her daughter should anything happen to her at a time when she was not covered by a company policy. Then, and just as important, she bought a modest major medical policy, with the largest deductible she could find, to guard against the occurrence of catastrophic uninsured medical expenses.

Then she cashed in her United States savings bonds, with their ruinous interest rate, and put the proceeds into a money market fund paying a much higher rate of interest and with greater liquidity.

She thinks she can save between $2000 and $4000 a year, as measured in current dollars, and perhaps more if she gets raises and promotions. Whatever she saves will be put into the money market fund during the year. Once a year, she will reevaluate her financial situation and decide whether or not to move some of her assets out of the fund into other investments. She is thinking about the possibilities inherent in such tax-advantaged vehicles as single-premium deferred annuities and about investing later in the stock of her own company, an investment she is in an excellent position to evalute. Whatever she does, she is likely to do well, having started the financial planning habit rather early in her career.

Sherman and Andrea Goldstein

Andrea and Sherman "have a little trouble saving." It doesn't bother them much, because they are both very successful, youngish New Yorkers on their way up in their chosen careers— but enough to cause them to seek some advice from their accountant, who took them to his investment advisor.

At 31, Andrea has become an excellent and widely sought freelance advertising copywriter. She earns about $55,000 a year and says that she could earn twice as much if she wanted to work at absolutely full capacity, seven days a week and 16 hours a day. The work is there, but she doesn't want to work that hard or to develop an organization to handle it. The odds are that, at some time in the next 5 to 10 years, she will develop that kind of organization, for her focus is very much on her career.

Sherman is 38 and a successful middle-range executive in television production with a major network. He earns $46,000 a year now and will probably be earning half again that much in today's dollars within a decade. Alimony and child support obligations from a first marriage do cut into his aftertax income somewhat, but he and Andrea together now gross more than $90,000 a year after allowing for the alimony and child support.

They have no children of their own and plan none. His parents are gone; hers are alive, well, and possessed of enough resources to take care of themselves for the rest of their lives. They do recognize that the time will come when they will want to contribute money for the education of Sherman's son, now 5 years old, but that is far off, and they are sure they will be able to handle it out of current income.

However, they have saved nothing and have invested almost nothing. All they have is some rather expensive personal property in their rented New York apartment, $2000 of cash surrender value in a straight life insurance policy Sherman bought some years ago, and about $1000 in cash in a joint checking account. They have $2000 to $3000 in short-term current credit card debts, that being roughly the amount they put on credit cards in a month. New York is an expensive place, and they live in it to the hilt. That means eating out a lot, taking a lot of taxis, summer rentals in the Hamptons, clothes, theater tickets, and a good deal more. It's all a lot of fun, and they are young people on their way up—but they do indeed have trouble saving.

Quite in keeping with their basic stance, they are not particularly interested in developing long-term investment plans at this point in their lives. What they want is a medium-range plan, for the next 10 or 12 years, that will enable them to develop enough capital to be able to do such things as buy a summer place and perhaps a cooperative apartment and travel widely, while continuing to live essentially in the same way they now live. Neither of them has ever begun to consider the possibility that crack young advertising writers like Andrea sometimes go stale or are vulnerable to competition from new talent on its way up—or that television is a very chancy kind of industry, one that faces a sea of new technology, which will soon transform it, creating new jobs and eliminating old ones in the process. Those who live at the crest of a wave seldom pause to consider that their environment may soon change.

To guard against sudden and catastrophic changes, Andrea and Sherman's advisors urged them to secure adequate life and major medical insurance coverage, beyond whatever either of them had through employer group plans.

Recognizing that their goals included two kinds of real estate investments—a summer place and a cooperative apartment—their advisors urged them to cut their current expenditure levels aggressively, so that they could save enough to put down payments on each. In such an instance as this, consuming goals involving the acquisition of real estate may be turned into powerfully motivated short-term savings plans. Once the down payments have been made and mortgage loans taken, which need periodic repayment, a forced investment situation has been created. Both the cooperative apartment and the summer place can reasonably be expected to grow in value over the years; as "growth" investments, both have good potential. Neither yields current income, but that is the last thing in the world Sherman and Andrea need. The truth is they would only spend it.

Beyond forced saving and investment, there is only the will—or the lack of it—to plan effectively the financial side of life. Their investment advisor made a number of other recommendations, mainly involving money market funds and several tax-advantaged investments, all of which can help Andrea and Sherman to build a sound financial base, and all of which require them to consume a little less, to reach for a little more freedom than is really available to those who are compulsive consumers. They have the analysis and the advice—now it is up to them.

Young Peter Field is about to do it all. Three years ago, he completed his Master of Business Administration degree, secured a fast-promotion-track executive trainee's job in the home office of a major Los Angeles firm, and started paying back the mountain of debts he had incurred during the course of his education. His family's modest finances saw him through the first two years of college, but after that he was on his own, and that meant piling up debts.

He will pay them off without any trouble, though. He switched from the Los Angeles company to a Chicago-based national consulting firm last year and at 27 is making $35,000 a year. Living alone and traveling a great deal at his firm's expense, he is able to pay the installments due on his education loans and to save $5,000 a year besides—and his salary will go up. He will not accelerate payment on his education loans to "get them out of the way"; he quite correctly feels that it makes more sense to invest the money he would have used to pay them off and thereby get a far better net return on investment, because of the very low interest rates carried by the education loans.

Peter expects to marry within the next few years; have children, a house, automobiles, and dogs; belong to country clubs; and travel—that is, to lead the kind of life lived by most of the older top executives he sees around him. He also very seriously intends to eventually go into business for himself and become chief executive of his own company, either in consulting or in one of the newer high-technology areas. In short, he is the prototypical young superachiever in a hurry to win fame and fortune.

Right now, he wants to start making some personal financial moves, to begin to build a personal financial basis for all that he hopes will come later. His impulses are to consume and speculate. Surrounded by all the indicia of corporate conspicuous consumption, and living much of the time on an expense account, he is inclined to buy expensive things—cars, clothes, and entertainment, all that goes with being "on the way up." He also wants to get into the investment game and "gamble with the big boys," pitting his speculative investment judgments against those of people who have been playing the game for decades. Both impulses—to consume and to speculate—are enormously seductive. He will succumb to both; in this he has much company.

At the same time, he will make a few moves aimed at securing his financial base. One will be to secure an adequate major medical insurance program outside his corporate coverage. Another will be to go into a money market fund, using that as a basic savings vehicle and evaluating at least yearly how much he can take out for investing purposes—in his case, that evaluation is more likely to be monthly than yearly. Another move will be to own, rather than to rent, housing, so that both tax advantage and growth can result.

Unless he discovers the joys of borrowing large amounts of money and "leveraging," Peter is unlikely to hurt himself too much in the investment market. He has excellent earning power, has covered himself against catastrophe, has a short-term emergency fund, and will soon own his own habitation. The main hazards he faces are personal, not financial, in nature.

Joan Hopkins

At 30, retirement planning is the farthest thing from Joan's mind. She is eight years out of college, past a near-disastrous early marriage, and dead set on a big career in New York publishing. Childless, she plans no children. Unmarried, she plans no further marriages, though she is now living with a man whom she likes very much. If it turns into something more, perhaps they will make permanent arrangements—but she is determined to keep her independence and develop her career, no matter what else happens in her life.

Right now, as the very young editor-in-chief of a medium-sized publishing house, she lives in a whirl of cocktail parties, business lunches, editorial conferences, meetings with writers and celebrities, and endless talk about money and contracts involving money. She spends a great deal of time nights and weekends reading manuscripts, keeping up with professional periodicals—and worrying whether or not anybody else knows how ill prepared she was by her college English major for most of her current work, especially that part of it involving money and contracts. She knows that she has come up very fast in a trade that can be very hard on bright young people and that many who assiduously court her now will drop her the day she becomes unemployed.

Joan knows about being unemployed, about eating peanut butter sandwiches for dinner, and about walking because bus money is scarce. Her divorced mother helped her through college, but for most of it Joan was on her own. In those years, she budgeted carefully as a matter of simple necessity: later on, in the early New York years, that budgeting experience proved very useful.

Now she does not have to budget that way. She makes $42,500 a year and, even after the considerable amount of taxes she pays on that income, has more than enough left over to live well. At the same time, she knows she is in a volatile trade and is quite conscious of the need to provide for the possibility of a long stretch of unemployment.

Beyond the question of unemployment, Joan is keenly aware that the financial independence she regards as essential will, in the long run, depend largely on how well she plans her financial future. As she puts it to her closest friends, "I want to be able to walk away from all this any time." She doesn't plan to change careers now or in the future, but for her freedom includes the ability to be able to make changes if and when they are indicated.

For example, she and the man she is living with, who is also in publishing, have discussed the possibility of going into partnership in a literary agency or even trying a small publishing company of their own. Either would require some starting capital and some economic staying power to enable them get through the first two to three years. For that matter, she has thought of taking a couple of years off to try writing the "Great American Novel" she started in high school. Like so many editors, she first thought she wanted to be a writer—and yet may be. But that, too, requires capital—and the ability to take a much lower paying job, if necessary, when coming back into the job market after years away.

Joan is rather young, and her affluence is very recent. Even so, she has saved $13,000 in the last five years, holding it in savings accounts and six-month bank certificates of deposit. She has bought no insurance, reasoning that she is covered by her company and that she would be able to convert her company group insurance to personal insurance if her employment were terminated. She recognizes that so far she has saved, rather than planned, and is now determined to embark on a long-term financial planning program, with the help of her accountant and a financial planner.

After talking with advisors, Joan decided that she needed to be better protected against personal catastrophe and bought a major medical insurance policy, guaranteeing coverage no matter what her employment situation.

Recognizing that her great concern about employment security is well founded, her advisors suggested that she transfer the money in her savings accounts into a money market fund, gaining much higher interest and retaining liquidity. As her bank certificates of deposit mature, she will move those assets into the money market fund as well, on the theory that, aside from very short-term and minor swings, the money market fund will pay as well as the certificates of deposit and will provide much better liquidity—liquidity she may need if unemployed for any substantial length of time.

She also thinks that she will take $5000 of her $13,000 and invest in something longer range, such as an equity fund or directly in common stock. She is beginning to know her own industry rather well and has some reservations about most publishing stocks, but is beginning to think that one or two may have considerable promise. And because as a single person her top combined federal and state tax bracket is well over 50%, she is seriously considering investing some portion of her accumulating capital in tax deferred instruments.

Once a year, Joan will sit down with her financial advisor and carefully discuss her entire financial planning situation. Out of that meeting will come the basic moves to be made with those assets currently being employed for savings and investment. And out of her developing involvement in such evaluations will come a set of indispensable financial planning skills that she will use successfully all her life.

THE LANGUAGE OF
FINANCIAL PLANNING

Not all professionals cloak their activities in private, rather mystifying jargon—but most do, and often quite unnecessarily. Some do so out of a real, though usually misguided, sense of precision; others because they quite correctly perceive that membership in a "guild" carries status and consequent psychic and material rewards. The professionals you deal with in the course of financial planning—bankers, lawyers, accountants, stockbrokers, insurance people, and financial advisors—all have developed jargons of their own, which interlock to form what often seems, to outsiders who must deal with them, an incomprehensible line of gibberish. This special language requires a certain amount of explanation and demystification.

To that end, we here include definitions of and comments on some of the key concepts, instruments, and techniques encountered in financial planning. What now follows is no substitute for a good investor's dictionary, which we strongly urge you to purchase and use routinely; we do not here define all of the specific and technical terms and phrases you might meet, although the Index at the back of the book is a handy reference to pages where specific terms are discussed. Rather, we have focused here on the techniques and the underlying concepts that will be of the most general use to you in your financial planning.

Advance refunding.   Advance refunding is a technique bond issuers use to avoid having to pay the face amounts of bonds prematurely, by offering to substitute new bonds for old at favorable rates at some time before- the redemption date of the old bonds. The offer normally occurs when interest rates are rising, causing the rates paid in previous years to be noncompetitive with current rates being offered by those selling bonds. The United States government has used the technique rather often, because the comparatively very low rates it has paid on its low-priced bonds—the classic consumer bonds it sells, from the "war bonds" of World War I to the bonds of today—have made those bonds harder and harder to sell to increasingly sophisticated low- and middle-income Americans, to whom even appeals to patriotism eventually proved to be ineffective selling devices. Significant effects of this long-term rise in government bond interest rates have been an equally long-term impact on the dollar amount of government debts and a substantial increase in the amount of interest the federal government has to pay on long-term debts out of current income and ever-increasing amounts of debt. It is one of several basic factors underlying the constant trend toward inflation that characterizes the American economy, and one of the reasons inflation will not just "go away" or prove itself amenable to short-term money supply manipulation.

Amortization.   When you repay a loan in installments, as when you repay a constant-payment mortgage loan over 30 years in 360 equal monthly payments, you normally include both interest and principal repayments in the same monthly sum sent to the mortgage lender. That part of each payment which represents repayment of principal is amortization, or lessening of the loan amount still owed.

The term has another major meaning as well, taking lessening or reduction in a different sense, and with much tax significance. When a fixed asset depreciates, that is, loses its stated value over a period of years—even though it may not, in fact, lose any real or resale value—it is amortizing over the period of years. Similarly, when it depletes—that is, when it is, for tax purposes, used up over a period of years, again not necessarily actually being entirely used up—it is amortizing, or lessening and reducing. In all senses, amortization is a lessening in value down to zero; however, in relation to depreciation and depletion, it is very much a legal and taxing fiction, while in loan repayment it is entirely literal, describing specific reductions in sums owed down to zero.

Annuity.   In the widest sense, an annuity has come to mean any sum paid over a number of years, as when a common stock purchased long ago has greatly increased in value, pays a handsome dividend, and gives every indication that it will continue to do so; then it is often admiringly described as "a real annuity." Somewhat more narrowly, it is a sum paid in equal installments over a period to recipients, called "annuitants," under the terms of a bequest or an insurance policy, called an "annuity policy."

As an insurance policy, the annuity is used by individual purchasers and financial planners for retirement planning and for the tax advantages involved in this type of policy. Annuity policies come in different types with multiple options, but all such policies are purchased from an insurance company, which is contractually committed to pay the annuitant, owner, or beneficiary certain dollars at a time specified under the policy provisions. No matter what the type, the amounts paid by the insurer will never be greater than the cash values and interest accumulated in the contract. An annuity may be purchased either by specified periodic payments over a period of time before the date on which the company is obligated to begin payments, or by a lump sum of money to the insurance company, with the annuity payments to commence immediately or at a specified date thereafter.

During the accumulation period, an annuitant who has deferred receiving payments until some future date may, if desired, withdraw the accumulated cash values; if the annuitant dies, the beneficiary of the policy will receive the proceeds. However, once annuity payments have begun, the annuitant no longer has the right to withdraw those monies and they remain irrevocably in the hands of the insurance company; the company's only obligation then is to make periodic payments as stated in the contract.

Some companies offer "variable annuities" under which the contract provisions are usually the same as for fixed annuities, but the periodic payments are variable, not fixed. The amount of the variable periodic payment to the annuitant is determined by the success of a special investment account in which are placed the monies of owners of this type of policy, to be invested by the company. Such policies generally provide for a "floor," or basic minimum, of payments to the annuitant.

A single premium deferred annuity is a relatively new type of annuity which has the basic elements of an "immediate annuity," but has some special characteristics. With a single premium deferred annuity, the deposit to the insurance company is not irrevocably given, but may be withdrawn by the owner of the policy at any time, partially or totally, before the date on which payments are to begin; in some contracts, this date can be as late as age 85 of the annuitant. The interest paid by the insurance company varies with the current interest rate, with a floor interest rate guaranteed in the contract. The interest is tax-deferred during the accumulation period, and upon withdrawal of funds, the annuitant or owner has no tax obligation until the sum withdrawn exceeds the sum initially deposited. The contract thus allows for a fixed dollar deposit, interest payments at current rates with a rate floor guaranteed by the insurance company, and tax-deferred yield during accumulation. And, since the single premium deferred annuity is an insurance contract, the proceeds are not subject to probate costs but on the death of the annuitant are paid directly to a named beneficiary. Another new variation, the flexible premium retirement annuity, is similar to the single premium deferred annuity except that payments into the insurance contract may be made periodically rather than in a single lump sum.

Another relatively new kind of annuity is the "wrap-around" annuity, which combines an insurance company annuity contract with a mutual fund sale, with the value of the annuity varying with that of the mutual fund component, and with tax deferral aspects much like those encountered in the single premium deferred annuity

transaction. The Internal Revenue Service as of this writing is contesting the tax deferral aspects of the transaction;
once tax aspects have been settled, so will the relative de-
sirability of the transaction

Appreciation potential.   This is investment-community jargon
for "It may go up!" Because this is a term used mainly by
those with something to sell, there is—quite understand-
ably—no opposite term, such as "depreciation potential."
A common stock is said to have appreciation potential
when those trading it feel that, for any or several reasons,
it may go up. If the rise in market price is thought to be
only for the near term, the stock is said to have "short-
term appreciation potential"; if only for the long term,
then "long-term appreciation potential." Less pretentious-
ly, a stock may be described as having "growth potential"
or its opposite, "downside risk."

Some people selling other assets and interests also use
these terms, such as those selling real estate and debt instruments such as bonds.

One need not necessarily be terribly wary of those who
use this kind of jargon, as in a very real sense it is the special language of their trade. On the other hand, if you can
find a sophisticated investment advisor who uses such
plain language as "I think it will go up," that person may
be well worth cultivating.

Arbitrage.   When a trader buys something in one market and
simultaneously, or very nearly simultaneously, sells the
same kind of thing in another market at a different price,
pursuing a profit resulting from the difference between
the two prices, that trader is practicing arbitrage. It is a
specialty among investment traders, with those participat-
ing normally engaging in very large transactions in two or
more widely separated markets at the same time, hoping
to profit from very small price differences between the
markets. The most common investments traded in by
these specialists, called "arbitrageurs," are currencies,

commodities, and several kinds of commodity and financial futures.

For example, a trader may find the British pound selling in Amsterdam at $2.30 and at the same time selling in Rio de Janeiro at $2.31—usually the differences are even smaller. By buying a million pounds in Rio at $2.31, the arbitrageur can make a penny on each pound, or $10,000, minus transaction costs. That is something of an oversimplification, but it accurately portrays the basic transaction.

In recent years, the term "risk arbitrage" has come to be used in connection with a branch of investment banking that has little or nothing to do with the kind of arbitrage just described. In common usage, the qualifying word "risk" is often dropped, leading to considerable confusion as to what arbitrage is. Risk arbitrage is that branch of investment banking concerned with realizing profit from trading the securities of companies involved in takeover situations. Traders involved take very substantial risks for very substantial possible profits, for example, by buying the common stock of a company that has just received a takeover bid from another company, which has offered considerably more per share than the current market price of the stock. By buying shortly after the takeover bid has been received, while the stock is on the way up toward the price offered, traders can, if the takeover goes through, make the difference between their own purchase prices and the takeover bid price of the stock. But if the takeover does not eventuate, then traders will probably lose the difference between what they paid for the stock and its market price at the time the takeover bid was received. The traders' risk of loss and possibility of gain becomes very great when much of the money used for this kind of speculation is borrowed money, as it so often is. Some traders speculate on the rumor of a takeover bid, rather than its actuality, magnifying the risk even more.

Assets.   In the widest colloquial sense, anything carrying any kind of positive value—from such tangibles as real estate to such intangibles as future royalties, love, and happiness—can be described as an asset. In the economic and financial sense, although assets can be as tangible as real estate or as intangible as a future interest in royalties, they must be capable of producing wealth that can be measured in financial terms now or at some future time— and that lets out love and happiness.

Assets can be liquid—that is, cash or near cash—such as notes minus an allowance for uncollectibles, or quickly marketable securities and commodities, including listed common stocks, some bonds, and gold. Some assets may be less liquid, such as real estate, furnishings, and business goods and equipment. Others may be extremely difficult to make liquid, such as future interests and equity in a wholly owned business that is not readily salable. Yet all of these are assets, to which a value may be attached, ultimately if by no one else than the taxing authorities.

For financial planning purposes, assets are sometimes hard to evaluate. The money spent on education by a woman reentering the work force after years or even decades of being away is in a very real sense investment money—yet it vanishes from a statement of net worth, even though $10,000 spent on that kind of education may result in additional earnings of $200,000 to $400,000 in the next 20 years. The $20,000 spent on going into business may be lost within the first year—or it may be well-spent investment money that results in the development of a million-dollar business asset. By all means, generate a statement of net worth periodically and use it as a tool to help you evaluate your assets—but try not to develop too narrow a view of what your assets really are, for it can impede the breadth of your forward planning.

Audit.   In accounting, auditing is the examination of records in order to attempt to substantiate the completeness and accuracy of books of account and of the transactions they record, with considerable attention paid to the internal consistency of the records being examined. That examination, or audit, is carried out by someone professionally trained to conduct such examinations: an auditor, who is usually also an accountant.

Most people encounter the term in relation to examinations of personal and business records carried out by taxing authorities. In that context, auditing is often carried out by an employee of a taxing authority, such as an IRS agent, who may or may not be professionally trained in accounting and whose auditing activities often take on some of the flavor of adversary proceedings.

Average.   In ordinary usage, an average is an arithmetic mean, reached by adding two or more figures and dividing by the number of figures; for example, the average of 3 + 3 + 6 is the sum of the three, which is 12, divided by 3, giving 4. In a wider arithmetic sense, an average can be any number expressing the center of or typifying a set of numbers of which it is part; for example, an average can be a median, or middle number in a group of numbers, or it can be a weighted average, which stresses some numbers more than others in a group, moving the average in their direction.

In securities markets, an average reflects the value of a group of selected stocks, which are thought to be representative of their markets as a whole and therefore indicators of market health, such as the Dow Jones industrial, Standard and Poor's, the *New York Times,* and the New York Stock Exchange averages.

The Dow Jones averages are actually three different current stock price averages, composed, respectively, of industrial, transportation, and utilities stocks. The best known and most frequently referred to of the three is the industrial average, composed of 30 well-known common stocks. It is also by far the best known of all the stock market averages, and its fluctuations are watched closely by people who follow stock market price trends, even though

the other major averages are composed of far larger numbers of stocks, fluctuate a good deal less, and are therefore
somewhat more statistically reliable for predictive purposes.

Averaging.   Averaging is a stock market investment technique
also known as "dollar cost averaging." It involves investing fixed sums of money in securities through periodic
purchases, as in the monthly purchase of $1000 in shares
of a specific common stock over a period of six months, ignoring short-term price fluctuations in that stock on the
theory that the long-term trend of that stock and indeed
of the whole stock market is up, and that the purchase of
sound stocks over the long term can only prove profitable.
The New York Stock Exchange's Monthly Investment
Plan, which provides for periodic small stock purchases by
small investors, with title to even fractional shares passing
to the investor on receipt of periodic payments, in essence provides this kind of averaging mechanism for small
investors.

This technique works out rather well for some investors
during periods of prolonged general stock market advance, such as the late 1960s. It has, however, come to be
seen as questionable under conditions of such protracted
stock market stagnation or decline as characterized the
1970s.

Balance.   "Balance" is a term with two quite distinct meanings
and several financial and investment uses.

In its first major sense, balance means remainder, that
which is left after other transactions have taken place. A
balance due is the remainder of what is owed. A bank balance is what you own in a bank account—again what is
owed, but this time by the bank to you. A balance of payments is a summing up of plus and minus payment transactions between countries, as a balance of indebtedness is
a summing up of debt obligations and a balance of trade a
summing up of trading transactions.

In its second major sense, balance deals with equilibrium. A tightrope walker keeps balance, or equilibrium, while traversing the rope in order to avoid falling off. An accountant brings books of account into equilibrium by equalizing the debits and credits in a double-entry accounting system and calls it "balancing the books."

A balance sheet is a statement, derived from a double-entry bookkeeping system, of the financial condition of a business entity as of a given moment, including all assets, liabilities, and ownership equities. For smaller entities, balance sheets may be quite detailed and therefore tell a great deal about the entity; for larger entities, such as major corporations, they may be very brief summaries, requiring that a great deal of additional data be added before they become very useful tools of financial analysis. In summary form or detailed, though, they are basic to any kind of financial analysis, by either professional analysts or investors.

Balanced fund.   A balanced fund is a diversely invested mutual fund, really a fund that from the start is so organized as to be able to invest in several kinds of stocks and bonds at the same time and to shift emphasis from one to another as fund managers' assessments of market situations change from time to time. Many mutual funds are not so organized, their choice being to move from one kind of investment, such as municipal bonds or common stocks or even a single kind of common stock, to cash and cash instruments, without the ability to move relatively freely among an assortment of stocks and debt instruments.

For investors, the net effect of a fund management's inability to move freely is that what is presumably being bought with a mutual fund investment—professional management and diversification of risk—is strikingly absent from many of the single-investment funds. A diversified or balanced fund may be badly managed, but its managers at least have a chance to move about professionally in several markets, rather than being forced to rush into cash when a single kind of specialized investment strikes a low period.

Balloon.   Like so many words in special languages, such as those of business and finance, "balloon," is yesterday's slang now become part of the language. A balloon is a bubble of material filled with gas that is lighter than air and that therefore rises and floats in air. So, too, is an item of value that is filled with tips, rumors, hopes, and unending talk of riches to come and that therefore rises in price extraordinarily far beyond its intrinsic value—so far, indeed, that some kind of price manipulation is suspected by investors and regulatory authorities. That is a classic investment balloon.

But it has another, more prosaic meaning as well. It is a final loan repayment sum, due at the end of the repayment period and larger than previous payments, as with a mortgage or other loan on which only interest is payable until the last payment, when the entire principal becomes due. A bond, which pays interest over a period of years and its face amount at maturity, is, in this sense of the word, a balloon.

Bank account.   A bank account is quite literally a store of value, and a bank its storehouse. However, a bank is in the business of selling money to others in the form of loans at a profit and therefore does not really store your money—it uses it to make money. It makes no economic sense at all to store money in a bank in a non-interest-bearing account, as are many checking accounts in commercial banks, when you can store it in an interest-bearing account in another commercial bank, a savings bank, a savings and loan association, or a money market fund, and make money with your stored money. If you do use a money market fund, which is, in this sense, really a kind of banking institution, be aware that, although you may earn higher interest on your stored money, much of that money is not federally insured, as it is in the other banking institutions; that can matter in a financial crisis.

Ordinary bank accounts are viewed as liquid assets, capable of being turned into usable cash immediately, with even long-term savings accounts yielding higher-than-normal interest rates capable of being withdrawn early, though at a loss of interest. However, that is not entirely true. A checking account is a demand deposit, with the balance in the account literally payable on demand, whereas a savings account is technically payable at a stated time after notice has been given to the bank of intent to withdraw funds—a requirement that is generally waived by banks, but not necessarily in all instances. During some recent periods of heavy demand for withdrawal of moneys from 6-month or longer certificates of deposit, some banks took advantage of the "fine print" of the transaction and refused to make those funds available to depositors until the maturity date of the certificates. Even demand deposits may not be readily available if a bank has closed its doors either because of individual bank failure or because of the kind of bank holiday declared in time of crisis, as in 1933.

Other generations of Americans, inured to panics and bank failures here and in their countries of origin, often tended to mistrust banks, and even currency, keeping some currency and some valuable goods stored away privately for a time of crisis. For a smallish portion of one's assets, that still may be a prudent course of action, even though it might be more psychologically reassuring than economically sound.

Bankruptcy. It happens. For whatever reason, every day business and personal debtors are declared insolvent by court proceedings, and their affairs administered by a court through a receiver or trustee. Bankruptcy may be involuntary or voluntary; it may be worked through with a court standing as a shield between creditors and debtor over a period of years, or it may be a matter of liquidation and forced sale of all business or almost all personal assets to satisfy creditors.

For individuals trying to do effective financial planning, it is obviously a disaster, signaling a wipeout of most kinds of personal assets and the need to start all over again, with credit rating impaired for many years. But some people and businesses do work through bankruptcies, and others come back after wipeouts.

Personal bankruptcy does not impair government Social Security, survivors', and disability payments; nor are pension assets or pension payments many years later impaired, although monies from pension funds, once payments to recipients start, may be subject to any obligations than remain after bankruptcy. At least the bedrock government and private pension payments survive bankruptcy; with these elements in place, financial planning can start anew.

Basis.   "Basis" is one of those rather frustrating terms that has several quite separate and distinct meanings, depending on the context within which it is used.

In taxation, basis refers to the cost of an asset to be deducted from a selling price in order to arrive at taxable capital gains, whether short or long term, as when you buy stock at one price and sell it later at a higher price.

It means the same thing in real estate transactions, but with the addition of the cost of improvements during the period of ownership and the subtraction of depreciation and some other minor deductions to arrive at taxable gain. (The depreciation computed is based upon buying price plus improvements.)

In bond markets, basis means something else—the rate of interest paid on bonds and other debt securities. In that context, a "basis point" means one-hundredth of 1%.

In stock analysis, it means the annual rate of return on stock, figuring the actual return as a proportion of the current market value of the stock.

In commodities trading, basis refers to the difference between current, or spot, prices and futures prices.

This term is a classic illustration of the need to listen hard to the context within which a term is being used, since a single word may occur in several different business languages.

Blue chip. "Blue chip" is a synonym for high-quality investment, now applied widely to many noninvestment items and matter of value. That is odd, in a way, for the term, which originated in gambling rooms, implicitly recognizes the element of risk inherent in all investment operations.

Blue-chip common stocks are the stocks of large, highly regarded companies, which have grown in value and paid dividends over a period measured in decades and which are therefore thought to be rather safe investments, with little chance of omitting dividends and losing value quickly and catastrophically. There is no accepted list of blue-chip stocks; even the *Fortune* lists of leading companies include companies that have grown swiftly, paid little or no dividends, and whose stocks fluctuate a good deal. Calling a stock a blue chip may help sell it, but only vigilance directed toward your own investments can save you from sharp financial reverses, whatever your investments. Those who did not properly watch the stock market as a whole in the early 1970s and those who failed to see properly what was happening to the American automobile industry in the late 1970s and early 1980s can testify to that; before the middle 1970s, the major American auto companies were the bluest of blue chips—and had been for decades.

Boiler room and bucket shop. These are really two investment-industry slang terms meaning the same thing—a fraudulent investment-selling firm. These are the kinds of illegal operations that give telephone selling a bad name. Their representatives sell mainly by telephone and will sell anything that is currently popular—as long as they can make a great deal of money doing it. During the stock market boom of the 1960s, they sold stocks, and either did not execute the customer orders taken, pocketed their customers' money and ran, or executed the orders late, to their own benefit. After the stock market declined and then went into a long period of stagnation, they moved into real estate syndication, gold futures, gold, silver, diamonds (which they "stored" for their customers and which their customers never saw), and whatever else was "going," or moving up in value rapidly, and therefore attractive to unsophisticated investors seeking to "make a killing."

When a stranger is heard on your telephone, with a wonderful, foolproof investment opportunity on which you cannot possibly lose and on which you will surely make a lot of money—don't.

Bond.   A tie that binds, and a word with a dozen different meanings and scores of uses. In finance, a bond is an instrument evidencing debt obligation; in insurance, a bond is a pledge of surety for another; in commerce, some goods held pending excise tax payments are said to be held in bond; in law, a bond is an agreement.

In financial planning, the term refers to a debt instrument issued by a corporation or government, in which the issuer promises to pay back the money borrowed from bond buyers with interest within a specified time. Usually, interest is payable in installments during the life of the debt obligation, and principal is repaid in a lump sum at the end of the period; sometimes, however, as in the case of some government bonds, interest accretes during the debt period and is paid with principal repayment at the end of the period. Bonds are usually medium- to long-term debt instruments, running five years or more.

You will often find bonds backed by the "full faith and credit" of their issuer. That sounds good, but it is merely a bare promise to pay and is only as good as the financial position of its issuer. If that issuer is the United States government, which backs its promise to pay with its taxing power and ultimately with the full force of the national state, then that promise is worth a good deal as long as that government continues in its present form, which seems rather likely for some considerable time to come. But even that is nothing to blindly take for granted. The world is full of government bonds worth little more than the paper they are printed on; governments come and go, and their obligations often go with them.

When bonds are issued by states, municipalities, or corporations, they should be evaluated just as a banker evaluates your capacity to repay a requested loan. When you buy a bond, the essence of the transaction is that you are lending your money to its issuer—you are banking its issuer. If the issuer offers no collateral, then you are very trusting, indeed, if you lend it money without investigation, at least in terms of how the bond is rated by rating services, such as Moody's, which are available at many public libraries and at stock brokerage offices.

A bond that is not backed by collateral is a kind of debenture, which is an instrument evidencing an unsecured promise of its issuer to pay, usually in the form of a bond. A bond that is backed by some kind of collateral may, in addition, be backed by its issuer's promise to pay. Collateralized bonds are often secured by liens on real property and equipment, such as first, second, and subsequent mortgages on real estate and equipment.

Bond fund. A bond fund is a mutual fund that limits its investments to either bonds or cash instruments, trading in bonds with the money invested in it by its mutual fund purchasers.

A special form of bond fund is the municipal bond fund, which limits its bond-trading activities to state and municipal bonds, thereby reaching for the tax advantages inherent in these kinds of debt obligations, which are usually exempt from federal taxes and sometimes from state and local taxes as well.

Bond market.   Bonds of all kinds are traded on many stock exchanges, but no exchange dominates the trading in bonds as the New York Stock Exchange dominates stock trading. Instead, bond trading proceeds over the counter, through a network of firms trading in these debt obligations, all of which make up the bond market. Most bond transactions are very large and represent trades between financial institutions, such as banks, pension funds, mutual funds, and insurance companies, buying and selling for their own accounts.

Book value.   Book value is an accounting concept, and a valuable one when trying to assess the intrinsic asset value of a business or a share of common stock. It is calculated a little differently for each. For a business, book value is the difference between all assets and all liabilities; putting it a little differently, it is the net of assets minus liabilities. Those assets are valued as part of a going business, rather than at their scrap or salvage value, which would be much less; and that is proper, for it is that going business that is being evaluated.

When assessing the intrinsic value of a share of common stock, any preferred stock outstanding must also be taken into account. To estimate the book value of a share of common stock, you would take the net of assets minus liabilities, subtract the value of any preferred stock outstanding, and divide the resulting net by the number of outstanding shares of common stock, with the result being book value. For example, if assets were $100 and liabilities $50, the net would be $50. If preferred stock were worth $10 and were subtracted from that $50, the result would be $40. If there were 40 common stock shares outstanding, their book value would be $1 per share.

That is an important figure, for if stock is selling below its book value, it may be the stock of a company in terrible trouble, perhaps in the process of being forced out of business with the resulting reevaluation of assets way down to salvage value, or it may be the stock of a company that is far undervalued and a very good buy. Conversely, if a stock is selling far above its book value, it may be a company with interesting growth and profit possibilities that has shown extraordinary results and that may soon show more, or it may be a company that is far overvalued, as were so many "glamour" stocks in the 1960s, and a very bad buy. Either way—and these are tendencies, with the truth being almost invariably less simple than this and lying between these polar opposites—book value is a concept well worth understanding.

Boom and bust.   Prosperity and depression—the rapid expansion of the 1920s followed by the Great Depression of the 1930s, after the Crash of 1929—are the classic boom and bust. We often think of the unrestrained operation of the "boom-and-bust" business cycle as a purely historical matter, living as we do in a far more managed economy. But recession is only a euphemism for depression, and there have been many depressions of lesser impact than the Great Depression, both before and after the 1930s. We are not yet done with the business cycle and its impacts; indeed, one of the major economic phenomena of our time is the fluctuation of a managed economy around stagnation, expanding as money supply is manipulated by governments and contracting as the resulting inflation causes governments to manipulate money supply differently. The main feature of the American economy before this current period was not the business cycle—it was prolonged, meteoric growth, punctuated by the recurrent temporary contractions. The main feature of this period is the economic stagnation around which the business cycle continues to move.

Bottom line.   Ah, the bottom line we hear so much about! In the widest sense, this financial term has moved right out into the language and become synonymous with net result.

In finance, it is literally the bottom line of a profit and loss statement—the net figure, after all else has been computed. But here, too, the term has come to be used more widely to mean the net result of a single action or financial transaction, as well as the net of all the transactions embodied in a profit and loss statement.

Break even.   Break even is a concept that is considerably more complex than it sounds. Straightforwardly, to break even is to conclude a transaction with neither profit nor loss. However, in personal financial planning, as in business, it is easy to leave out some factors that should be figured into an assessment of whether what occurred was a breaking even or a real loss. Very often, such factors as inflation, transaction costs, and time spent are not properly considered.

For example, common stock purchased now for $10,000 and sold two years from now for $10,000 seems to break even, but in reality will probably be sold at a very considerable loss. Assuming an inflation rate of 10 to 11%—and that may be low—$10,000 two years from now may be worth only $8000 in today's dollars, the dollars paid for the stock now. That is a very real loss of $2000, to which must be added the brokerage costs involved in buying and selling the stock, as well as the foregone earnings the money might have yielded in a fixed-dollar investment during those two years.

In business, break-even analysis tries to take into account all relevant factors by analyzing alternative cost and price factors before making projected business moves, especially in new product areas. Using several different sets of cost and price assumptions, planners seek to represent graphically, in a break-even chart, where costs and prices intersect in order to set optimal prices and specifications for new products. Planners factor in a series of standard business costs, such as production, marketing, and overhead costs, and also include such factors as inflation assumptions and financing costs, often using computer assistance. Individuals cannot do all that, but certainly can try to see, at least roughly, the real effects of current financial actions.

Bubble. In finance, a bubble is an investment vehicle that has become the object of irrational expectations on the part of investors, who push its price far beyond any possible intrinsic value until confidence is eventually shaken, inflation becomes apparent, and panic selling takes over. Such investments are often thought later to have been intrinsically worthless, but that is not always true; quite sound investments can become enormously popular and be pushed far higher than their worth.

Some seeming bubbles are hard to assess: for example, gold's meteoric rise in value during the late 1970s and early 1980s seemed to many to be little more than a bubble. Yet, though gold did fluctuate, its historic rise has—as of this writing—turned out not to be a bubble at all. At the same time, silver, which is subject to international manipulation, was indeed a short-lived bubble, with many investors joining the rush to buy at inflated prices only to find very quickly that the bubble had burst and that they had lost a good deal of their money. Not that bubbles depend on manipulation—some historic bubbles have grown and flourished on little more than rumor and the price rises developed from that rumor, the rises then feeding upon themselves as more and more investors rushed to get on the bandwagon.

Budgeting. Unfortunately, budgeting has, for many individuals, somehow come to be identified with counting pennies and self-denial, both processes at considerable variance with American dreams, though not necessarily with current American realities. The process really has little to do with either; whether done by organizations or individuals, budgeting involves an estimate of future income and costs for a specified period and a serious attempt to live within the bounds of that estimate.

One significant difference exists between public and private budgeting efforts. Public budgeters talk about living within their means and incur deficits; private budgeters sooner or later live within their means or go bankrupt. For those individuals trying to do effective financial planing, realistic, flexible budgeting is a habit that is indispensable. Without capital to invest, no financial planning is possible, and without budgeting there is all too often no capital to invest.

Bull and bear.   Put simply, a bull is an optimist and a bear a pessimist. It makes a good deal more sense to describe these states of mind as tendencies, rather than as fixed positions, for as tendencies, they may move and change with shifting perceptions of reality, while as fixed states of mind, "bullish" and "bearish" could only describe abnormalities. "Bull" and "bear" are traditional stock market terms that have now moved out into the general language. One can be optimistic or pessimistic about anything, and the terms are encountered in a wide range of connections, from an assessment of the possibility of peace in our time to whether or not it will rain tomorrow, the city dweller normally being pessimistic, or bearish, when predicting rain, the farmer normally taking the opposite view.

In the financial world, a bull thinks a specific stock or debt obligation, or a whole market or set of markets, is likely to go up and buys now in anticipation of that rise. Bulls often buy on margin, that is, on borrowed money, and hold the securities or commodities in brokers' margin accounts in an attempt to maximize the impact of their investments, holding on as long as possible in a falling market.

A bear thinks that a single investment or group of investments will go down and sells rather than buys. While bulls often buy long and hold, bears often do the opposite; they sell short—that is, they sell stocks they do not yet own, planning and hoping to buy stocks to cover their sales later at lower prices, profiting from the difference between the two sets of prices.

Markets fluctuate; one who is a bull today may be a bear tomorrow. Views as to long-term trends change less quickly than that; one can be properly described as a bull or a bear for a whole market period lasting years. But one who is pessimist or optimist too long, failing to recognize changing circumstances, leaves analysis behind, and with it a sizable portion of invested assets.

Capital.   Capital is tangible wealth that can be used to produce more wealth. It need not be so used; money stored away in a safe-deposit box is capital, as is money invested in a business or used to purchase securities. Often, such intangibles as skills and goodwill are called capital; although not capital in a rigorous accounting or economic sense, they may be as important as capital for financial planning. For example, creating a body of skills by the investment of capital in education uses up the capital invested without the production of tangible wealth, but may be the most lucrative use of that capital.

Capital gains.   Capital gains are the profits resulting from sale of an asset. For example, when securities or realty worth $10,000 are sold later for $15,000, the difference of $5000 may be capital gain—and therefore taxable, for that is the main significance of the concept.

At this writing, profits from sale of assets held for less than one year are short-term taxable gains for tax purposes and are taxed as ordinary income. Profits from sale of assets held for a year or more—and that means anything sold the first day after the end of a full year, such as the sale of something on August 1 that was bought on July 31 of the previous year—are treated as long-term capital gains and receive more favorable tax treatment, the specifics of which are best left to your tax preparer.

No allowance is made for inflation, so that taxes are paid on "gains" even when they may, in fact, be losses. For example, if the assets just cited were sold with a $5000 taxable gain 10 years after purchase, when the dollar might be worth less than half of what it was worth in the year of purchase, that "gain" might have been a very real loss of much more than $5000, made even larger by the taxes that must be paid on the "gain" realized.

Capital stock.   Capital stock is all the stock representing ownership of a corporation, including common and preferred stock issued and outstanding, that is held by the public and all that has been issued and is owned by the corporation itself, as when stock has been sold to the public and then repurchased by the corporation.

The underlying or intrinsic value of the total capital stock of a corporation is its book value, or the net of all assets minus all liabilities, that net being one measure of the total ownership equity in the corporation. Another measure of the current value of the ownership equity in a corporation is often supplied by the market value placed on publicly traded stock of that corporation, which is one reason corporate managements pay so very much attention to the price of their publicly traded stock. One hazard faced by corporate managements is the development of a situation in which publicly traded stock is selling considerably below book value, making acquisition of the corporation very attractive to others and sale of stock held very attractive to its current holders when they are offered a price higher than its current market price.

Cash flow statement.   The cash flow statement is a prime planning tool for individuals trying to accomplish effective financial planning, as it is for businesses. As a record of what happened, it traces the flow of cash through the hands of an individual or business, literally showing where cash came from and where it went. As a forward planning device, it forecasts where money is expected to come from, in what quantities, and when, and where money is expected to go, in what quantities, and when.

Like companies, individuals should routinely lay out in chart form a realistic cash flow statement and forward projection; this will show you when you will have money to invest; when you will need to borrow; how much you need to hold in short-term forms for coming cash needs; what major expenditures will need to be financed—or, if discretionary, should not be made; and what the impact of your lifestyle will be upon your available cash. As you make new cash flow statements periodically, you can also assess whether your previous predictions have indeed been realistic and modify your planning accordingly. In short, a good cash flow statement is a map of the cash side of your financial life, and an indispensable one.

Cash surrender value.   If you own a life insurance policy that includes both savings and insurance components—usually called a "whole life," "permanent life," or "straight life" policy—that policy includes a sum you can claim on cancellation of the policy. That sum, called the "cash surrender value," consists of the savings you have accrued in the policy plus a very small interest payment on the money.

Most often, people do not cancel life insurance policies to obtain the cash surrender value in them; nor do insurance companies encourage the practice. Instead, at modest interest rates—but higher than the rates the insurance company pays its policyholders—you may borrow from the insurance company right up to the full value of the money you have lent it, thus keeping the insurance in force and still having the use of your own money. If you have, in previous years, bought this kind of life insurance policy, the ability to borrow against the savings in it can be important; this kind of policy is usually written on a level premium basis, with the insurance you purchase at an early age costing much less per year than insurance purchased later. It is also possible that you were insurable when you bought the policy, but that you might have trouble qualifying for insurance now, as a result of health problems that have developed in subsequent years.

On the other hand, it does not sound much like effective financial planning to tie up savings in life insurance policies yielding low interest when inflation makes its absolutely necessary to work hard to stay even and when other, far better opportunities exist.

Certificate of deposit.   A certificate of deposit is a document evidencing the existence of a deposit in a bank, issued by a bank to the owner of the deposit; a passbook is the same kind of instrument, in a different physical form.

They are widely called "CDs" and occur in two basic forms. One form, widely sold by commercial banks to individuals as a means of attracting depositor money at somewhat higher interest rates than those permitted under existing laws, is that of a demand certificate of deposit, which specifies that the depositor can withdraw the deposit on demand, although suffering substantial interest rate penalties for premature withdrawal. Because of its demand nature, this kind of certificate of deposit is not tradable in investment markets.

The second form is that of a time certificate of deposit, which is payable at some specified future time. Such certificates are widely traded in money markets, as they are usually direct obligations of highly regarded banks, although not as safe as direct federal debt obligations.

Some time certificates of deposit are issued in denominations so high as to place them outside the normal buying range of all but the wealthiest individuals. But individuals can reach them—and their sometimes attractive rates— through mutual funds, notably money market funds, which routinely include them in their portfolios.

Collateral.   Something of value that is used as security for a loan is collateral. Normal collateral consists of real or personal property of determinable value belonging to the borrower or to one guaranteeing the loan for the borrower, which on default will become the property of the lender. When a lender and borrower enter into a home mortgage loan, the property mortgaged is collateral for the loan. When a borrower formally pledges any property, such as stocks and other financial instruments or automobiles and other personal possessions, as security for a loan, that which is pledged is collateral. When a borrower gives the lender physical possession of property so pledged, to be returned on repayment of the loan, the loan is called a collateral loan.

Although collateral usually consists of tangibles of determinable value that can be fairly easily sold, it may be anything recognized by a lender as having value; for example, a future interest in an estate or indeterminate future royalty payments may be accepted by a lender as collateral. Such collateral will not be accepted by your bank, though—and those lenders who will accept it are speculative, and their rates of interest are very high.

Collectibles. In the widest investment sense, collectibles have come to mean all tangibles bought, held, and traded for which any kind of market exists. Antiques, works of art, old and rare books, stamps, and jewelry have been joined by bottle tops, comic books, glass, barbed wire, matchbook covers, and hundreds of other items so bought, held, and traded. Lively formal and informal markets in these kinds of items have sprung up all over the United States and in many other parts of the world; these often function to push trading prices up far beyond intrinsic values and inflation rates and have become arenas of considerable speculative activity.

At the same time, the terms "art" and "antique" have tended to become ever more imprecise, reflecting a general tendency on the part of traders to add negotiable luster to the collectibles they have to sell. Art surely is in the eye of the beholder, and the products of the minor arts are, in this sense, works of art; when the description "work of art" is used as a selling phrase, however, the investor/collector should view the designation with considerable skepticism, unless accompanied by unimpeachable attribution.

"Antiques," in investment terms, are simply old collectibles, in which age and condition play a considerable part in the assessment of value. If an item is less than 100 years old, it is not likely to be viewed by most expert collectors as an antique, although many sellers and dealers would have unwary buyers believe otherwise.

Comaker.   There is only one better way to lose a friend than to lend that friend money—and that is to become your friend's comaker. Yet many of us become comakers, and in a stagnating economy, children, other relatives, and close friends are hard to turn down when they ask for your cosignature on a loan instrument that may help them to secure a down payment on a house or a needed automobile or to meet current expenses.

A comaker, also known as a "cosigner," is responsible for repayment of a loan made to another, but receives none of the proceeds of that loan. If the borrower defaults, then the comaker must legally complete payment. This is not a responsibility to be undertaken lightly, as those needing comakers often are poor credit risks, and the possibility of default therefore is considerable. Even if the borrower makes all payments, and in a timely way, the credit standing of the cosigner reflects the existence of the cosigned loan, much as if it were the comaker's loan, except for the drain on the borrower's current income caused by repayment. Comakers, applying for loans of their own, are often surprised to find that lenders take existing comade loans into account in deciding whether or not to extend loans to them; in some cases it can prove the difference between obtaining a loan or not.

Commercial paper.   In the widest sense, commercial paper includes all short-term debt instruments issued by businesses of all kinds. Such notes are negotiable and may be
traded and used as collateral. Some such debt instruments
are traded widely, are rated for safety, and have become
part of the money market. These are the instruments issued by major businesses, which stand behind them, essentially as they do for any unsecured longer-term
instrument, such as a bond, with their full faith and credit, which is a promise to pay. The instruments are as good
as the businesses issuing them, which in the case of a major oil company may be very good indeed, and in the case
of a troubled automobile company not very good at all.

Because the instruments are normally issued in denominations of $100,000 to $1 million, very few individuals can
trade in them. However, money market mutual funds do,
and that is the way individuals can reach for their yields,
which are higher than, though generally not as safe as,
federally issued and federally insured debt obligations.

Commodities.   Commodities are those items of value that are
tradable, but in an investment-market sense they are
those kinds of goods traded on commodities exchanges,
such as gold, silver, platinum, other precious metals and
resources, coffee, tea, sugar, lumber, cotton, wool, corn,
pork bellies, and wheat.

Both current, or spot, commodity contracts and commodity futures contracts are traded on commodity exchanges,
the contracts, rather than the commodities themselves,
being the instruments traded. A commodities future contract specifies all the terms of an agreement to deliver a
specific amount of a commodity at a specified place on a
future date. It is so constructed as to be tradable, since
each contract is identical with all other contracts of a like
kind.

Common stock.   Common stock is an unrestricted ownership
share in a corporation and is the kind of stock that is nor-

mally traded in investment markets. Common stock is by far the main form such ownership shares take, its owner sharing fully in risks and opportunities and voting its proportion of ownership in the issuing corporation. In this, it contrasts with preferred stock, whose owner may share less risk, but shares in opportunities to only a limited degree. When a stock is reported as rising or falling in market value, it is a common stock that is being described, unless otherwise noted.

Conservative investment.   A conservative investment is literally an investment aimed primarily at conserving assets safely, as in highly rated bonds, rather than at growing them swiftly, but at higher risk, as in commodity futures. However, the investment world has indeed turned upside down since the 1960s, and yesterday's conservative investment may be today's high-risk investment. Moreover, yesterday's conservative investment may today still be conservative and yet higher yielding than far riskier investments. For example, some "blue-chip" common stocks, purchased many years ago and held through all market fluctuations since then, may no longer be at all safe—some automobile stocks, for example—and may yield very small dividends as well. Some long-term bonds, purchased for safety and modest yield when interest rates were low, may today be selling at very deep discounts, leaving their holders two disagreeable options— sell now at a large loss or hold to maturity, taking low interest until then, and thus take the loss gradually by foregoing the higher interest the money in the bonds would command today. On the other hand, short-term federal debt obligations, some of the safest investments available in the world, in some periods pay far better than do all but a very few common stocks—and to find those common stocks the investor must take high risks all the way.

In investment, conservatism is, then, very much in the eye of the beholder.

Constant dollar value.   If you buy something now for $1000 and sell it for $1000 some years in the future, when inflation has caused the dollar to lose half its present value, do not plan to congratulate yourself on having held the money you put into it, for in fact you will have sold it for half what you paid for it. In terms of dollar value now, also called constant dollar value, you will have actually sold it for $500. If you sold it at a seeming profit and paid capital gains taxes on that profit, you may have actually sold it at a loss and paid taxes that increase that loss.

It is impractical to suggest that you keep a running score on what your assets are worth in terms of their constant dollar values, purchased as they are in different years, carrying different yields, and having different tax treatments. But you can periodically reevaluate your major assets in constant dollar terms, using the Consumer Price Index (CPI) as a guide for rough estimating. It is an extremely valuable exercise, which enables you to make an independent estimate of how your investment planning is working out in terms of real asset growth, especially so because we tend to hold on to most of our major assets as part of our long-term planning.

For example, one who has owned a home for the past 20 years may find that home's fair market value now to be 500% of, or five times, its purchase price then. However, the Consumer Price Index may have risen by 400% in that period, and thus the house is not worth five times what it was worth then, as so many people choose to believe; it is worth 20% more than its purchase price. Suppose the house was purchased 20 years ago for $30,000. In dollars as they were then, the house is now worth $37,500. Prices have skyrocketed since then, and the $30,000 paid for the house is now $120,000, while the current value is $150,000. The difference in value is $30,000, which is worth $7500 in dollars 20 years ago. The example is simplified, of course, omitting closing and mortgage costs, tax payments, and tax deductions. But it certainly makes the point.

That kind of increase in value, though far from what it seems, is most unusual. Very few investments have held up that way, or have even gained. The savings portion, or cash surrender value, of a "straight life" insurance policy, with its very low interest factor, may have lost more than half its value in that period; a share of common stock, selling at the same price at which it traded 10 years ago, has lost considerably more than half its value, as measured in real, or constant, dollars.

Constant dollar value is a very useful concept; it can help you cut through a maze of conflicting claims and selling talk to reach the underlying facts of an investment situation.

Consumer Price Index. The Consumer Price Index, maintained by the Federal Bureau of Labor Statistics and updated monthly, used to be called the "Cost of Living Index" and is just that. Economists have some dispute as to whether or not it accurately reflects the real pace of increase in the cost of living, and there is considerable reason to believe that it does not; for example, it makes no serious attempt to allow for hidden inflation, which is a matter of cutting the quantity and quality of goods sold, as opposed to raising prices, which is more obvious. However, this index is the best tool we have for rough measurement of the cost of living, which, in turn, can be used for measuring our own individual situations.

For example, if your aftertax personal income—aftertax, not gross, income—rises by 5% in a year in which the Consumer Price Index has risen by 15%, you have not gained 5%, but have lost the difference between the 5% and the 15%, which is 10%. If your aftertax income remains the same, you have lost the whole 15%. If you seem to have gained 20%, you have actually gained a little.

Contract.   Much of the civil law governing our relations with one another is contract law, and we enter into many contracts during our lives, from marriage, which is in part a contract, to purchase and sale of a wide number of assets. A contract is any legally enforceable agreement, written or oral, in which two or more parties, for something of value considered in law to be adequate, make or accept promises to perform or not to perform that which was promised. When in writing, a contract is also the instrument evidencing the agreement.

In finance, one such writing that takes on special significance is the commodities contract, which is a contract to buy or sell commodities or commodity futures, with the written contract itself becoming that which is traded on commodities exchanges.

Convertible.   Some bonds and preferred stocks that are issued carry the privilege of conversion over to a stated number of shares of common stock at a stated price within a stated period after issue. Their purchasers may hold these convertibles in their purchased form until maturity or may exercise the privilege of converting them, depending upon whether or not the stated amount of common stock is worth more than the bond or preferred stock at some time before the conversion privilege expires.

In a sharply rising stock market, such as that last experienced in the mid-1960s, convertibles are quite popular instruments. Investors liked them then because they offered significant profit opportunities along with seemingly safe debt instruments; companies liked them because it was often possible to raise money more easily with a debt instrument than with a common stock issue. But in the stock market investment climate of the 1970s and early 1980s, with the real values and net yields of most common stocks far lower than those available in other instruments, convertibles became unpopular, and they await another stock market boom, in which popularity may be restored.

Credit.   Buy now, pay later; to a considerable extent credit is what makes the economic world go 'round. Credit comes in many forms, from a simple promise to pay, unsecured by collateral and resulting from an undocumented telephone conversation, to a complex mortgage document covering every contingency and fully secured by a lien on the property being mortgaged.

Businesses have for centuries used the credit line, which is the ability to borrow up to a certain limit, sometimes not a very sharply defined limit, from a financing organization, such as a commercial bank. Moneyed individuals have done the same. Not-so-moneyed individuals have done so, too, as anyone who has run up a bill at a grocery store will attest. In recent years banking institutions and credit card companies have extended credit line privileges, also called "overdraft privileges," to much larger groups than ever before, with a resulting enormous expansion of consumer credit in the United States.

But beware such consumer credit, especially if you have tended to use it, as businesses often do, as a rolling body of short-term debt, keeping the principal owed basically the same and paying interest charges on that principal. For, as the experience of the credit crunch of 1979 proved, credit offered can be credit frozen or withdrawn, even if your own credit and credit repayment record are excellent. If you are rolling credit around in that fashion, it may be withheld just when you need it most—at the depths of a recession, during a credit crunch, or both—and the impact on your financial condition under those circumstances can be severe.

Credit rating.   Your credit rating is an evaluation of the kind of credit risk that will be taken by one lending to you, whether you are an individual or a business organization. It is also often described as an assessment of creditworthiness, which is the same thing.

When the assessment is made formally, as when a credit evaluating organization such as Dun and Bradstreet examines the creditworthiness of a business, it will be expressed by a letter or number rating scale (such as from A to D), by evaluative comments, or by both. When less formal, as it is for most individuals, it will result from examination of credit investigation reports in the files of credit bureaus, from checking of credit references you have given, and from any other information in the possession of a lender.

Your credit rating is only one element in the decision as to whether or not to extend you a requested loan. If it is a low rating, it may knock you out of consideration for the loan, but not always—even a very bad rating can often be bypassed by the provision of adequate collateral or of an acceptable comaker. Other elements a lender will consider are your character and reputation; your estimated ability to repay, based upon the size of the loan requested; your current income and other debt obligations; your future prospects; the lender's own economic situation and willingness to extend credit; and the current general economic situation.

Cyclical stocks.   Cyclical stocks are the traded stocks of companies thought to be quickly affected by the ups and downs of the economy, the prices of such stocks therefore fluctuating more directly than most stocks as the business cycle moves between prosperity and depression or recession. For example, companies manufacturing consumer goods and therefore depending wholly or largely on discretionary consumer purchases, such as automobiles, furniture, and appliances, may feel the impact of a recession very sharply, while also being the beneficiaries of pent-up demand as a period of prosperity unfolds.

The general observation that a company's stock is more affected than most by cyclical swings must, however, be tempered by the knowledge that other factors can also strongly affect the price of that stock, among them the health of the individual company, foreign competition, and comparative currency values. For example, a sick automobile company may be in no position to withstand foreign and domestic competition even during a period of prosperity, and a company breaking new ground in entertainment technology may do extraordinarily well even during a deep recession.

Debt monetization.   Debt monetization is a debt-paying technique that is not available to individuals, although most of us have wished it were at some time or another. All national governments do it at least sometimes, and the United States government has done it very often; though they deny that it has any real significance in causing inflation, it is, in fact, one of the basic and long-term causes of inflation throughout the world. It is the payment of government debts by the issuance of new money, thereby increasing the national money supply and further depressing the value of each currency unit.

Debt service.   Debt service is what it costs to pay back what is owed, including both principal and interest during a given period. The term can be used to describe payments made on a single loan, the total of a group of loans, or all loans outstanding during the period. This can be an important element in many cash flows and is an element often neglected or underestimated by individuals doing forward planning. It can be disastrous to those who find it necessary to incur new and increasing debt in order to keep their heads above water; then debt service can get entirely out of hand as a proportion of cash need and can lead straight to bankruptcy.

Defensive investment.   A defensive investment is one aimed at attempting to hold on to whatever you have, resisting the erosion caused by inflation, while trying to minimize the risks involved in doing so. It can be best described as a stance and a tendency, rather than as investment in a specific group of investment vehicles; it is really a willingness to err on the side of caution, rather than on the side of risk.

What constitutes a defensive investment varies considerably with time and circumstance. During periods of sharp swings in many investment markets, only investments in the safest of short-term federal securities may be properly defensive, while during periods of protracted boom, the definition may widen a good deal, to include several kinds of bonds and common stocks. During periods of national economic crisis, many have felt—and still feel—that the only properly defensive investments are portable commodities that can be easily moved from country to country, such as precious stones.

One thing is sure in this area—defense implies constant attention. It is strikingly unwise to make what is intended as a defensive investment and then to forget about it, as so many do. Every investment must be watched, reevaluated as circumstances change, and, when necessary, converted into something else more in tune with the needs of the times.

Depletion allowance.   Natural resources, such as deposits of coal or metals, pools of oil, bodies of natural gas, and stands of timber, are capable of being used up. To put it differently, they are depletable. National policy, as embodied in tax law, reflects the view that those extracting and otherwise taking such resources should be tax advantaged in that taking, to make up for the depletion of those resources by use. Depletion allowances therefore exist for most such natural resources; these allowances enable those taking the resources to subtract substantial sums from their income taxes. Like the depreciation deductions allowed in real estate taxation, depletion allowances provide durable tax-shelter opportunities for some individual taxpayers, as well as, in practice, providing substantial subsidies to many companies and individuals involved in extractive industries.

Depreciation.   Depreciation itself is a simple-enough matter. It is an accounting estimate—made period by period, usually year by year—of the extent to which an asset loses its value because of age and use. Ordinary depreciation, often called "straight-line depreciation," takes an asset, such as a house, industrial plant, or machine tool, and reduces its value by a fixed amount from the time of purchase and for a number of years. Generally the number of years is fixed by taxing authorities, for depreciation is a tax deduction when business property is involved. A business asset worth $100, depreciated on a straight-line basis for 20 years, will lose $5 per year in value and will therefore generate that $5 per year in tax deductions.

However, a legal and taxing fiction is involved here, reflecting an enormous tax break extended to property owners of all kinds and enshrined as national and statutory policy. When an asset is sold, the whole depreciation process begins again, with the sale price as the new starting point for beginning depreciation and with the same 20-year depreciation period. Since a property may later be sold for as much as, or even more than, it did originally, it is not at all unusual for a property to depreciate fully several times during the course of its actual useful life.

"Accelerated depreciation" is a set of elaborations and magnifications of this fiction and of the tax break involved. Several ways of figuring depreciation of fixed assets that yield even greater tax deductions for business property than will ordinary or straight-line depreciation are acceptable to taxing authorities and courts. The net effect of such methods often is that two to three times as much in tax deductions is yielded during the first few years of new ownership than would have resulted from ordinary depreciation.

Those who appraise real estate use depreciation somewhat differently, by attempting to estimate the real loss of value occurring from age and use, taking depreciation into account, along with other factors, to come up with a realistic appraisal of the current fair market value of a property.

Discretionary spending and discretionary income. Discretionary spending and discretionary income are more useful as economic concepts and classifying constructs than as concepts for personal financial planning. Discretionary spending is consumer spending that is not required—spending beyond what is necessary for basic life support. Discretionary income is income that need not be spent for such necessities as food, housing, clothing, debt service, and taxes and that therefore may be used, if desired, for such things as savings, investments, recreation, and luxury goods.

For planning purposes, the main question posed by these concepts is the style and scale of life adopted. Housing is a necessity—but a big, expensive house and many of the expenses accompanying it are not. Although some of those accompanying expenses may be classifiable as discretionary, they go with the big house as surely as if they were necessities and can greatly reduce the owner's range of real financial discretion.

Earnings per share. Earnings are profits. Earnings per share, a very important indicator of the economic health of an enterprise, are profits minus taxes and preferred stock dividends, divided by the number of shares of common stock outstanding. For example, if earnings are $1000, and taxes are $400, net aftertax earnings are $600. Assuming subtraction of preferred stock dividends totaling $100, leaving $500, and 500 common shares outstanding, net earnings per share are $1 each.

Earnings per share are not to be confused with dividends, as it would be highly unusual for all net earnings to be distributed to shareholders. That would leave no earnings to be put back into the business to help it grow, an essential for the development of any business. Dividends should be expected to be lower than earnings per share, though in some instances companies in a low-earnings or even a loss position will maintain dividend payouts, at least in the short term.

Easy and tight money.   Quite simply, easy money is easy-to-get credit, and tight money is hard-to-get credit. Before manipulation of the federal money supply became a dominant feature of the economic landscape, money was easy to borrow during a period of booming expansion, although interest rates tended to rise, reflecting the exuberance of the economy and the optimism of the time. Then, during a period of economic contraction—whether labeled a "depression," "recession," or, as it was often called before 1929, a "panic"—money became very hard to borrow, although lenders tended to lower interest rates somewhat in order to attract those who were still good lending risks and who wanted to borrow.

In recent years federal intervention has changed that pattern considerably. Money is still relatively easy to borrow during a period of relative prosperity, although that is often not a period of real expansion, but rather a period of high inflation rates. However, money can become very hard to borrow and can feature skyrocketing interest rates because of federal manipulation of the money supply and of interest rates late in such a period, as the federal government makes an attempt to diminish the rate of inflation. Then, as that manipulation helps develop the recession phase of the cycle, further manipulation can cause interest rates to fall and money to become much easier to borrow during that recession, in an attempt to bring about relative prosperity.

Economic indicators.   The economy fluctuates between prosperity and recession, whether in the context of a sustained long-term expansion, such as between 1945 and 1968, or a period of economic stagnation, such as in the 1970s. In an attempt to help track and predict the course of fluctuations, the federal government has identified a substantial number of economic factors, which, when measured, are thought to be helpful in indicating the direction of economic fluctuation; such economic indicators include construction starts, prices, wages, profits, industrial capacity used, and scores of others. Those factors thought to give indications well in advance of major cyclical economic fluctuations are called "leading indicators"; those thought to move at the same time as those fluctuations are called "coincident indicators"; and those thought to move after fluctuations are called "lagging indicators."

These indicators do not, however, indicate quite as well as they might, because they do not allow for sudden, sharp swings up and down within a stagnant economy, caused by federal manipulation of the economy in pursuit of the economic goals of the moment—which are all too often deeply affected by the political goals of the moment.

Equity.   In finance, equity is the value of an ownership share. That sounds rather straightforward, but it is often very difficult to determine. If a company has issued stock that is publicly traded, and you own some of that stock, its market price rather easily determines the value of your ownership share, or equity, at any given time and also indicates the total market value of the company at that time. On the other hand, the same company may sell for more or less than the total of all its shares outstanding, and the shares themselves will soon reflect the difference in a sale situation. Similarly, you can estimate the value of your ownership interest in a dwelling by estimating fair market value and subtracting outstanding mortgage debts, but you will not be able to find the real worth of that equity until an actual sale. In taxation, the value of a closely held business is often a hotly disputed matter between taxing authorities and heirs, much affecting the taxes levied on many estates.

Fiduciary. Some relationships specifically state or imply by their very nature that one acting as an agent or representative of another in matters concerning money or property is acting from a position of trust and is therefore legally prohibited from acting in any but the best interests of the principal represented. Such relationships are fiduciary in nature, and those agents or representatives are acting in fiduciary capacities. Some who are considered to be acting in fiduciary capacities are trustees, executors, bankers, brokers, sales agents, lawyers, and accountants.

Financial futures. These are like commodity futures contracts, but involve contracts for the future delivery of financial instruments, rather than commodities. Financial futures contracts specify prices, terms, and future delivery dates for such financial instruments as short-term federal bills and notes; the contracts themselves are traded on financial futures markets.

Financial statement. Quite often, the terms "financial statement" and "balance sheet" are used as synonyms. However, a financial statement is actually any of several documents and attached materials illuminating the financial condition of an individual or organization. Among the several kinds of financial statements are balance sheets, cash flow statements, and profit and loss statements.

Fixed income. Fixed income constitutes one of the great retirement traps in an economy characterized by a long-term, inexorable tendency toward inflation and consequent currency value loss. The truth is that income at fixed dollar levels, with no provision built in to adjust those levels up as inflation rises, is not fixed income at all, though that is what it is called. Such income is really diminishing income, as its real value lessens every year. Even in periods with low inflation rates, the impact is substantial as the years go by and as people live longer. In periods of rapid inflation, the impact is catastrophic. Although it is true that in a period of deflation the reverse would be true, and the dollar would gain value, the last such deflation occurred during the Great Depression of the 1930s and is not likely to come again in our time.

Social Security payments have been, in a practical sense, indexed to inflation, reflecting political pressure on legislators to move them up in response to rapid inflation. But they will not necessarily keep up with inflation as counterpressure builds to limit payments in a no-longer-so-affluent United States. Private pension plan payments, with rare exceptions, are fixed. Most annuity payments are fixed, although variable payments, which may give some opportunity to try to keep up with inflation, have been growing in popularity. Medium- and long-term bond income is fixed, although reinvestment of principal at higher interest rates at maturity is often possible.

Most of us have long carried the idea that fixed income investments are somehow safer than those providing varying amounts of income, on the theory that, with fixed income investment, "At least you know what you have coming in." Alas, that is an error. Fixed income is diminishing income, and safety need not be equated with this kind of diminishing income. You cannot do much about Social Security or private pension plan payments, but you certainly can buy shorter-term bonds, variable annuities, highly regarded common stocks, some rental properties, and other similar conserving investments, while keeping long-term financial planning funds away from volatile securities and such outright gambles as commodity futures.

Flexible interest rates.   Flexible interest rates, also called "variable rates," are rates that are not fixed for the full term of a debt obligation, but instead vary from time to time as stated conditions occur. They may be rates paid to you, as when you buy a variable annuity and the interest paid on it depends, at least partly, on the investment success enjoyed by the insurance company's investment managers.

More often, they will be rates that you pay to others, as when interest rates are related to changes in the Consumer Price Index or in the prime mortgage-lending rate of interest. Especially in home mortgage lending, there is a growing trend toward the flexible-rate mortgage, in which a mortgage loan is extended for a longer term—usually the now standard 30 years—but the rate of interest is re-evaluated in terms of the prime mortgage-lending rate, as frequently as yearly, but usually in three- to five-year periods. This enables lenders to offer mortgage loans in some periods at somewhat lower rates than would be possible on 30-year fixed-interest mortgages; such loans can therefore become very attractive to borrowers, but they can be very dangerous for borrowers, as well.

The British experience is instructive here. In Great Britain variable-rate mortgages have been widely used for many years, with lenders and borrowers therefore tied to a very high, but quite erratic, inflation rate. One result is that many who might otherwise not be able to buy homes can do so when the inflation rate and interest rates are relatively low—as when a temporary freeze or a set of brakes is placed by government on the pace of inflation; however, these same people find it very difficult to hold on to those homes when inflation hits hard again and interest rates skyrocket. For Americans, too, variable mortgage interest rates pose considerable hazards.

Forecasting. Attempting to predict the course of future economic and financial events and trends is not unlike modern weather forecasting, in that it is systematic, uses a set of analytical tools that include computer models, and is far, far better on long-term trends—the further away the better—than on short-term trends and specific events. Like everyone in the prediction business, forecasters understand well that, to stay in business, they must hedge their predictions in as many ways as possible while seeming to make hard, specific forecasts—and they must be prepared to call attention to those forecasts that turned out well, while ignoring those that proved inaccurate.

One observation that may be useful in trying to assess who to believe or whose investment advisory service to buy—when someone claims to have a foolproof analytical method, it isn't.

Fundamentalist and chartist.   The market prices of securities fluctuate—and a whole industry has been built around attempts to predict the future course of securities price fluctuations. Securities analysts, investment advisors, and market forecasting services all claim expert knowledge, advise, predict, hedge their claims and bets, and seek the fruits of successful prediction—or at least seek to be recognized by investors as successful forecasters. There are two major schools of thought as to how to approach securities fluctuation forecasting, along with a number of other approaches and variations.

One major approach to forecasting is that of the fundamentalists, who believe that basic economic, social, political, and specific company facts and trends must be understood and assessed on the way toward successful prediction. They want to know a great deal about specific company managements, balance sheets, cash flow statements, industry trends, and national and international factors that may have an impact—in short, about all the facts underlying an investment.

Another major approach is that of the chartists, many of whom want to know very little about those things that concern the fundamentalists. Chartists want to know about how a graph showing the past performance of a market or group of investments can be used to predict the future course of price fluctuation in those investments.

As is usually true, seeming polar opposites are often only tendencies. Most fundamentalists will also study charts of previous price movements, while continuing to ask basic economic questions. Chartists also—though many are purists—will ask basic questions, while focusing on their charts.

Other theories, some rather eccentric, also exist, among them the sunspot theory, which holds that substantial sun-

spot activity tends to drive the stock market down by depressing investor attitudes and thereby generating selling.

Futures.   When "futures" are being traded, the specific instruments of value being traded are really uniform contracts.
When a future is bought or sold, ownership of the tangibles or intangibles that are the subject of the contract
does not change hands; all that passes is the contract itself. That contract details the specifics of a future transaction, including quality, quantity, and terms identical with
those of all other contracts trading the same kinds of items
on the same organized exchanges. Futures contracts are
traded on several commodities and financial futures exchanges, with trading available in a considerable variety of
tangible goods, including gold and other precious metals,
and in such intangibles as government debt obligations
and currency. Although futures trading is very popular in
some periods, it is generally highly speculative.

Glamour stocks.   "Hot" stocks, "glamour" stocks, stocks that
"everybody is buying and you can't miss"; these are the
stocks that dreams are made of. That is not reality, however; reality is a glamour stock that has lost its glamour
just after you have bought it at an inflated price. Glamour
stocks are those that are extremely popular for a time, far
more so than is usually justified by performance or prospects. They go up basically because more and more people are buying them in hope of quick profits. Often that
hope of profit is spurred by a real, though temporary,
surge or an anticipated surge in profits, as was true of
some gambling stocks in the late 1970s. Sometimes a new
technology that seems to offer enormous profit potential
spurs popularity, as was true of some computer and elec-
tronic stocks in the 1960s.

Gold shares.   Gold shares are stocks representing ownership
shares in companies that are mainly in the gold-mining
business. During times of historic runs up in the world
price of gold, such shares are often enormously popular,

since their profits considerably reflect the rising price of gold.

Many of them are South African companies, as they are by far the largest suppliers of newly extracted gold to the world market. Leaving aside the question of whether or not you wish to invest in a South African company—which is an ethical question we consider outside the scope of this book—the question of company stability in a highly volatile political atmosphere is raised. South Africa's political stability, while at this writing not in immediate serious question, is in the long run likely to be precarious, and investments in South African gold shares are, in our view, very high risk investments.

Gross national product.   The gross national product, or GNP, as it is often abbreviated, is a major indicator of national economic health. It is the market value of all goods and services produced within a nation in a given period; usually the reporting period adopted is one year, without allowance for the using up of capital goods or for depreciation. Adjustment is made for inflation and deflation, to achieve a figure really comparable with those of other years. In periods of real economic growth, the gross national product can be expected to rise substantially year after year. In periods of stagnation, it can be expected to rise a little in some years, decline in others, and show very little real net change.

Growth investment.   Any investment oriented primarily toward securing growth in the value of the investment itself, rather than toward immediate financial return, is a growth investment.

The concept is often encountered in stock trading, when a company is described as a "growth company," meaning one that is experiencing rapid growth in net asset value, in sales, and often in total ownership equity as the value of its stock appreciates, that stock then being called a "growth stock." However, such stocks rarely pay much in the way of dividends, since much of what might otherwise be profits and dividends is being plowed back into the company to spur future growth. Unfortunately, many such stocks that were highly touted during the boom years of the 1960s lost their attractiveness when they began to stagnate along with most of the rest of the stock market, in many cases losing even more than market averages because of their failure to pay dividends.

In those years, "growth funds" were also often popular. These are mutual funds focusing on the acquisition of stocks thought to be growth stocks and looking for rapid appreciation in total fund asset value, rather than for income to be passed along to fund participants. Similarly, there were "growth portfolios," individual investment portfolios geared to the acquisition of growth stocks. All were casualties of market stagnation.

The concept had and has some limited validity, however, for those of considerable current income who want to invest in common stocks, but who have little need or desire for additional highly taxable current income. For example, when faced with a choice as to which stock of two to buy, both reasonably equivalent in net yield, one consideration may very well be which is more oriented toward growth and which toward current income.

Hidden inflation.   It is really true that "things aren't made as well as they used to be." That is what hidden inflation is all about. Unfortunately, hidden inflation is a major feature of the American landscape, one that is not reflected by the government's Consumer Price Index. For example, a 2 by 4 inch piece of lumber is still called a "two-by-four," but has for some years been considerably smaller than 2 by 4 inches. That is a fact that all builders and carpenters must take into account when measuring work, but it is also an indication of hidden inflation. If the price of an item goes up by 10%, and the amount of material in it—exactly the same material as what used to be in the item—goes down by 10%, you experience a real price increase of 20%, not the 10% that shows.

Such hidden inflation has been occurring throughout the American economy for well over a decade. Prices go up, while quality and quantity go down. We see the price increase as inflation, but fail to take the quality and quantity downgrading into account; as a result, we very seriously understate the real inflation rate we are experiencing, which is a combination of acknowledged and hidden inflation.

That is not merely a matter for economists to consider, since it can substantially affect some of the major buying decisions that are such an important part of effective financial planning. A used house built 40 to 60 years ago, especially a well-maintained one, may be a far better buy than a new house in terms of price and quality. Some foreign cars may be far better buys than some American cars in terms of price, materials, and workmanship largely because of hidden inflation. Actually, American workers are rather good at their jobs, in comparative world terms; it is scarcely their alleged laziness and inefficiency that causes American-made goods to be quite justifiably losing their reputations for high quality, but much more the operation of hidden inflation, which so seriously attacks the quality of many American-made goods.

Hot money. In popular use, and certainly in television detective series, "hot money" is synonymous with money illegally acquired, such as the proceeds of robbery, prostitution, or illegal gambling. In the financial world, however, hot money is investment money, usually large amounts of it, that moves from investment vehicle to investment vehicle, and from country to country, in search of the highest possible rate of return. It is speculating money, which may one week be found in currency trading, the next week in gold, and the week after that in commodity futures. It is most emphatically *not* to be followed on its adventurous way; small investors who speculate almost inevitably find themselves buying too late to buy low and selling too late to make profit or even to stem substantial loss.

Income fund.   Income funds are mutual funds aimed primarily at securing current income for their participants, and therefore toward the puchase of securities yielding cash payout rather than growth. They are far from recession-proof, but they tend to be somewhat recession-resistant, in that companies consistently paying substantial dividends over a long period tend to be some of the most stable and best regarded current "blue chips" available in investment markets. Because it is the business of fund managers to watch fund investments, the likelihood is considerably diminished that yesterday's blue-chip investment, which may be today's troubled company, will be kept in the fund too long. For people in retirement, income funds may be appropriate investments in periods of stock market resurgence.

Income property.   Income property is shorthand for income-producing property. A major attraction inherent in income property is that the right property can both appreciate in value and yield increasing net income. Such a combination of appreciation and income stands a fair chance of equaling or even bettering the rate of inflation—something very few other investments can reach for in these years.

As a practical matter, many people mix living and income property functions in a single property, themselves occupying one portion of a house or one house on a property and renting out the rest. For such people, the effort involved in being an owner-manager is much like being in a part-time business—which is exactly what is occurring. Others make substantial investments in real estate, developing a series or group of rental properties either as a sideline or as a full-time occupation.

Inflation.   We must define inflation in terms of what we see, rather than attempt to analyze its causes, which are in considerable dispute among economists and others who daily attempt to understand causation and prescribe cures for what is perceived as a severe economic malady.

What we see is that inflation is an overall rise in price levels accompanied by a lowering of the purchasing power of currency—in the United States, of the dollar. It may be accompanied by losses in the purchasing power of consumers, who very often will find that their dollar incomes do not keep up with the rate of inflation, as, for example, when average prices increase by 15% in a year, average wages by 8%, and the net dollar loss to wage earners is therefore 7%. Average wages may, at times, keep up with or even surpass the inflation rate, as happened throughout most of the 1960s. However, many seeming gains on the inflation rate, as measured by a comparison of average income increases with the Consumer Price Index, utterly fail to take into account the impact of lessened quality and diminished quantity in many goods and services, called "hidden inflation"; if factored into inflation/income comparisons, the effect of hidden inflation would change the comparisons considerably and further clarify the real impact of inflation.

In times of very rapid inflation, which almost inevitably brings rapid erosion of real incomes and investment values, many look for inflation hedges—that is, for investments that can yield enough to keep up with or better the rate of inflation. In the late 1970s, for example, real estate and gold were widely bought as inflation hedges. The problem is that investors tend to move increasingly into speculative areas in the attempt to beat inflation. More conservative investors hedge by putting their investment money into short-term federal securities, which often combine safety, relatively high yield, and flexibility.

Interest.   Money paid for the use of money is interest. It is usually stated as a percentage of the amount borrowed, that percentage being the rate of interest. If you deposit money in a bank, and the bank pays you an annual rate of interest of 6% compounded monthly, what essentially happens is that you lend your money to the bank for a month and get interest on that money for the amount; if you leave the interest in the account, you are now lending the bank that interest as well as the original principal, and the next month you will get interest on both the original principal and last month's interest. What you have done by leaving both the interest and principal in the bank account is to compound the interest, which is the payment of interest on interest. On the other hand, if you lend money to a friend and charge your friend 6% annually only on the principal, you are charging simple interest, which in the long run amounts to a good deal less.

A bank or other money lender is in the business of buying and selling the use of money, whatever else it does. It pays interest to those who lend it money, and it sells that money to others at a higher rate of interest, the difference between the two rates of interest being the main source of the money lender's income.

Investment. Practically speaking, any attempt to derive economic profit from the use of valuables is investment. There is no real difference between using owned land to produce crops for sale and using an amount of money equal to the value of that land to buy common stocks in another business. Both are investments. Either or both may involve the use of borrowed money; either or both may not make money—it is the intent that defines the act of investment, not the success or failure of the act. One may involve personal labor as well, but that does not in any way affect the act of investing; a small business involves investment, even if it employs no one but its owner.

Some expenditures that may result in economic benefits later and some that may result only in noneconomic benefits later are also often called investments, such as an investment in a career, which may later turn out to be the best-yielding money ever spent in economic terms, or an investment in learning, which may yield lifelong psychic benefits. They are indeed investments in the widest sense; although so indeterminate a return makes them difficult to assess in terms of success or failure, they nonetheless may require the same kind of attention that any other major investments require.

Investment advisor. One who is in the business of offering and charging for investment advice is an investment advisor. Such an advisor is required to be registered with the United States government. The advice offered is often in published form, such as stock market publications that offer advice on buying, selling, and holding specific securities; it may be in the form of charges for investment counseling with a specific investor; or it may be some combination of publication and individual counseling.

As a practical matter, many others also offer investment advice, including bankers, brokers, insurance sellers, accountants, and a friend met on a street corner, but do not directly charge for that advice; the difference lies in the registration with the government and the charges for the advice. It should also be noted here that government or private regulatory bodies impose no particular quality standards on those who register as investment advisors, other than requiring evidence of moral character and a clean record.

Leverage. "Leverage" has come to be widely used to mean making money on borrowed money, but that widens the use of the term so much as to make it not nearly as useful as it was in its original financial-market sense. In that sense, leverage is the possibility of making or losing money with somebody else's money, whether borrowed or otherwise acquired.

When a company carries a very heavy debt load, the market price of its common stock can swing considerably more widely in response to profit and loss than without that load. When that company is making money, it often makes money both on owner's equity and on borrowed funds, therefore yielding more return overall and driving common stock prices up; when it is losing money, the converse occurs, and the common stock of the company may be driven far down. The common stock of such a company is said to be heavily leveraged. Similarly, when income-producing real estate is heavily financed, its partnership shares may be said to be heavily leveraged.

In a slightly different way, but following the approach of making money with money borrowed or otherwise acquired from others, a company buying another company for cash may buy with very little of its own available cash if it can borrow the cash for the purchase and repay it wholly or mainly out of the cash reserves and cash flow of the acquired company; then the acquisition is described as heavily leveraged.

Limited partnership.   Limited partnership is a partnership form very often encountered in real estate investment, in which the tax-shelter benefits inherent in the partnership form of real estate investment are allowed to pass through to investors, while liability is limited for those wishing only to invest, rather than taking an unlimited profit and liability share in a partnership. Limited partners share partnership liability exposure only up to the dollar value of their original investments, take profits if available only within previously stated limits, and therefore own only financial shares. Those who participate in an unlimited fashion are called "general partners."

Liquidity.   Liquidity is the extent to which assets are in liquid form, meaning in cash or very quickly marketable securities, assuming relatively normal economic conditions. In estimating one's own liquidity, current liabilities should be subtracted from total liquid assets.

Cash includes demand deposits in banks, although under some circumstances those deposits may not be available to you, reducing your liquidity sharply. For that matter, such near-cash equivalents as federal securities may not be available in crisis conditions. Liquidity is a concept that rests within the context of a working society; under certain conditions, the only liquid assets that are worth anything at all might be such barterable goods as food and fuel.

Many assets are entirely salable under normal conditions, but are not liquid, such as real property and equipment, which may take considerable time to sell. As a practical matter, some assets may be salable but only at a fraction of their value under conditions in which they would need to be sold, as when a small business with unsolvable cash flow problems is forced to sell equipment to raise cash to pay creditors, effectively forcing itself out of business and reducing the value of the equipment to or near its salvage value.

Listed and unlisted.   By far the majority of publicly owned stocks are traded in over-the-counter markets, that is, directly between brokers rather than through the medium of an organized stock exchange. Such stocks are "unlisted," and they include many well-known and highly respected American companies. Those stocks that meet the rules of an organized stock exchange, in terms of the size and financial condition of their issuing companies and the number of shares outstanding and tradable, may be "listed" by one or more exchanges as tradable on those exchanges.

A stock may be listed simultaneously on the New York Stock Exchange, the largest stock exchange in the world; on the American Stock Exchange; and on several regional exchanges. That a stock is listed on a major exchange, such as the New York or American exchanges, means only that it is likely to be easily tradable. Some unlisted securities are as easily tradable as any company listed on the New York Stock Exchange, but many others, often the stocks of little-known and relatively small companies, may be difficult to trade when you wish to do so. Similarly, some unlisted stocks may be, for example, difficult to trade at a fair price; some thinly held stocks, which are stocks with relatively few shares in public hands, may be exceedingly responsive to even slight selling pressure and may lose value dramatically when a few substantial holders decide to sell at once, something far less likely to happen with stocks that are widely held.

Load. In finance and insurance, a load is a sales charge. The term is sometimes applied widely to include all sales charges and commissions, but is usually applied to sales charges on mutual fund and life insurance and annuity purchases. Many mutual fund and some life insurance annuity purchases do not have sales charges attached to them. They are called "no-load funds and policies." That is a competitive selling matter, especially in the mutual funds industry, where for many years most large funds charged substantial sales charges, but found themselves competing with smaller funds that did not. Although the trend is away from such sales charges, charges still exist and should be noted when considering purchase of a mutual fund.

Some investments and insurance contracts do not have front-load charges, but may have "back-load" charges or expense factors that are beyond the norm and act as a load.

Loan. Any property owned by one person and temporarily passed to another for use is a loan. In finance, a loan may be for a fixed or an indeterminate period, may be of money or of other valuables, and usually is repaid with interest. Usually money is what is lent, as when you lend a bank money for interest and the bank relends it to others at higher rate of interest; however, other valuables, such as stocks, may also be lent, as when a short seller of futures borrows contracts from a broker to meet buying obligations and returns the same number of contracts later, usually accompanied by a payment of interest. A loan may be secured—that is, wholly or partly backed by some kind of collateral—or it may be unsecured—that is, backed solely by its borrower's promise to pay and sometimes by the general assets of the borrower.

Long and short. When you buy securities or commodities "long," you are buying them at current market prices and holding them in hopes of making money as those prices rise. One who buys long is an optimist, or a "bull," as to the profit prospects of that which has been bought, but anyone who buys is likely to have bought in anticipation of gain, so this widely used characterization is insufficient. More to the point, most people who describe themselves as holding long positions are investors who have bought in anticipation of sharp, short-term upward price swings; who have bought on margin, that is, partly with borrowed money; and who expect to sell at or near the top of a short-term movement for quick profit, having made enough money to pay for interest due on the margined purchase and still come out substantially ahead.

One holding a long position is always a buyer hoping to make money from market price rises. One holding a short position is always a seller, hoping to make money from market price declines. The short seller sells securities or commodities not owned, hoping to be able to buy later at lower market prices than those at which the sale was made, for later delivery to their buyer. Sometimes the seller will borrow securities or commodities through a broker, paying interest on the borrowings; deliver the borrowings to the buyer; and then later buy enough to replace the borrowings. All this is often done in a margin account, and interest must also be paid for the money borrowed in that account. If all goes as hoped, and the securities or commodities go down, the short seller makes enough money to pay interest and still profit. But if the securities or commodities sold short go up, the short seller must eventually buy at higher prices and then loses the difference between buying and selling prices, plus any interest paid, and, if much borrowed money was used in an attempt to maximize the impact of gain, much of what was invested. As always, leverage works both ways—and short selling with borrowed money is speculation doubled.

Make a market. A securities dealer who is a trader in a specific stock either on the floor of an organized stock exchange or in the over-the-counter market may "make a market" in that stock. Such a dealer matches buy and sell orders from other brokers and dealers and often carries something of an inventory of the stock for limited periods, with which to respond to buy and sell orders, attempting to minimize the sharpness of price fluctuations in that stock.

Margin. Securities trading in a "margin account" is trading that is conducted partly with the money of the trader and partly with borrowed money. Margin is the amount of ownership actually held by a buyer, expressed as a percentage; one who has purchased stock on 80% margin has purchased 80% of the stock with his or her own money and 20% with money borrowed from the brokerage firm handling the margin account. The brokerage firm, in turn, has usually not financed the 20% loan itself, but has used the securities purchased as collateral for a short-term bank loan to cover the amount lent to the brokerage customer. The margin customer, in turn, pays interest to the brokerage firm to cover the cost of the borrowed money.

Federal regulations specify what credit percentage a broker may lend a customer in a margin account and have done so ever since the 1930s, in reaction against the unrestrained margin buying that helped trigger the stock market crash of 1929. Should a decline in stock prices cause the value of stock held on margin to become lower in relation to the amounts borrowed than is allowed by current regulations, the broker must issue a "margin call" to the investor, requiring that more cash be supplied to bring the investor's stake in the margin account up to mandated levels. Failure to meet the margin calls in a specified time under the securities regulations forces the broker to sell the customer's stock. During a serious downturn in the market, failures to meet margin calls and the subsequent sale of customers' stocks creates a greater supply of the stocks in the marketplace, further decreasing their value.

Market.   A market is an arena within which valuables are traded. That is a broad-enough definition to include retail stores, bazaars, organized and over-the-counter stock markets, and worldwide commodities and currencies markets. Rather confusingly, all those involved as specialists in specific markets refer to their own area of special interest as "the market," much as those deeply involved in a particular line of work invariably refer to their own businesses as "the business."

"How did the market do today?" is a widely encountered question among brokers and investors. It is usually answered, "It went up—or down—X points." In that instance, the market referred to is almost always the New York Stock Exchange, and the "it" that went up or down is the Dow Jones industrial average, the most widely followed and quoted American index of stock prices.

Merger and acquisition.   In business, merger and acquisition are, with very few exceptions, the same thing. Very rarely, a merger of two business organizations results in the equal merger of two hitherto separate interests. Usually it involves the taking over, or acquisition, of one business organization by another, by the taking of at least working control of the acquired organization by the acquiring organization, whether or not the acquired organization keeps its identity in terms of public image.

Money market.   Institutions and monied individuals all over the world trade in short-term debt obligations, such as the United States government's Treasury bills, bank certificates of deposit, and commercial paper of all kinds. The sum of all those who trade and their trades is the world money market, which is really a series of interlocked markets operating simultaneously in many countries.

As many of the obligations traded are issued in denominations of $100,000 and up, most individuals were, until recent years, effectively barred from participation in these markets, even though many of the obligations traded were and are attractive investment opportunities. In the past several years, however, the growing popularity of money market funds, which are mutual funds organized to invest in these and similar instruments, have made them accessible to smaller investors—who have flocked to them, especially under conditions of high short-term interest rates and otherwise unstable financial markets.

Municipal bond. The word "municipal" is somewhat misleading here. Municipalities are any self-governing units of government other than county, state, and federal governments; municipal bonds, however, include all government debt obligations other than those of the federal government, including county and state government obligations.

"Municipals," as they are often called, have for decades been favored by high-income investors because of their inherent tax advantages, which for those in very high income tax brackets have tended to outweigh their somewhat smaller yields than those available in corporate bonds. Municipals are exempt from federal income taxes, and some from state and local taxes as well.

Mutual funds focusing on municipal bond investments were quite popular during the mid-1970s, until it became evident that municipals were not without two kinds of risks. One kind of risk was that of bankruptcy on the part of some of their municipal issuers. The other was that of sharp decreases in value as medium- and long-term municipal bond prices declined sharply on bond markets, when the net aftertax interest available from other instruments, some safer, became much higher than that available from most municipal bonds and municipal bond funds.

Mutual funds.   The same concept is embodied in all mutual funds: By pooling their funds and paying professional fund managers, small investors can profit from their investments and simultaneously diversify those investments far better than they can alone. Any mutual fund, however invested, is a pool of investors' money; investors buy shares and may or not pay sales charges. A fund may consist of a limited number of shares, in which case it is called a "closed-end fund," or it may be as large as the number of shares it succeeds in selling to the public, in which case it is called an "open-end fund." Investors in open-end funds can sell their shares back to the fund at any time, which is called "redemption." Closed-end funds are sold on the over-the-counter market, much like stocks.

Mutual fund pools of investment money can focus on many kinds of investments, including money market instruments, several kinds of stocks, and bonds; they can specialize in one kind of investment or attempt to balance among several. In the 1960s, at the height of the bull market of the time, there was even a Fund of Funds, which bought only the shares of other mutual funds.

Opportunity cost.   Opportunity cost is a concept widely used in business and accounting; although it is seldom used in personal financial planning, it deserves careful understanding and earnest consideration. The concept is simple enough. The difference between what you actually earn on an investment and what you might have earned with reasonably equivalent safety is seen as a cost, thereby accentuating the importance of paying close and fruitful attention to investment decisions. For example, if you put $5000 into a savings account and earn $300 per year on that money, when you might have put the same $5000 into equally safe short-term federal government securities and earned $450 on it, your opportunity cost is $150 a year, highlighting the cost of failing to make even as simple and obvious a choice as where to put what are essentially savings dollars. When you include tax implications and longer-term investment considerations, failure to give sufficient attention to such decisions can result in enormous long-term opportunity costs. Note that there is a trap here, too—the concept is useful only if the investments considered are of reasonably equivalent safety and liquidity.

Option. In the widest sense "option" is synonymous with choice; that choice may or may not be something of value, and it may or may not be legally enforceable. In finance, an option is something of value and is legally enforceable; it is the right to buy or sell something at a set price at a stated time, with the option buyer often betting that a price will go up and the seller betting the opposite. That kind of option is almost always in writing, although it may or may not have involved some kind of consideration. For example, an option to buy a piece of real estate will almost always have cost something, whereas an employee's option to buy company stock or a stockholder's option to buy additional stock will usually not have cost anything. Stock and some commodity purchase and sale options are actively traded on American financial markets.

Several kinds of option arrangements have different names, which can sometimes cause investor confusion. Commodity options are simply called options; but stock options are variously called stock options, puts and calls, rights, and warrants. When a corporate employee has an option to buy company stock at a favorable price within a stated period, that is a "stock option." When an option to buy a certain stock at a fixed price within a specified time is traded on financial markets, that is a "call." When the same kind of stock option, but to sell rather than to buy, is traded, that is a "put." When the option to buy additional shares of stock at a stated price within a stated time is attached to a new stock issue by a company, that stock purchase option is a "right." When the same kind of option is attached to a new bond or preferred stock issue, that is a "warrant."

All are different kinds of options. None need be exercised; that is the nature of an option—it is a choice. Some, such as commodity options, puts, calls, rights, and warrants, are themselves valuable and are actively traded. Others, such as employee stock options, have no intrinsic value of their own and are not tradable. Still others, such as real estate options, may have intrinsic value, depending on whether or not they are negotiable.

Overextension.   When so much has been borrowed that lenders must seriously question whether or not the loans will be paid back, and must consider refusing further loans without substantial additional payment guarantees, such as the provision of new collateral or acceptable comakers, the borrower is in a condition of overextension. Overextension does not necessarily mean a condition in which liabilities exceed assets. An individual or a business may have assets 10 times the total of all outstanding loans, but may have those assets in illiquid form, and have very little cash or cash equivalents with which to pay debts. For example, a heavily indebted landowner may have assets consisting almost entirely of land that cannot be sold, or that can be sold only on very unfavorable terms, and may therefore be overextended.

Overextension is also loosely used as a synonym for being overdue or in default on obligations, as when one overdue on bank loan installment repayments is described as "overextended at the bank."

Par value.   The par value of an instrument is the value printed on its face. For common stocks, that face, or par, value is, from original issuance, usually far less than market value, so as to minimize documentary taxes paid on such instruments. For preferred stocks and bonds, that par value is very close to issuance value, with trading markets then setting fluctuating market prices. For negotiable instruments, such as checks, par value is the value of the instrument before such subtractions as discounts and handling charges.

Portfolio. A portfolio is a container; an investment portfolio is a bag of investments of a single owner, whether that owner is an individual or an organization, and whether the portfolio is self-managed or in the hands of a professional investment manager. The word may be used to describe all investments of every kind held, including stocks, bonds, real estate investments, and even savings; more often it is used to describe that body of tradable investments held.

Preferred stock. Preferred stock is a form of ownership share issued by a corporation, in which the stock is literally preferred over common stock in terms of the issuance of dividends, which must be distributed to preferred shareholders before dividends can be distributed to common shareholders. It sometimes also carries a preferred position in voting on some corporate affairs. Preferred stock dividend amounts are specified by the terms of original issue; they may be cumulative—that is, payable in subsequent years if not paid in a given year or years—or noncumulative—that is, if a dividend is "passed," or not paid, in a given year, it is lost. Some preferred stocks can, to a limited extent, share profits beyond stated dividends with common stocks, which have neither guarantees nor limits placed on their shares of profit participation.

As a practical matter, most preferred stocks today represent equity ownership and what amounts to a debt obligation, since almost all corporate boards must pay them before common stocks and at the same time literally must pay some dividends to common stockholders. However, preferred stocks generally present neither the profit nor the growth possibilities inherent in common stock ownership, which is why the overwhelming majority of stocks traded are common stocks.

Premium. A premium is generally "something more," as when a lender demands more than the interest stated in a mortgage loan instrument, as when additional "points" of interest are paid at the start of the mortgage repayment period, or as when a seller demands a somewhat higher price than what is normally charged because of the allegedly higher quality of goods or services being supplied.

In the financial industries, the word has other related, but somewhat different, meanings. The market price at which a commodity option sells is called a premium. The amount at which a security or commodity is selling above its face value is called its premium. The amount at which a new stock issue is selling above its issue price is called its premium, even though its issuing price normally has nothing at all to do with its face, or par, value. In insurance, the payments made on an insurance policy are called premiums.

Pretax dollars. A dollar of income without allowance for income taxes is a pretax dollar. It is not entirely pretax even then, as deductions for payroll and self-employment taxes are unavoidable, but it is still a far larger dollar than it will be after income taxes have been levied on it. That is the essence of the nationwide movement toward tax avoidance, which is so conspicuous in the growth of tax-shelter consciousness and of a whole tax-shelter industry. That dollar, as the inexorable mathematics of compound interest are worked out over the years, may later be worth many times what it might have been worth if it had not been taxed in the year it was earned. Investor interest in real estate, natural resource extraction, and several other tax-related investment vehicles is largely spurred by a sincere, heartfelt, overwhelming desire to avoid income taxes and to invest pretax, rather than aftertax, dollars.

Prime rate. This is "the prime" that is so carefully monitored by all who watch and worry over the American economy, including bankers, borrowers, and economists, as well as generation after generation of politicians, who are aware that substantial variations in the prime lending rate can have considerable impact on their political futures. The prime rate is that rate of interest charged by commercial banks to their largest, most reliable, and therefore most favored borrowers, a rate that tends to vary very little from bank to bank and region to region, as marketplace competition tends to substantially equalize lending rates to these kinds of borrowers.

A different "prime" is the prime lending rate set by mortgage lenders for those they consider their best credit risks; this should not be confused with the main prime lending rate.

As that main prime rate changes, so do other lending interest rates throughout the American economy. An increase or decrease in that prime rate has substantial impact on the availability and cost of money throughout the country and therefore on the fluctuation of the business cycle around the economic stagnation that is the main feature of the American economy in this period.

Profit and loss statement. A profit and loss statement, often called an "income statement," is a basic accounting of income and expenses and consequent profits and losses for a given period. Like the balance sheet and the cash flow or flow of funds statement, it is one of the basic financial documents that must be studied when trying to assess the economic health of any business. Profit and loss statements are rarely prepared less frequently than yearly; they are often prepared monthly and quarterly.

Note that a profit and loss statement is a record of what has happened in a given period. A profit and loss projection is entirely different, even though it may look quite the same and be entirely logical, for a projection is a forecast of what its makers are predicting will happen. Logical predictions are easy to make, and numbers are easy to work up—but the assumptions underlying sets of numbers contained in forecasts of future results may be very faulty indeed, reflecting the hopes, rather than the sober analyses, of their makers.

Profit sharing.   Profit sharing is an element of employee compensation that is tied to the current profit performance of a business. Quite often it takes the form of a straightforward monthly, quarterly, or year-end bonus, with the year-end by far the most common form of bonus given.

However, the American tax system invites tax-avoidance and tax-deferral efforts, and such bonuses are entirely taxable as current income. Therefore, many businesses are heavily involved in tax-deferred profit-sharing arrangements, in which portions of current profits are held in tax-deferred, IRS-qualified profit-sharing plans until retirement or termination of employment.

Public and private corporations.   A public corporation is either a corporation owned or controlled by the government or a privately owned corporation that has sold all or part of its equity to the general public in the form of stock, which may be freely traded by its owners. The latter is the main form to which the term applies. What can be somewhat confusing is that such a corporation, owned by private citizens, is called a public corporation, whereas a closely held corporation, which is one that has not issued stock to the general public, is commonly referred to as a private or privately held corporation. In fact, both closely held private corporations and privately owned corporations whose stock is traded publicly are owned by private citizens.

Pyramiding.   Pyramiding, leveraging, building a house of cards or matchsticks—all involve the same basic techniques. In some situations, pyramiding, which is the building of a financial structure essentially on air, is fraudulent. In other situations, it is hailed as nothing short of acquisition or investment genius—if it works. In personal financial planning terms, it is legal, may work very occasionally (and usually accidentally if it does), and is usually merely a foolish error, sometimes made into a catastrophic one by the relative size of the commitments made and the consequent size of the losses later endured.

In business, illegal pyramiding is like any other illegal pyramid game. It involves the selling of franchises, dealerships, and "agencies" of all kinds for resale to others. The promoters do extraordinarily well and may succeed in disappearing before the whole promotion goes sour and the law catches up with them. Early investors usually do well, too, because of their sales of the same kinds of schemes to others further down in the pyramid. Those who come later do not do well at all—they lose their investments, which sometimes also amount to all or most of the money they have in the world.

In the world of corporate acquisitions, the technique involves acquiring at a great rate, using the assets of each corporation acquired as part of the basis for future acquisitions—and usually a great deal of borrowed money as well. Lenders, including the officers of many major banking institutions, have all too often proven extraordinarily eager to jump on such acquisition bandwagons, being as blinded by the action as gullible small investors. There need be nothing illegal in these kinds of situations, and they sometimes work out very well for all concerned. But one usually hears only about the victories, not the defeats.

In investments, each generation of investors discovers anew the joys of investing on margin—that is, partly on borrowed money—and of using the paper profits made on stocks or commodities in margined accounts as additional collateral with which to buy more stocks and commodities. The position on paper looks better and better, with the investor "leaving the profits in"—until the stocks or commodities decline, making it necessary to come up with more margin or to sell part of the holdings. Then the paper profit tends to disappear, plus a good deal of the original investment, since stocks and commodities have an unfortunate habit of coming down faster than anticipated, often fed largely by the selling needs of those holding such margin accounts. That is especially true of the kinds of stocks and commodities normally held by those who adopt this means of building a paper pyramid.

Real cost of borrowing. The apparent cost of borrowing, which is the interest dollars paid for the borrowing made, must be adjusted in two most significant ways before you can understand what the borrowing is really costing you, and that real cost must be estimated, at least roughly, before the borrowing decision can properly be made. If you do not have a fairly good idea as to the real cost of borrowed money, it is almost impossible to assess whether or not an investment decision that involves borrowed money, such as the purchase of income-producing property that will be mortgaged, is a good one.

Roughly—and you should get your accountant's help in calculating this for substantial decisions—you must determine the true interest you are paying for borrowing and subtract an estimated rate of inflation over the period of repayment to form an estimate of the true cost of borrowing. The federal truth-in-lending laws will help on the former, as will your accountant. You will need your own estimates, obtained with your accountant's help, to arrive at the latter. It may take some time and work on the part of both you and your accountant to make the estimate, but it will be time well spent and work well worth paying for.

Real income. Real income is actually only comparative income—income for a given period as compared with income for a previous period. The computation done involves taking the Consumer Price Index level for a given period and the average wage of a group and comparing changes in both. For example, when the Consumer Price Index goes up 20 points during a period, and the average wage of a group goes up 25 points, real income is said by the federal government, which keeps these figures, to have gone up 5 points, the difference between the two. That is not 5%, though, unless the Consumer Price Index and the average wage both started out at 100. It is more likely to be in the 4 to 5% range. In the 1970s and 1980s, the Consumer Price Index will more likely have gone up faster than the average wage level, indicating a loss in real income as measured by government figures.

It should be noted that the government figures are highly suspect. Those figures fail to take into account hidden inflation, which involves deterioration in quality and diminution in quantity; the decline suffered by American and most other world goods and services in the last two decades has been enormous and is a very large and real element in inflation.

Realize. "To realize," in financial terms, is to turn something of value into something else of value, usually cash. The term is usually used in connection with appreciation in value; you can realize a loss on a transaction, but most people speak of a loss as "taken," while gain is "realized," or money is "made." Until gains are realized, they are "paper" gains, although such paper gains do have increased real value as collateral.

Refinancing. Refinancing is the redoing of one or more loans in order to provide more loan proceeds, to extend repayment periods, to provide smaller current loan payments, or to hold off repayment of principal. It involves the redoing of loan instruments, which also often involves substantial one-time transaction and tax costs, as with redoing mortgages and corporate bonds. Corporations often refinance bonds and such other debt obligations as bank loans in order to avoid current repayment of principal on maturation, continuously rolling over a large body of loans, in effect extending them indefinitely. Individuals often do essentially the same with both personal and mortgage loans.

Reinvestment.   Reinvestment is the placing of proceeds or profits from one investment back into more of the same
investment or the placing of them into some other investment, rather than taking them for personal consumption
use or putting them into savings. The term is somewhat
misleading, in that it implies that all the money realized
by an investment sale is available for further investment,
when, in fact, very substantial provision must often be
made for taxes on investment gain. On the other hand, reinvestment is a very useful approach; that is, if gain is realized, but is not put back to work the result is often no
better than the pace of inflation and usually a good deal
worse, especially after tax impacts.

It is important, however, not to reinvest blindly. It is
quite natural for a securities salesperson, for example, to
assume that you will invest stock sale proceeds in more
stock, but that should not be your assumption. At the
point at which you have made any investment liquid, that
is, turned it into cash, all options are once again open,
and you should freshly examine them.

Return on investment.   A concept widely used in business, return on investment has even achieved a generally used
abbreviation—ROI. In large companies it is a central accounting and profit-planning concept, often accompanied
by complex computer-assisted analysis. But conceptually
it is simple, entirely adaptable to the needs of people attempting to do effective financial planning, and useful
even when relatively rough estimates must be made rather than the complex, more precise estimates used in large
companies.

When you invest $100 in a common stock, get $3 in dividends during the year after purchase, and sell it at the
end of that year for $107, you have gained $10 and have
a roughly estimated return on investment of 10%. This is
only a rough estimate because it does not take into ac-

count the operation of inflation during that year and two consequent facts—that the dollars you received in dividends were worth progressively less as the year advanced and that the dollars you received at the end of the year were worth even less. Also, the estimate does not make any allowance for tax impact, which must be calculated individually. So ROI is a rough estimate, but a useful one, especially for comparisons.

For example, if the same $100 were put into short-term debt obligations yielding 8% for that year, it would yield only that 8%—and at ordinary income tax rates, at that, unless they are tax-free municipals. Of course, the 8% is sure, and the 10% is not; that is some of what investment decisions are made of. If that $100 had been coupled with borrowed money—as in a margin account, through personal loans, or as part of a real estate mortgage—it might have purchased $200 worth of investments. Then if you had received the same 10% yield, you would have gained $20. If you had paid back the loan with $8 interest, your gain would have been a net of $12 before taxes, or 12% instead of 10%. Or—and this is the seductive aspect of the currently popular practice of leveraging or pyramiding— you may have borrowed $400 on top of your $100 and used the resulting $500 in investment money to secure a 15% return. Then you would have made $75, paid back 8% of $400, or $32, for the money you borrowed—and come out of it all with $43. That's a whopping 43% return on your money, right?

Not so fast. You might also have gained not at all, or even lost money on your investments. Then you would have to pay interest on the borrowed money, with no gain to offset it. Had you lost $10 on your $100 investment, you would have lost $40 more on the borrowed $400 and would have had to pay $32 in interest as well. Your net would be $82 lost out of $100 invested—82%. So, beware. Return on investment is an extremely useful concept for evaluating alternative investment opportunities, as long as it is not used for self-entrapment.

Rights. Rights are a kind of stock option. When a corporation authorizes a new stock issue, it may also give current stockholders the right to buy some portion of the new issue at a discount, proportional to the amount of stock currently held in the corporation. These options to buy are "rights." Rights may be exercised up to a specified date; until that date, they are valuables, and as such, are actively traded.

Savings. That portion of net aftertax income not spent currently, but instead held for accumulation and investment, is savings. Savings may be held with no attempt to use them to earn, as in a non-interest-bearing bank account or in a hole in the ground, in which instances they remain entirely savings, or they may be used to help create earnings, as when held in an interest-paying debt obligation or when invested in a business. Money in a savings account in a commercial bank, savings and loan association, or savings bank is, in financial terms, quite the same as money put into a federal bill or a money market fund. In all these instances, you have lent your savings to another in hope of profit, within whatever bounds of safety you deem appropriate. Money used to buy an ownership interest in a business is transformed into the equity purchased, rather than remaining savings.

Senior and junior obligations. Bonds, mortgage loans, and other debt instruments carry an order of priority with them as to the standing of the call they can make upon that which is collateral for them. That obligation with the prior call is the senior obligation; that with the lesser call is the junior obligation.

These are relative terms. A first mortgage, under most circumstances, is senior, which means that it has higher priority for payment than all other mortgages, and a first mortgage holder therefore must be satisfied in full before other mortgage holders can be paid anything. A second mortgage is junior to the first mortgage, but is itself senior to a third mortgage, which is junior to both the first and second mortgages. A bond secured by a first mortgage on corporation-owned land and buildings is senior to a bond secured only by second mortgages.

In a wider sense, any lien upon property that takes payment precedence over other liens is senior to those liens, as when one mechanic's lien on an automobile is senior to another because it was filed with a court earlier.

Special situation.   "Special situation" is a stock market term used to characterize a security thought to have unusual profit possibilities. For example, a stock that is selling for considerably less than its underlying asset value may be thought of as ready for a rebound because of impending profitable operations or because another company is about to purchase it at a per-share price far higher than its current market price. A company that is losing money may be under new management and be ready to be "turned around," with consequent increases in the market price of its stock. A company owning desert land may be thought to be sitting on a pool of highly profitable oil.

It should be noted that most situations so assessed are not so special. Acquisition plans can fall through; new management may prove as unable as old management to solve intractable long-term problems; a huge pool of oil can turn into a trickle of oil, a lot of water, and considerable talk on the part of its promoters. There is no simple measuring device with which you can separate truly special situations from quite ordinary, usually losing situations. Special situations are therefore properly regarded as speculations and should be treated with extreme skepticism.

Speculation.   To speculate is to take high risks in the hope of earning very high profits, as when raw land is purchased in expectation of a new superhighway interchange, which may or may not come, or of a long-term commercial development, which may be blocked by a combination of local opposition and bad times. Speculation is also the purchase of commodity futures or highly volatile common stocks with the hope of great gain and the risk of considerable investment loss; the risk can be made even higher by the use of borrowed money in such investments. Speculation is much like betting on horses, rolling dice, or playing slot machines, and for most small investors, it is just about as informed. If you must gamble, by all means do so; that is part of being free for many people. And by all means try to cut your risks by securing as much information as possible about the objects of your speculative investments. But don't fool yourself and call it investment. Try to do it as little as possible—and don't use needed long-term financial planning dollars for speculation.

Stagflation. "Stagflation" is a term that was coined by the Swedish economist Gunnar Myrdal in an attempt to characterize what he believed to be the main economic trend of the current period in most Western economies, including that of the United States. The word combines "stagnation" and "inflation," because he believed that the business cycle no longer operates quite as it did during the sustained growth that characterized the first 60-some years of this century. Instead, the main feature of the economy is believed to be stagnation, the impact of which is magnified by persistent and so far unsolvable inflation, which waxes and wanes as recessions come and go, but without prosperity or any real economic growth.

Standard of living. Every politician trying for office sooner or later extols the virtues and trumpets his or her impassioned defense of the "American standard of living." Without defining what it is, of course. It is, in truth, undefinable.

What is generally meant by standard of living is the quantity of goods and services consumed at current income

levels by the consumers in a given economy. It is basically, then, a strikingly imprecise measure of the quantity of
consumption, with little or no reference to the quality of
life. To the extent that real wages go down, meaning that
average incomes go down relative to the Consumer Price
Index, the standard of living can be said to have gone
down. To the extent that real wages go down even further
than so indicated, because of the severe deterioration in
the quality and quantity of most goods and services in the
United States, the standard of living can be said to go
down even further. For effective financial planning, the
real challenge in this area is not in the maintenance of a
high-consumption personal economy; rather, it is in the
development of adequate, healthy living standards, which
at the same time allow savings for investment—that is, for
capital formation.

Stock split.   When a corporation divides the number of its outstanding ownership shares, thereby creating a larger number of shares without directly affecting the total market
value of outstanding shares, it is executing a stock split.
For example, a corporation with 100,000 shares outstanding, currently selling at $100 each, may split 2:1, or two
new shares for one old share, creating 200,000 shares at
$50 each. As a practical matter, corporations executing a
stock split often accompany the split, which is usually
aimed at securing a wider distribution of shares, with
good news for shareholders, such as an increased dividend
coupled with optimistic forecasts. Therefore, total share
value is likely to go up at the time of the stock splitting,
with the $100 share going up in anticipation of the split
and the resulting $50-plus shares sometimes going up
even more after the split.

Sometimes, a split works in reverse, with a corporation
consolidating, rather than expanding, outstanding shares,
by the device of calling in an existing stock issue and re-
placing it with an issue containing fewer total shares; that
is called a "reverse split."

Store of value. The phrase "store of value" becomes fashionable when hard and uncertain economic times are upon
us. All it really means is anything of value that can be
traded—not necessarily easily traded, but traded. It is
used to expand the range of acceptable tradables when
valuables normally traded, such as most stocks and many
bonds, have lost their appeal to investors.

In that context, collectibles of all kinds, precious stones,
precious metals, land, and other items of real and personal property previously thought of more as hobbies and
speculations by the main body of American investors became "stores of value" in the 1970s and 1980s. They had
always been so; the application of the term simply helped
make them acceptable investment alternatives in a period
of fear and uncertainty.

Tax avoidance and tax evasion. No, they are not quite the
same things. Tax avoidance is legal minimization of taxes,
and it is enshrined in public policy, statute, court decision, and massive national practice. It applies to a wide
number of tax-planning devices and employs an army of
accountants, lawyers, investment advisors, and bankers,
among others. Like baseball, it is a national pastime. Tax
evasion is different, in that it is usually accompanied by an
intent, whether a conscious one or one that will be implied by law, to defraud the government of taxes due. No,
they are not identical; yes, the distinction in practice is often a fine one.

Tax fraud. Tax fraud involves a good deal more than an argu-
ment over whether a single meal was really deductible for
business purposes or whether something received as a gift
should really have been reported as income. There must
be intent to defraud, whether conscious or court-con-
structed. Intent stems from substantial provable actions,
such as failure to report thousands of dollars of income, or
through the existence of a pattern of false business-
expense reporting that can be proved to the satisfaction of

a court. Where intent to defraud government is successfully alleged against a taxpayer, there is no statute of limitations on prosecution.

Tax haven.   Some countries and areas within countries impose
little or no income tax on noncitizens, hoping thereby to
attract savings and investment from abroad by providing a
means for some businesses and individuals to avoid paying
taxes that might otherwise be due their own countries. In
essence, they attempt to provide a safe and tax-advantaged haven for assets—therefore the term "tax haven."

Although many large American companies and wealthy individuals do successfully and legally enjoy the tax-avoidance possibilities offered by some tax havens—though not
always without federal challenge—those individuals attempting to use them may run into considerable difficulty, if only because of the costs made necessary by defense
against Internal Revenue Service challenge. That is at
best; at worst, the nature of many such arrangements can
raise the question of prosecution for tax fraud, which,
even if successfully resisted, may make less adventurous
tax-avoidance moves seem more desirable. If you do indeed decide to investigate the use of tax havens, do so in
close consultation with your accountant and probably a
competent tax lawyer as well.

Tax selling.   Tax selling is the selling of securities in the most
advantageous way to establish gain or loss for tax purposes. It usually involves securities to which long-term
capital gains tax rules apply and occurs before year-end,
when most tax-avoidance planning and maneuvers take
place.

Tax shelter.   Tax shelters are quite literally transactions that are
aimed at sheltering income from taxation. They are means
of securing greatly accelerated growth through the avoidance of taxes on current income and the consequent ability to reinvest and compound far greater pretax sums than
would be possible from the investment of aftertax income.

Real estate, pension and profit-sharing plans, and natural resource extraction are major examples among a variety of sheltering devices that are always under consideration by those attempting to shelter income from taxation.

United States government securities. The federal government issues a wide range of debt obligations, including short-, medium-, and long-term bills, certificates, notes, and bonds. The Treasury Department is by far the largest single issuer, but many other federal agencies also fund their operations through debt obligation issuance.

In uncertain times, investors have heavily invested in short-term Treasury bills, reasoning quite correctly that they were as safe as any securities sold anywhere in the world, bore what in some periods were quite high rates of interest, and offered an excellent way to stay liquid, make money, and wait for safer times. Somewhat longer-maturing, but still short-term, Treasury issues are called "Treasury certificates," these maturing in one year or less. Medium-term issues are called "notes"; longer-term issues are "bonds." Other federal agency debt issues run the same range of description and length of term.

Usury. One state's usury is another state's quite legal lending rate. In one state a pawnbroker may legally charge less interest than what a very respectable bank effectively and legally charges in another state. Usury, which is the imposition of illegally high rates of interest, is a matter of state law; and state laws on usury are a patchwork quilt. As a result, in times of very high interest rates, home and personal loans may be quite available in one state, as lenders continue to make these kinds of loans—at very high rates—and not available at all in another state, as those lenders change their focus entirely over to higher-interest commercial loans.

Even states with relatively strong usury laws, in which the permissible interest rate is relatively low, often allow higher rates by default, as when a bank charges three or even four extra "points" as an origination fee in advance on a mortgage loan. The "points" are not regarded as interest; a set of legal and regulatory fictions converts what is very obviously extra interest, often beyond that allowed by state usury laws, into an "origination fee."

Vested interest. In financial planning, a vested interest is a person's interest, or equity, in receiving payments from a pension plan or profit-sharing plan, which covers that person even if employment or association with the organization providing the plan is terminated before retirement. For example, an employee covered under a pension plan may go to work with a company at the age of 30, stay for 10 years, leave at age 40, retire 25 years later at age 65, and still be legally entitled to a modest, continuing pension payment from the company's pension plan after 65. Given that example, the payments will indeed be modest, taking into account the amount of time worked and the impact of inflation after a quarter of a century—but payments will be legally due then. If the employee had stayed 25 years, until age 55, and then moved on, the payments due 10 years later, at age 65, might be quite substantial.

Warrant. A warrant is a kind of option, in this instance a valuable right to purchase stock, and one that accompanies a new bond or preferred stock issue. That option allows its holder to buy a specified amount of stock at an established price within a specified time or in perpetuity; if within a specified time, it is usually a period measured in many months or years, in contrast to a stock right, which is usually for a shorter period. When the warrant is issued standing physically alone, it is a negotiable instrument; when attached to another instrument, as a coupon to a bond, it is not negotiable.

Yield. "Yield" is synonymous with "rate of return." It is the actual return, as when a bond pays an interest rate of 8%, compared with the price originally paid for that bond. It is the rate of return, therefore, on the money invested, rather than bearing any relationship to any later value of the investment. It should not be confused with the concept of "return on investment," which provides a far better assessment of investment results.

The "true yield" is the interest received as a function of the market value of the investment instrument; the amount received remains constant, but the true yield changes in direct proportion to the market value of the underlying instrument.

SOURCES OF
INFORMATION

Here is a substantial selection of information sources that are useful for a wide variety of personal financial planning purposes. We have included key newspapers, magazines, directories, newsletters, business services, and books. Some will prove so useful that you may want to subscribe to them; others will, because of expense and occasional use, be best used in libraries and brokerage offices. Some may be accessible only to people living in or near large cities, but are worth listing for those who can gain access to them.

Let us stress that, although this is a substantial list, it is still only a selection. Most of the following sources are drawn from *Where to Find Business Information* (by David M. Brownstone and Gorton Carruth, Wiley, 1979), itself a compilation of more than 5000 sources of business and investment information drawn from all over the English-speaking world, which is available in most business and investment libraries and in most substantial public libraries as well. It, and books like it, should be your second line of inquiry when seeking financial-planning-related information.

The kind of information you want and need will depend on your interests, planning approaches, means, and stage of life. We have tried to provide a selection wide enough to satisfy most such wants and needs. You should review the list with your personal situation in mind, selecting those sources that seem most likely to give you the strong base of information and understanding you need in your future planning.

Please note that the prices of most of the following information sources have undoubtedly risen since the information herein supplied was gathered—alas, that is what inflation does to us all.

American Board of Trade Options Market. American Board of Trade, 286 5th Ave, Suite 506, New York, NY 10001. Telephone (212) 736-9740.

Booklets. Offers puts and calls options market price lists. Covers gold, silver, platinum copper, plywood, British pound, Swiss franc, German mark, Canadian dollar, and Japanese yen. Price free of charge.

American Exchange Stock Reports. Standard & Poor's Corp, 345 Hudson St, New York, NY 10014. Telephone (212) 924-6400.

Quarterly reports revised twice a week. Cover stocks listed on American Stock Exchange. Analyze company activities and financial results and provide statistics on earnings and dividends. Price $440.00 per year (daily edition); $300.00 per year (weekly edition).

American Investors Service. Chestnutt Corp, 88 Field Point Rd, Greenwich, CT 06830. Telephone (203) 622-1600.

Weekly service. Analyzes current stock market activity and shows changes over a two-week period for selected stocks. Ranks stocks by percentage strength and provides charts indicating industrial group stock trends. Price available on request.

American Journal of Small Business. University of Baltimore, 1420 North Charles St, Baltimore, MD 21201. Telephone (301) 727-6350.

Quarterly magazine. Discusses small business management and finance. Notes the activities of the Small Business Administration and includes book reviews. Price $10.00 per year. ISSN 0363-9428.

America's Fastest Growing Companies. John S Harold, Inc, 35 Mason St, Greenwich, CT 06830. Telephone (203) 869-2585.

Monthly publication. Provides data and comments on growth stocks. Charts and tables. Price $78.00 per year.

Andrews Newsletter. R E Andrews and Assocs, 25743 N Hogan Dr, Valencia, CA 91355. Telephone (805) 259-3742.

Monthly newsletter. Covers stock market cycles, interest rate trends, and economic and industrial developments. Price $100.00 per year.

Babson's Investment & Barometer Letter. Babson's Reports, Inc, Wellesley, MA 02181. Telephone (617) 235-0900.

Weekly newsletter lists buy, hold, and sell options on promising stocks. Reports on current market activity and reviews companies in the news. Subscription includes an annual forecast issue. Price $72.00 per year.

Babson's Washington Forecast Letter. Babson's Reports, Inc., Wellesley Hills, MA 02181. Telephone (617) 235-0900.

Weekly newsletter. Interprets and forecasts the impact of federal legislation in economic, environmental, social, and other areas. Price $9.00 per three months.

Barron's. Dow Jones & Co, Inc, 22 Cortlandt St, New York, NY 10007. Telephone (212) 285-5000, 5243.

Weekly newspaper. Provides financial and investment news. Includes information on commodities and international trading. Contains tables on New York Stock Exchange transactions. Price $32.00 per year.

Baxter. Baxters, 1030 E Putnam Ave, Greenwich, CT 06830. Telephone (203) 637-4559.

Weekly bulletin. Offers advice concerning investments. Covers such areas as inflation and currency markets. Price $108.00 per year.

Better Investing. National Assn of Investment Clubs, 1515 E Eleven Mile Rd, Royal Oaks, MI 48067. Telephone (313) 543-0612.

Monthly magazine. Offers investment advice. Recommends specific stocks and groups of stocks and comments on tax issues. Price $6.00 per year. ISSN 0006-016X.

Black Enterprise. Earl Graves Publishing Co, Inc, 295 Madison Ave, New York, NY 10017. Telephone (212) 889-8220.

Monthly magazine geared to black people in business and professions. Provides information on money, management, and marketing. Price $10.00 per year.

Boardroom Reports. Boardroom Reports, Inc, 500 5th Ave, New York, NY 10036. Telephone (212) 354-0005.

Semimonthly magazine for executives. Discusses new ideas about such subjects as advertising, investments, law, management, personnel, selling, and taxes. Price $39.00 per year.

Bond Guide. Standard & Poor's Corp, 345 Hudson St, New York, NY 10014. Telephone (212) 924-6400.

Monthly report. Gives data on 3900 corporate bonds, including current yield, registered and coupon bonds, bond quality ratings, municipal bonds, and convertible bonds. Price $80.00

Business & Capital Reporter. National Counselor Reports, Inc, Task Bldg, Kerrville, TX 87028. Telephone (512) 257-5050.

Monthly newsletter. Lists nationwide lending and investment opportunities ranging from $10,000 to $10,000,000. Includes such ventures as those involving agriculture, trade, and land development. Price $100.00 for 12 issues.

Business Week. McGraw-Hill, Inc, Publications Co, 1221 Ave of the Americas, New York, NY 10020. Telephone (212) 997-6375. Telex TWX 7105814879 WUI 62555.

Weekly magazine. Reports on US and international business and economic topics. Is aimed at business management personnel. Includes industrial, European, international, and five US regional editions. Price $26.00 per year.

Caveat Emptor. Consumer Education Research Group, 620 Freeman St, Orange, NJ 07050. Telephone (201) 675-8474.

Monthly magazine. Discusses consumer issues, with emphasis on frauds, dishonest medical behavior, deceptive advertising, and government conflict-of-interest cases. Price $8.00 per year.

Changing Times. Kiplinger Washington Editors, Inc, 1729 H St NW, Washington, DC 20006. Telephone (202) 298-6400.

Monthly magazine. Offers advice on personal finances, including saving, investing, shopping, taxation, housing, and other topics. Price $12.00 per year.

Chartcraft Commodity Service. Chartcraft, Inc, 1 West Ave, Larchmont, NY 10538. Telephone (914) 834-5181.

Weekly service. Supplies point and figure charts on commodity futures. Includes charts for actively traded over-the-counter gold stocks and futures. Price $180.00 per year.

Chartcraft Weekly Service. Chartcraft, Inc, 1 West Ave, Larchmont, NY 10538. Telephone (914) 834-5181.

Weekly loose-leaf report provides point and figure technique for analyzing stocks listed on New York and American stock exchanges. Graphs and charts. Price $180.00 per year.

Commodities. Commodities Magazine, Inc, 219 Parkade, Cedar Falls, Iowa 50613. Telephone (319) 277-6341.

Monthly magazine provides information on commodity futures and trading. Price $34.00 per year.

Commodity Chart Service. Commodity Research Bureau, Inc, One Liberty Plz—47th floor, New York, NY 10006. Telephone (212) 285-4660.

Weekly loose-leaf service. Charts cover all actively traded commodities. Price $245.00 per year.

Commodity Journal. American Assn of Commodity Traders, 10 Park St, Concord, NH 03301. Telephone (603) 224-2376.

Bimonthly magazine. Presents data on commodity market trends. Analyzes raw data in detail. Offers articles by experts. Price $12.00 per year.

Commodity Year Book. Commodity Research Bureau, Inc, One Liberty Plz—47th Floor, New York, NY 10006. Telephone (212) 285-4660.

Annual book. Statistical tables and charts are used to appraise commodity market trends. Price $22.95 each.

Commodity Yearbook Statistical Abstract Service. Commodity Research Bureau, Inc, One Liberty Plz—47th floor, New York, NY 10006. Telephone (212) 285-4660.

Three times yearly. Statistical data for commodity market are presented with charts and tables. Intended to update the Commodity Year Book. Price $35.00 per year.

Common Stock Reporter. Media General Financial Services, Inc, PO Box 26565, Richmond, VA 23261. Telephone (804) 649-6586.

Weekly report. Gives stock information for private investors. Price $32.00 per year.

Comparative Investment Analyses (CIA). Wright Investors' Service, Wright Bldg, 500 State St, Bridgeport, CT 06604. Telephone (203) 377-9444.

Weekly service. Provides data on all New York Stock Exchange stocks by industry group. Offers comparative investment evaluations. Includes updated earnings and dividends. Price $500.00 per quarter.

Consensus. Consensus, Inc, 30 W Pershing Rd, Kansas City, MO 64108. Telephone (816) 471-3862.

Weekly newspaper. Reports on commodity futures. Includes statistical section, tables, and graphs. Price $243.00 per year.

Consensus of Insiders. Consensus of Insiders, PO Box 10247, Fort Lauderdale, FL 33305. Telephone (305) 566-1091.

Weekly newsletter. Provides information on insiders' stock trading. Indicates transactions of stock exchange members, specialists, and traders. Includes data on pension and mutual funds, foreign funds, and banks and insurance companies. Price $180.00 per year.

Consumer Newsweekly. Consumer News, Inc, 813 National Press Bldg, Washington, DC 20045. Telephone (202) 737-1190.

Weekly newsletter. Reports on consumer issues, including advertising, product safety, and consumer legislation. Includes product ratings. Price $15.00 per year.

Consumer Reports. Consumers Union of US, Inc, Blaisdell Rd, Orangeburg, NY 10962. Telephone (914) 359-8200.

Monthly magazine. Gives comparative shopping information, product testing results, advice on goods and services. Price $11.00 per year.

Consumers Digest. Consumers Digest Inc, 4401 W Devon Ave, Chicago, IL 60646. Telephone (312) 286-7606.

Bimonthly magazine. Offers test reports, ratings, and recommendations on variety of consumer goods. Extra issue in January. Price $10.00 per year.

Consumers Digest Guide to Discount Buying. Consumer's Digest, Inc, 4401 W Devon Ave, Chicago, IL 60646. Telephone (312) 286-7606.

Annual book. Gives digest of test reports, ratings, and recommendations for variety of consumer goods. Price $2.95.

Consumers' Research. Consumers' Research, Inc, Washington, NJ 07882. Telephone (201) 689-3300.

Monthly magazine. Provides consumers with information, including test results, on many products and advice about purchase of services. Includes annual Handbook of Buying. Price $10.00 per year.

Cycli-Graphs. United Business Service Co, 210 Newbury St, Boston, MA 02116. Telephone (617) 267-8855.

Quarterly set of charts. Provides monthly price ranges, relative market performance, volumes, earnings, and dividends for 1105 stocks. Includes industry group and selected business charts. Price $37.00 per year.

Daily Bond Buyer. Bond Buyer, One State St Plz, New York, NY 10004. Telephone (212) 943-8200. Telex 12-9233.

Daily newspaper (except Saturday and Sunday). Reports on municipal bond news. Tables and charts. Price $732.00 per year.

Daily Commodity Computer Trend Analyzer. Commodity Research Bureau, Inc, One Liberty Plz—47th floor, New York, NY 10006. Telephone (212) 285-4660.

Daily report. Covers trends and changes as well as current data of the commodity market. Price $595.00 per year.

Daily Graphs. American Stock Exchange/OTC. William O'Neil & Co, Inc, PO Box 24933, Los Angeles, CA 90024. Telephone (213) 820-2583.

Weekly information service. Provides daily charting of 718 common stocks on American Stock Exchange and 50 selected over-the-counter stocks. Lists 64 facts per stock, including daily price and volume activity. Price $290.00 per year.

Daily Graphs—NY Stock Exchange/OTC. William O'Neil & Co, Inc, PO Box 24933, Los Angeles, CA 90024. Telephone (213) 820-2583.

Weekly information service. Charts provide 64 facts, including daily price and volume activity, for nearly all New York Stock Exchange common stocks and 50 selected over-the-counter stocks. Price $290.00 per year.

Daily Graphs Stock Option Guide. William O'Neil & Co, Inc, PO Box 24933, Los Angeles, CA 90024. Telephone (213) 820-2583.

Weekly information service. Presents statistical data on all listed call and put options, plus daily chart on each underlying stock. Price $98.00 per year.

Daily Stock Price Records. Standard & Poor's Corp, 345 Hudson St, New York, NY 10014. Telephone (212) 924-6400.

Quarterly books. Give data on over 2100 issues on New York Stock Exchange. Price $165.00 per year.

Daily Trader's Guide. Donald L Jones, Editor, Commodity Information Service Co, 33 W Ridge Pike, Limerick, PA 19468. Telephone (215) 489-4188.

Weekly report and daily hot line. Trading recommendations on "standard unit" of ten futures for trading in commodities futures. Price $750.00 per year.

Data Base Service. Ford Investor Services, PO Box 99131, San Diego, CA 92109. Telephone (714) 270-7290.

Monthly service. Provides computerized data base for 1400 common stocks, or any portion of it, on magnetic tape. Price $480.00 per year.

Directory of Franchising Organizations. Pilot Books, 347 5th Ave, New York, NY 10016. Telephone (212) 685-0736.

Annual book. Lists nation's top money-making franchises. Offers concise descriptions and facts about franchising. Price $2.95.

Dividend Record (Daily). Standard & Poor's Corp, 345 Hudson St, New York, NY 10014. Telephone (212) 924-6400.

Daily loose-leaf report. Contains dividend information on over 9800 listed and unlisted issues. Includes a notice of dividend meetings and the tax status of dividend supplements. Price $200.00 per year.

Dow Jones Commodities Handbook, 1977 edition. Dow Jones & Co, Inc, 22 Cortlandt St, New York, NY 10007. Order from Dow Jones & Co, Inc, PO Box 300, Princeton, NJ 08540. Telephone (212) 285-5000.

Book. Reviews commodities futures trading in 1976. Anticipates key factors in 1977 markets. Charts. Price $5.95. ISBN 0-87128-528-2.

Dunn & Hargitt Commodity Service. Dunn & Hargitt, Inc, 22 N 2nd St, Lafayette, IN 47902. Telephone (317) 423-2626.

Weekly newsletter. Advises on the commodity futures market. Analyzes the price outlook for major commodities. Charts of most active contracts. Price $95.00 per year.

Dunn & Hargitt Market Guide. Dunn & Hargitt, Inc, 22 N 2nd St, Lafayette, IN 47902. Telephone (317) 423-2626.

Weekly newsletter. Provides investment advice on stocks and options based on analyses for 1000 leading stocks. Price $95.00 per year.

Dunn & Hargitt Trust Investment Advisory. Dunn & Hargitt, Inc, 22 N 2nd St, Lafayette, IN 47902. Telephone (317) 423-2626.

Monthly report. Analyzes the quarterly earnings growth for blue-chip stocks. Price $250.00 per year.

Earnings Forecaster. Standard & Poor's Corp, 345 Hudson St, New York, NY 10014. Telephone (212) 924-6400.

Weekly newsletter. Provides new and revised earnings estimates for over 1600 companies. Price $220.00 per year.

Economic Week. Citibank, Economics Dept, 399 Park Ave, New York, NY 10022. Telephone (212) 559-4022.

Weekly newsletter. Reports on US economic trends. Includes such issues as consumer prices, construction activity, exchange rates, and inventories. Price $85.00 per year.

Enterprising Women. Artemis Enterprises, Inc, 525 West End Ave, New York, NY 10024. Telephone (212) 787-6780.

Monthly magazine. Addresses itself to women's role in the economy and professions. Discusses taxes, insurance, and personal finances as well as management issues. Price $18.00 per year.

EVM Stock Option Letter. EVM Analysts, Inc, 1001 Gayley Ave, Suite 208, Westwood Village, Los Angeles, CA 90024. Telephone (213) 478-3693.

Weekly newsletter. Covers listed stock options, market conditions, and trading methods. Price $130.00 per year.

Executive Woman. Executive Woman, 747 3rd Ave, New York, NY 10017. Telephone (212) 688-4601.

Monthly (except June and July) newsletter for business and professional women. Contains information on credit, investments, education, career opportunities, and business trends. Price $24.00 per year.

F & S Index of Corporations and Industries. Predicasts, Inc, 200 University Circle Research Center, 11001 Cedar Ave, Cleveland, OH 44106. Telephone (216) 795-3000.

Weekly report with monthly and quarterly cumulatives. Provides abstracts of articles on US business information, including mergers, investments, legislation, and new products. Price $325.00 per year.

Financial Analysts' Handbook, 1975. Dow Jones-Irwin, 1818 Ridge Rd, Homewood, IL 60430. Telephone (312) 798-3100.

Two books. Discuss the theory and practice of investment management. Price $30.00.

Financial Analysts Journal. Financial Analysts Federation, 219 E 42nd St, New York, NY 10017. Order from Financial Analysts Journal, PO Box 8021, New York, NY 10049. Telephone (212) 557-0065.

Bimonthly magazine. Presents articles on investment and stock issues. Includes book reviews. Price $24.00 per year.

Financial Handbook. Jules Bogen and Samuel Shipmen, John Wiley & Sons, Inc, 605 Third Ave, New York, NY 10016. Telephone (212) 867-9800.

Book. Covers corporate finance, money, and banking. Price $22.00. ISBN 0-8260-1160-8.

Financial Planner. The Financial Planner, 5775 Peachtree Dunwoody Road, Suite 120-C, Atlanta, Ga., 30342. Telephone (404) 257-0110.

Covers such financial planning matters as pension planning, insurance, investments, estate planning, and money management, as well as providing news on industry developments and legal and regulatory matters. Price $24.00 per year.

Financial Trend. Equity Media, Inc, 7616 LBJ Fwy, Dallas, TX 75251. Telephone (214) 239-0161.

Weekly newspaper. Covers industry and investments in Texas, Oklahoma, Arkansas, Louisiana, and New Mexico. Includes such topics as corporate finance, business management, equity investment, commercial banking, venture capital, energy companies, and securities regulation. Price $23.00 per year.

Financial World. Macro Communications, 919 3rd Ave, New York, NY. Telephone (212) 826-4360.

Weekly report. Investment analysis and forecasts for specific companies and industries as a whole. Price $32.00 per year.

Fitch Corporate Bond Ratings Book. Fitch Investors Service, 12 Barclay St, New York, NY 10007. Telephone (212) 571-1415.

Annual loose-leaf book with monthly supplements. Rates bond offerings of banks, finance companies, and other corporations. Price $60.00 per year.

Fitch Investors Municipal Bond Reports. Fitch Investors Service, 12 Barclay St, New York, NY 10007. Telephone (212) 964-4500.

Loose-leaf reports. Evaluates municipal bonds. Include a daily inquiry privilege with a subscription. Tables. Price $95.00 per year.

Fixed Income Investor. Standard & Poor's Corp, 345 Hudson St, New York, NY 10014. Telephone (212) 924-6400.

Weekly loose-leaf report. Covers developments in the debt securities market, including bonds, commercial paper, and preferred stocks. Statistical analysis of convertible bonds. Price $385.00 per year.

Forbes. Forbes Investors Advisory Inst Inc, 60 5th Ave, New York, NY 10011. Telephone (212) 675-7500.

Biweekly magazine. Covers general economic and financial news. Reports on various corporations, executives, stocks, and industries. Price $21.00 per year.

Forbes Special Situation Survey. Forbes Investors Advisory Inst Inc, 60 5th Ave, New York, NY 10011. Telephone (212) 675-7500.

Monthly loose-leaf report. Discusses and recommends the purchase of one speculative equity security in each issue. Price $250.00 per year.

Forecaster. Forecaster Publishing Co, Inc, 19623 Ventura Blvd, Tarzana, CA 91356. Telephone (213) 345-4421.

Weekly newsletter. Suggests ways to increase personal capital, such as starting a coin collection, making real estate purchases, and using tax loopholes. Provides economic forecasts. Price $90.00 per year. ISSN 0095-294X.

Fortune. Time, Inc, Time & Life Bldg, New York, NY 10020. Order from Time, Inc, 541 N Fairbanks Ct, Chicago, IL 60611. Telephone (212) 586-1212.

Semimonthly magazine. Covers business and economic developments. Evaluates specific industries and corporations and notes banking and energy news. Price $20.00 per year.

Franchising. Matthew Bender & Co, 235 E 45th St., New York, NY 10017. Telephone (212) 661-5050.

Two-volume set of books. Provides a guide to franchising. Includes such topics as contracts, trademarks, taxation, and equipment provisions. Price $97.50.

Fraser Opinion Letter. Fraser Management Assoc, Box 494, 309 S Willard St, Burlington, VT 05401. Telephone (802) 658-0322.

Semimonthly newsletter. Looks at current economic trends in business and finance. Price $35.00 per year.

Futures. IPC Business Press Ltd, 205 E 42nd St, New York, NY 10017. Telephone (212) 889-0700. Telex 421710.

Bimonthly. Covers methods of long-term forecasting in areas such as economics, population, and technology. Price $72.80 (company rate); $57.20 (individual rate). ISSN 0016-3287.

Futures Market Service. Commodity Research Bureau, Inc, One Liberty Plz— 47th floor, New York, NY 10006. Telephone (212) 285-4660.

Weekly newsletter. Covers the fundamental developments influencing price changes in the futures markets. Price $95.00 per year.

Goldsmith-Nagan Bond & Money Market Letter. Peter S Nagan, Editor, Goldsmith-Nagan, Inc, 1120 19th St NW, Washington, DC 20036. Telephone (202) 628-1600.

Newsletter. Covers the bond and money markets. Price $148.00 per year.

Grand Trading Plan. Dennis D Dunn and Edwin F Hargitt, Editors, Dunn & Hargitt, Inc, 22 N 2nd St, Lafayette, IN 47902. Telephone (317) 423-2626.

Weekly newsletter. Gives specific buy and sell points for trading of a $25,000 commodity account. Price $1000.00 per year.

Granville Market Letter. The Granville Market Letter, Inc., Drawer O, Holly Hill, FL. 32017. Telephone (800) 874-0977.

Newsletter. Forty-six issues per year. Stock market advisory service, making specific trading recommendations. Price $250.00 per year.

Growth Stock Outlook. Growth Stock Outlook, Inc, 4405 E-W Hwy, Bethesda, MD 20014. Order from PO Box 9911, Chevy Chase, MD 20015. Telephone (301) 654-5205.

Semimonthly newsletter. Reports on selected stocks with vigorous growth. Includes such stock data as earnings per share, prices, year's growth, and revenues. Price $42.00 per year.

Holt 500 Trading Portfolio. T J Holt & Co, Inc, 277 Park Ave, New York, NY 10017. Telephone (212) 758-2410.

Portfolio published at irregular intervals. Instructs participants on high-rish stock market moves. Stresses rapid rather than long-term growth. Price $1000.00 per year.

Holt Investment Advisory. T J Holt & Co, Inc, 277 Park Ave, New York, NY 10017. Telephone (212) 758-2410.

Semimonthly information service. Discusses the economy and stock market for investors concerned with long-term capital growth. Price $144.00 per year.

Holt Trading Advisory. T J Holt & Co, Inc, 277 Park Ave, New York, NY 10017. Telephone (212) 758-2410.

Weekly information service for stock and option traders. Provides market averages, stock price ranges, projected option values, and other stock indicators. Offers an analysis of selected companies. Price $260.00 per year.

How and Where to Get Capital: Dollars in Your Future. National Counselor Reports, Inc, Task Bldg, Kerrville, TX 78028. Telephone (512) 257-5050.

Annual book. Lists over 2500 sources of capital, loans, and grants. Notes hundreds of government assistance programs. Price $25.00.

How to Handle Tax Audits, Requests for Rulings, Fraud Cases and Other Procedures Before IRS. Panel Publishers, 14 Plaza Rd, Greenvale, NY 11548. Telephone (516) 484-0006.

Two loose-leaf books with quarterly supplements. Discuss procedures involved in handling tax audits and fraud cases before Internal Rev-

enue Service. Reflect Tax Reform Act of 1976 changes. Price $75.00.
ISBN 0-916592-08-1.

How to Plan for Tax Savings in Real Estate Transactions. Panel Publishers,
14 Plaza Rd, Greenvale, NY 11548. Telephone (516) 484-0006.

Loose-leaf book with quarterly supplements. Explains taxation of real
estate under Tax Reform Act of 1976. Furnishes information on depreciation, financing, and installment sales. Price $75.00. ISBN 0-916592-
11-1.

*How to Save Taxes and Increase Your Wealth with a Professional Corpora-
tion.* Panel Publishers, 14 Plaza Rd, Greenvale, NY 11548. Telephone
(516) 484-0006.

Loose-leaf book with quarterly supplements. Discusses all aspects of
professional corporations, including tax advantages, life and health insurance, and medical expenses. Price $75.00. ISBN 0-916592-09-X.

*How to Set Up and Run a Qualified Pension or Profit-Sharing Plan for a
Small or Medium Size Business.* Panel Publishers, 14 Plaza Rd,
Greenvale, NY 11548. Telephone (516) 484-0006.

Loose-leaf book with bimonthly supplements. Provides information
needed to establish and administer pension or profit-sharing plan for
small or medium sized business. Includes Keogh and individual retirement plans. Price $75.00. ISBN 0-916592-10-3.

How to Take Money Out of a Closely Held Corporation. Panel Publishers, 14
Plaza Rd, Greenvale, NY 11548. Telephone (516) 484-0006.

Two loose-leaf books with quarterly supplements. Discuss methods of
transferring closely held corporate money to stockholders under current tax rules. Price $75.00. ISBN 0-916592-02-2.

How to Use Tax Shelters Today. Panel Publishers, 14 Plaza Rd, Greenvale,
NY 11548. Telephone (516) 484-0006.

Loose-leaf book with quarterly updates. Discusses tax shelters. Analyzes Tax Reform Act of 1976 and various forms of investment. Price
$75.00. ISBN 0-916592-25-1.

Indicator Digest. Indicator Digest, Inc, Indicator Digest Building, Palisades
Park, NJ 07650. Telephone (201) 947-8800.

Fortnightly digest. Surveys stock market, business, and monetary trends. Focuses on various stock groups. Reviews stock market indicators. Charts and graphs. Price $78.00 per year.

IndustriScope. Media General Financial Services, Inc, PO Box 26565, Richmond VA 23261. Telephone (804) 649-6586.

Monthly report. Lists stocks by industry group. Notes monthly activity. Price $85.00 per year.

Industry Forecast. S Jay Levy, Box 26, Chappaqua, NY 10514. Telephone (914) 238-3665.

Monthly newsletter. Offers economic predictions 6 to 18 months into future. Includes forecasts of production, sales, corporate profits and prices. Price $50.00 per year.

Institutional Investor. Institutional Investor Systems, Inc, 488 Madison Ave, New York, NY 10022. Telephone (212) 832-8888.

Monthly report. Discusses issues and developments in investment management. Price $52.00 per year. ISSN 0020-3580.

Institutional Investor International Edition. Institutional Investor Systems, Inc, 488 Madison Ave, New York, NY 10022. Telephone (212) 832-8888.

Monthly magazine. Covers news of international finance, including government and corporate finance, currency, and economic conditions. Price $73.00 per year.

International Investment Trends. International Investment Trends, PO Box 40, 8027 Zurich 2, Switzerland.

Newsletter issued 17 times per year. Reports on international investment and political trends. Emphasizes gold investments and South African politics. Notes stock market activity and world monetary developments. Price $95.00 per year.

International Monetary Market Yearbook. Chicago Mercantile Exchange, 444 West Jackson Blvd, Chicago, IL 60606. Telephone (312) 648-1000.

Yearbook. Contains data on trading futures in international currencies, US treasury bills, US silver coins, gold bullion, and copper. Price $4.50.

International Reports. International Reports, Inc, 200 Park Ave S, New York, NY 10003. Telephone (212) 477-0003. Telex RCA 223139 ITT 422963 WU 147101.

Weekly report. Covers international finance, including liquidity fore-casts, exchange rate projections, evaluations of Eurobond market, in-terest rate trends, and prospects for gold, silver, and other commodities. Tables. Price $495.00 per year.

International Stock Report. Standard & Poor's Corp, 345 Hudson St, New York, NY 10014. Telephone (212) 924-6400.

Monthly report. Analyzes European, Japanese, South African, and Australian securities and investment opportunities. Price $52.00 per year.

Investment Advice & Analysis (IAA). Wright Investors' Service, Wright Bldg, 500 State St, Bridgeport, CT 06604. Telephone (203) 377-9444.

Weekly service. Provides investment recommendations, model trust portfolios, stock market analyses, and data on 100 industry groups. Price $500.00 per quarter.

Investment Bulletin. American Inst Counselors, Inc, Great Barrington, MA 01230. Telephone (413) 528-0140.

Semimonthly newsletter. Features reports on investments, securities, and business trends. Price $25.00 per year.

Investment Dealers' Digest. Investment Dealers' Digest (IDD), Inc, 150 Broadway, New York, NY 10038. Telephone (212) 227-1200.

Weekly magazine. Covers investment news, including common stocks, municipal bonds, and foreign securities. Notes corporate financing and market developments. Price $70.00 per year.

Investment Management Report. Ford Investor Services, PO Box 99131, San Diego, CA 92109. Telephone (714) 270-7290.

Monthly report. Tabulates computerized information for 1400 common stocks. Provides standard value and earnings trend analysis. Includes buy/hold/sell evaluations. Price $180.00 per year.

Investment Quality Trends. Value Trend Analysis, 7440 Girard Ave, Suite 4, LaJolla, Ca 92037. Telephone (714) 459-3818.

Semimonthly report plus quarterly reviews. Provides investment ad-vice on 350 selected blue-chip stocks. Tables and charts. Price $125.00 per year.

Investors Intelligence. Investors Intelligence, Inc, 2 East Ave, Larchmont, NY 10538. Telephone (914) 834-5181.

Semimonthly report. Evaluates stock market trends, recommends specific stocks, summarizes various investment advisory services' recommendations, and notes insider transactions. Price $72.00 per year.

Investors Research Service. Investors Research Co, PO Box 30, 1900 State St, Santa Barbara, CA 93102. Telephone (805) 965-7078.

Weekly report. Provides stock market analyses. Price $135.00 per year.

Journal of Financial Planning. Panel Publishers, 14 Plaza Rd, Greenvale, NY 11548. Telephone (516) 484-0006.

Quarterly magazine. Covers business and personal financial planning, including estate planning, taxation, investments, securities, and insurance. Price $36.00 per year.

Journal of Portfolio Management. Institutional Investor Systems, Inc, 488 Madison Ave, New York, NY 10022. Telephone (212) 832-8888.

Quarterly report. Contains articles on stocks, bonds, and other aspects of investment portfolio management. Price $56.00 per year.

Kiplinger California Letter. Kiplinger Washington Editors, Inc, 1729 H St, NW, Washington, DC 10006. Telephone (202) 298-6400.

Monthly newsletter. Supplies information on business and investment in California. Notes developments in Washington that affect California. Price $32.00 per year.

Kiplinger European Letter. Kiplinger Washington Editors, Inc, 1729 H St, NW, Washington, DC 10006. Telephone (202) 298-6400.

Weekly newsletter. Analyzes recent European developments and their potential effect on business and the economy. Price available on request.

Kiplinger Florida Letter. Kiplinger Washington Editors, Inc, 1729 H St, NW, Washington, DC 20006. Telephone (202) 298-6400.

Monthly newsletter. Concerns money making in Florida. Notes population trends, new industries, planned roads, taxation, land prices, and tourism. Price $32.00 per year.

Kiplinger Tax Letter. Kiplinger Washington Editors, Inc., 1729 H St, NW, Washington, DC 20006. Telephone (202) 298-6400.

Bimonthly newsletter. Contains business tax information and advice. Price $42.00 per year.

Kiplinger Washington Letter. Kiplinger Washington Editors, Inc, 1729 H St, NW, Washington, DC 20006. Telephone (202) 298-6400.

Weekly newsletter. Supplies briefings on business trends. Includes pertinent government policies and information on employment, investment, and interest rates. Price $42.00 per year.

Liquidity Report. Amivest Corp, 505 Park Ave, New York, NY 10022. Telephone (212) 688-6667. Telex ITT: 422851.

Monthly service. Measures investment dollar value traded per each percent of price variation. Lists stocks alphabetically by industry and rank. Price $650.00 per year.

Market Chronicle. W B Dana Co, 25 Park Pl, New York, NY 10007. Telephone (212) 233-5200.

Weekly newspaper. Covers stock prices, company news, and other related information. Price $20.00.

Market Rhythm. Investors Pub Co, PO Box 36171, Grosse Pointe Farms, MI 48236. Telephone (313) 821-3738.

Book. Describes methods of recording, measuring, and analyzing stock and commodity market trends. Evaluates short- and long-term changes. Price $100.00.

MBH Weekly Commodity Future Trading Letter. MBH Commodity Advisors, Inc, Box 353, Winnetka, IL 60093.

Weekly newsletter. Reviews commodity market trends. Offers advice on specific commodities. Graphs and charts. Price $240.00 per year.

Money. Time, Inc, Time & Life Bldg, New York, NY 10020. Order from Money, Time-Life Bldg, 541 N Fairbanks Ct, Chicago, IL 60611. Telephone (212) 586-1212.

Monthly magazine. Reports on personal finance. Includes topics on stock market trends, estate planning, taxes and tax shelters, and consumer affairs. Price $14.95 per year.

Money Manager. Bond Buyer, 1 State St Plz, New York, NY 10004. Telephone (212) 943-8207. Telex 12-9233.

Weekly newspaper. Interprets international financial and economic news. Covers money markets; government, municipal, and corporate bond markets; and stock market. Price $126.00 per year.

Money Market Directory. Money Market Directories, Inc, 370 Lexington Ave, New York, NY 10017. Telephone (800) 446-2810.

Annual directory. Contains information on investment management, including tax-exempt funds, investment services, and research departments. Price $162.00 per copy.

Money Strategies. Alexander Hamilton Inst, 605 3rd Ave, New York, NY 10016. Telephone (212) 557-5207.

Biweekly report. Offers advice on personal investments such as stocks, bonds, precious metals, real estate, commodities, and collectibles. Price $36.00 per year.

Moody's Bank and Finance Manual and News Reports. Moody's Investors Service, Inc, 99 Church St, New York, NY 10007. Telephone (212) 267-8800.

Two books plus twice-weekly reports. Gives ratings and other information about banks, insurance companies, mutual funds, closed-end investment companies, mortgage and finance companies, and real estate investment trusts. Price $350.00 per year.

Moody's Bond Record. Moody's Investors Service, Inc, 99 Church St, New York, NY 10007. Telephone (212) 267-8800.

Monthly report. Gives rates for over 22,000 bond issues, including US, corporate, muncipal, and convertible bonds, commercial paper, and industrial development revenue bond. Price $80.00 per year.

Moody's Bond Survey. Moody's Investors Service, Inc, 99 Church St, New York, NY 10007. Telephone (212) 267-8800.

Weekly loose-leaf newsletter. Covers factors that may affect bond values. Gives ratings and rationale for fixed-income market. Price $475.00 per year.

Moody's Commercial Paper Reports. Moody's Investors Service, Inc, 99 Church St, New York, NY 10007. Telephone (212) 267-8800.

Semiannual report. Gives ratings and facts about companies, including operating information and financial statements.

Moody's Dividend Record. Moody's Investors Service, Inc, 99 Church St, New York, NY 10007. Telephone (212) 267-8800.

Semiweekly loose-leaf newsletter. Gives information about dividends on approximately 10,000 issues, including common and preferred stocks, nonpaying issues, income bonds, mutual funds, and foreign securities. Price $110.000 per year.

Moody's Handbook of Common Stocks. Moody's Investors Service, Inc, 99 Church St, New York, NY 10007. Telephone (212) 267-8800.

Quarterly book. Contains information on over 900 stock issues. Describes companies' business, operations, 10-year statistical history, and classification. Price $90.00 per year.

Moody's Industrial Manual and News Reports. Moody's Investors Services, Inc, 99 Church St, New York, NY 10007. Telephone (212) 267-8800.

Two-volume manual plus twic-weekly reports. Gives ratings for and details on all firms listed on New York and American stock exchanges, plus those listed on regional exchanges. Price $350.00 per year.

Moody's Municipal and Government Manual and News Reports. Moody's Investors Service, Inc, 99 Church St, New York, NY 10007. Telephone (212) 267-8800.

Two books plus twice-weekly reports. Covers 15,000 municipalities that have long-term debts of over $1 million. Includes federal and state agencies. Ratings. Price $440.00 per year.

Moody's Over-the-Counter (OTC) Industrial Manual and News Reports. Moody's Investors Service, Inc, 99 Church St, New York, NY 10007. Telephone (212) 267-8800.

Manual plus weekly loose-leaf reports. Offers ratings for and details on 3200 firms not listed on major exchanges. Price $320.00 per year.

Moody's Public Utility Manual and News Reports. Moody's Investors Service, Inc, 99 Church St, New York, NY 10007. Telephone (2120 267-8800.

Book plus twice-weekly loose-leaf reports. Gives vital data on more than 550 public and private utilities. Ratings. Price $300.00 per year.

Moody's Transportation Manual & News Reports. Moody's Investors Service, Inc, 99 Church St, New Y ork, NY 10007. Telephone (212) 267-8800.

Book plus twice-weekly loose-leaf reports. Covers domestic transportation companies. Include maps and details of ownership and operation. Price $280.00 per year.

Municipal Bond Selector. Standard & Poor's Corp, 345 Hudson St, New York, NY 10014. Telephone (212) 924-6400.

Bimonthly report. Gives quality ratings and statistical information for about 6500 municipal bonds. Groups bonds according to issuing states and divides them into general obligations bonds and revenue bonds. Price $90.00 per year.

Munn's Encyclopedia of Banking and Finance, 7th Edition. F L Garcia, Editor, Bankers Pub Co, 210 South St, Boston, MA 02111. Telephone (617) 426-4495.

Book. Contains 4000 alphabetically arranged entires on banking and finance, with illustrative examples and statistical tables. Includes technical terms, federal regulations, business laws, and abbreviations of listed securities. Price $49.75. ISBN 0-87267-019-8.

Mutual Fund Director. Investment Dealers' Digest, 150 Broadway, New York, NY 10038. Telephone (212) 227-1200.

Semiannual report. Contains statistics on individual mutual funds. Price $29.00 per year.

Mutual Fund Fact Book. Investment Company Inst, 1775 K St, NW, Washington, DC 10006. Telephone (202) 293-7700.

Annual book. Presents data on US mutual fund industry, including trends in sales, assets, distributions, accumulations, and withdrawal plans. Tables and charts. Price $1.00 per copy.

Mutual Fund Performance Review. Computer Directions Advisors, Inc, 8750 Georgia Ave, Silver Spring, MD 20910. Telephone (301) 565-9544.

Monthly report. Covers results and rankings for 400 open-end funds. Includes statistics on performance. Price $300.00 per year.

Mutual Funds Almanac, 8th edition, 1977. Yale Hirsch, Editor, Hirsch Organization, Inc, 6 Deer Trail, Old Tappan, NJ 07675. Telephone (201) 664-3400.

Annual book. Provides directory to over 600 mutual funds. Looks at 10-year performance. Statistics, tables, charts, and graphs. Price $15.00.

Mutual Funds Scoreboard. Yale Hirsch, Editor, The Hirsch Organization, Inc, 6 Deer Trail, Old Tappan, NJ 07675. Telephone (201) 664-3400.

Quarterly newsletter. Reports on mutual funds industry. Ranks funds. Subscription includes Mutual Funds Almanac. Price $24.00 per year.

National Forecast. National Securities & Research Corp, 605 3rd Ave, New York, NY 10016. Telephone (212) 661-3000.

Annual report. Presents general economic and stock market forecasts. Examines outlook for different groups of stocks. Graphs, charts, and tables. Free of charge.

National Tax Shelter Digest. National Tax Shelter Digest, 9550 Forest Lane, Suite 604, Dallas, Texas, 15243. Telephone (214) 343-9218.

Monthly. Reports on tax shelter field, including industry developments and legal and regulatory matters. Price $30.00 per year.

New York Stock Exchange NYSE) Fact Book. New York Stock Exchange, 11 Wall St, New York, NY 10005. Telephone (212) 623-2013.

Annual book. Gives statistics on New York Stock Exchange members, listed issues, market activity, shares, and other data. Price $.50.

New York Times. New York Tiems, 229 W 43rd St, New York, NY 10036. Telephone (212) 556-1234.

Daily newspaper. Contains articles on business, financial, and economic news, along with general news coverage. Includes securities price statistics. Price $150.00 per year.

Over-the-Counter Growth Stocks. John S Herold, Inc, 35 Mason St, Greenwich, CT 06830. Telephone (203) 869-2585.

Quarterly publication. Furnishes data and comment on fast-growing over-the-counter stocks. Charts. Price $30.00

Over-the-Counter Stock Reports. Standard & Poor's Corp, 345 Hudson St, New York, NY 10014. Telephone (212) 924-6400.

Daily and weekly loose-leaf reports. Cover issues traded over the counter and on regional exchanges. Describe company activities. Asses financial results. Price $440.00 per year (daily); $300.00 per year (weekly).

Personal Finance Letter. McGraw-Hill Publications Co, 1221 Ave of the Americas, New York, NY 10020. Telephone (212) 997-6375. Telex TWX 7105814879. WUI 62555.

Biweekly newsletter. Discusses personal finance topics, including tax planning, tax shelter, real estate, and estate planning. Price $49.00 per year.

Perspective on Aging. National Council on the Aging, Inc, 1828 L St, NW, Suite 504, Washington, DC 20036. Telephone (202) 223-6250.

Bimonthly magazine. Discusses aging. Reports on related executive decision, legislation, and specific programs. Price $35.00 per year (includes membership in NCOA).

Pick's Currency Yearbook. Pick Pub Corp, 21 W St, New York, NY 10006. Telephone (212) 425-0591.

Yearbook. Provides monetary information, including exchange rates and foreign exchange controls, free- and black-market gold prices, and Eurocurrency market conditions. Tables. Price $120.00. ISBN 0-87551-275-5. ISSN 0079-2063.

Pick's World Currency Report. Pick Pub Corp, 21 W St, New York, NY 10006. Telephone (212) 425-0591.

Monthly report. Reivews currency rates, international monetary developments, and gold and silver markets. Lists metal and diamond prices. Charts. Price $350.00 per year. ISBN 0-87551-176-7. ISSN 0048-4113.

Poor's Register of Corporations, Directors & Executives. Standard & Poor's Corp, 345 Hudson St, New York, NY 10014. Telephone (212) 924-6400.

Annual directory with three supplements. Lists 390,000 company officials with brief biographies and 37,000 companies with vital statistics. Includes banking and law firms. Price $185.00 per year.

Powell Gold Industry Guide & International Mining Analyst. Reserve Research Ltd, 63 Wall St, New York, NY 10005. Telephone (212) 943-3620.

Book. Assesses gold and other mining stocks. Price $25.00.

Powell Monetary Analyst. Reserve Research Ltd, 63 Wall St, New York, NY 10005. Telephone (212) 943-3620.

Biweekly newsletter. Contains advice about investment opportunities in gold and other mining industries. Price $115.00 per year. ISSN 0146-7190.

Private Investors Abroad. Matthew Bender & Co, 235 E 45th St, New York, NY 10017. Telephone (212) 661-5050.

Annual book. Analyzes private investment opprotunities abroad. Discusses international business transaction methods. Price $28.50.

Real Estate Investing Letter. United Media International, Inc, 306 Dartmouth St, Boston, Ma 02116. Telephone (617) 267-7100.

Monthly newsletter. Covers real estate investments, including tax strategies, depreciation, and real estate syndication. Price $35.00 per year.

Real Estate News. Real Estate News, 720 S Dearborn St, Chicago, IL 60605. Telephone (312) 922-7220.

Weekly magazine. Provides articles about real estate marketing trends. Contains listings of investment opportunities and classified advertising. Price $12.50 per year.

Reigstered Bond Interest Record. Standard & Poor's Corp, 345 Hudson St, New York, NY 10014. Telephone (212) 924-6400.

Weekly report. Contains list of payments, stock exchange rulings, and 10-day calendar for more than 5900 bond issues. Price $438.00 per year.

Register of Corporations, Directors and Executives. Standard & Poor's Corp, 345 Hudson St, New York, NY 10014. Telephone (212) 924-6400.

Three books. Contain an alphabetical listing of US and Canadian companies with brief descriptions, lists of company directors and executives, and indexes by geographic location and SIC number. Price available on request.

Rundt's Weekly Intelligence. S J Rundt and Assoc, Inc 130 63rd St, New York, NY 10021. Telephone (212) 838-0141.

Weekly newsletter. Examines world trade markets and currencies. Notes international economic conditions. Price $485.00 per year.

Savings and Loan Investor. Savings and Loan Investor, PO Box 7163, Long Beach, CA 90807. Telephone (213) 427-1905.

Semimonthly report on savings and loan associations. Includes buy/sell/hold recommendations and earnings-per-share estimates. Graphs and charts. Price $75.00 per year.

Security Charts. United Business Service Co, 210 Newbury St, Boston, MA 02116. Telephone (617) 267-8855.

Monthly set of charts. Supplies weekly price ranges, relative market performance, volumes, earnings, and dividends for 1105 stocks. Industry group charts and commentary. Price $59.00 per year.

Selected Interest and Exchange Rates. Federal Reserve System, Board of Governors, Washington, DC 20551. Order from Publication Services, Div of Adm Services, Board of Governors of the Federal Reserve System, Washington DC 20551. Telephone (202) 452-3245.

Weekly publication. Depicts spot and forward exchange rates, Eurodollar and foreign money market rates, bond yields, stock indexes, and gold prices. Series of charts. Price $15.00 per year.

Select Information Exchange (SIE) Guide to Business & Investment Books. Select Information Exchange, 2095 Broadway, New York, NY 10023. Telephone (212) 874-6408.

Book. Serves as a source finder for publications offering business and investment advice in the US and abroad. Price $12.95.

Silver Data. American Bureau of Metal Statistics, Inc, 420 Lexington Ave, New York, NY 10017. Telephone (212) 867-9450. Telex 14-7130.

Monthly report. Consists of silver-refining statistics for the US and other countries. Price $75.00 per year.

Smart Money. Yale Hirsch, Editor, The Hirsch Organization, Inc, 6 Deer Trail, Old Tappan, NJ 07675. Telephone (201) 664-3400.

Monthly newsletter. Covers stock market conditions and outlook. Graphs. Price $50.00 per year.

South African Gold Service. Indicator Digest, Inc, Indicator Digest Bldg, Palisades Park, NJ 07650. Telephone (201) 947-8800.

Weekly publication. Reports on South African gold indicators. Shows the activity of various gold companies and includes gold-mining news items. Charts. Price $90.00 per year.

Standard Corporation Records. Standard & Poor's Corp, 345 Hudson St, New York, NY 10014. Telephone (212) 924-6400.

Six loose-leaf volumes plus regular revisions. Provide financial information on over 5600 corporations. Price $512.00 per year (monthly); $436.00 per year (daily); $877.00 per year (daily and monthly revised.)

Standard New York Stock Exchange (NYSE) Stock Reports. Standard & Poor's Corp, 345 Hudson St, New York, NY 10014. Telephone (212) 924-6400.

Daily and weekly looseleaf reports. Profile companies listed on the New York Stock exchange. Forecast sales and earnings. Price and volume charts. Price $520.00 per year (daily); $350.00 per year (weekly).

Stock Guide. Standard & Poor's Corp, 345 Hudson St, New York, NY 10014. Telephone (212) 924-6400.

Monthly book. Offers investment data on over 5100 common and preferred stocks, listed and over the counter, for the New York and American stock exchanges. Price $49.00 per year.

Stock Market Research Library. Securities Research Co, Div of US Business Service Co, 208 Newbury St, Boston, MA 02116. Telephone (617) 267-8860.

Monthly charts, quarterly graphs, and wall chart. Present a record of prices, volume, earnings, and dividends for 1105 stocks. Price $79.00 complete annual service.

Stock Summary. Standard & Poor's Corp, 345 Hudson St, New York, NY 10014. Telephone (212) 924-6400.

Monthly report. Gives earnings and dividends rankings, price-earnings ratios, and institutional holdings for listed and over-the-counter stocks. Price $24.00 per year.

Stock Trader's Almanac, 11th edition, 1978. The Hirsch Organization, Inc, 6 Deer Trail, Old Tappan, NJ 07675. Telephone (201) 664-3400.

Annual book. Presents a memo calendar book with stock tips and information for the year. Tables, charts, graphs, and statistics. Price $9.95.

Tax Sheltered Investments. Clark Boardman Co Ltd, 435 Hudson St, New York, NY 10014. Telephone (212) 929-7500.

Loose-leaf book periodically revised. Discusses laws affecting tax-sheltered investments, with emphasis on the Tax Reform Act of 1976. Covers real estate investments, oil and gas investments, equipment leasing, cattle feeding and breeding, farmland, and motion pictures. Price $42.50. ISBN 0-87632-093-0.

Tax-Sheltered Investments. Inst for Business Planning, Inc, IPB Plz, Englewood Cliffs, NJ 07632. Telephone (201) 592-2040.

Loose-leaf books with monthly supplements and semimonthly letters. Discuss tax-sheltered investments in real estate, livestock, life insurance, oil and gas, farmland, and other areas. Price available on request.

Technical Stock Reports. Indicator Digest, Inc, Indicator Digest Bldg, Palisades Park, NJ 07650. Telephone (201) 947-8800.

Monthly reports. Provides comments on 1000 leading common stocks and brief market forecasts. Figures. Price $60.00 per year.

Technical Trends. Merrill Analysis, Inc, Box 228, Chappaqua, NY 10514. Telephone (914) 238-3641.

Weekly report. Gives a graphic summary of stock market barometers. Includes an analysis of selected growth companies. Price $50.00 per year.

Trading Cycles. R E Andrews and Assoc, 25743 N Hogan Dr, Valencia, CA 91355. Telephone (805) 259-3742.

Monthly newsletter. Carries buy-sell instructions for long-term investors. Indicates topping signals and major lows of various stock market cycles. Price $50.00 per year.

Trendline Service: Current Market Perspectives. Standard & Poor's Corp, 345 Hudson St, New York, NY 10014. Telephone (212) 924-6400.

Monthly publication. Provides information on over 1000 issues for a four-year time span. Charts and statistics. Price $92.00 per year.

Trendline Service: Daily Basis Stock Charts. Standard & Poor's Corp, 345 Hudson St, New York, NY 10014. Telephone (212) 924-6400.

Weekly service. Plots stock market behavior, including technical indicators, earnings, and dividend statistics. Charts. Price $280 per year for weekly listing; $87 per year for monthly.

Trendline Service: How Charts Can Help You in the Stock Market. Standard & Poor's Corp, 345 Hudson St, New York, NY 10014. Telephone (212) 924-6400.

Book. Describes and interprets classic stock chart patterns. Price $10.00.

Trendline Service: OTC Chart Manual. Standard & Poor's Corp, 345 Hudson St, New York, NY 10014. Telephone (212) 924-6400.

Bimonthly publication. Presents charts on unlisted stocks. Price $75.00 per year.

United Mutual Fund Selector. United Business Service Co, 210 Newbury St, Boston, MA 02116. Telephone (617) 267-8855.

Semimonthly report. Evaluates mutual funds, including bond and municipal bond funds. Notes industry developments. Tables and charts. Price $49.00 per year.

United States Master Tax Guide. Commerce Clearing House, Inc, 4025 W
  Peterson Ave, Chicago, IL 60646. Telephone (312) 236-2350
  Book. Covers federal income taxes for individuals, partnerships, corpo-
  rations, estates, and trusts. Rate tables and checklists. Price $7.00.

Value Line Convertible Strategist. Arnold Bernhard & Co, Inc, 5 E 44th St,
  New York, NY 10017. Telephone (212) 687-3965.
  Weekly loose-leaf newsletter. Supplies investment information, including material on options, convertibles, and warrants. Price $120.00 per
  year.

Value Line Investment Survey. Arnold Bernhard & Co, Inc, 5 E 44th St,
  New York, NY 10017. Telephone (212) 687-3965.
  Weekly loose-leaf booklet. Covers the business activities of corporations in a variety of industries. Charts and graphs. Price $285.00 per
  year.

Value Line OTC Special Situations Service. Arnold Bernhard & Co, Inc, 5 E
  44th St, New York, NY 10017. Telephone (212) 687-3965.
  Bimonthly loose-leaf newsletter. Contains information for investors on
  stocks and business trends. Price $250.00 per year.

Venture Capital. Capital Publishing Corp, 10 S LaSalle S, Chicago, IL
  60603. Telephone (312) 641-0922.
  Monthly loose-leaf magazine. Covers the venture capital field. Offers
  information on investments, trends, and companies. Price $295.00 per
  year.

VNR Dictionary of Business and Finance. Van Nostrand Reinhold Company,
  135 West 50th St., New York, NY, 10020. Telephone (212) 265-8700.
  Book. Contains over 4,500 definitions of terms drawn from all areas of
  business and finance, with examples of modern usage. Price $18.95.

VNR Investor's Dictionary. Van Nostrand Reinhold Company, 135 West 50th
  St., New York, NY 10020. Telephone (212) 265-8700.
  Book. Contains over 2,200 definitions of terms drawn from all invest-
  ment areas, with examples of modern usage. Price $16.95.

Wall Street Advisor. Wall Street Advisor, PO Box 2591, Ormond Beach, FL
  32074. Telephone (800) 824-5120.
  Semimonthly newsletter. Surveys the stock investment market. Presents a technical review and digest of professional opinion. Tables and
  charts. Price $100.00 per year.

Wall Street Journal. Dow Jones & Co, Inc, 22 Cortlandt St, New York, NY 10007. Telephone (212) 285-5000.

> Daily newspaper. Contains news articles on business and finance and includes statistics on securities, commodities, and exchange rates. Price available on request.

Wall Street Letter. Institutional Investor Systems, Inc, 488 Madison Ave, New York, NY 10022. Telephone (212) 832-8888.

> Weekly report. Covers news and trends in the securities trade, including new regulations and changes in brokerage businesses on Wall Street. Price $395.00 per year.

Weekly Insider Report. Stock Research Corp, 55 Liberty St, New York, NY 10005. Telephone (212) 964-2440.

> Weekly report. Supplies information on the stock transactions of 500 or more shares by corporate officers, directors, and 10% holders who buy or sell shares in their own companies. Price $50.00 per year.

Where to Find Business Information. John Wiley & Sons, 605 3rd Ave, New York, NY 10016. Telephone (212) 867-9800.

> Directory. Lists and describes over 5000 sources of business information drawn from entire English-speaking world. Includes sources covering all business subject areas and complete ordering information.

Wiesenberger Financial Services. Warren, Gorham & Lamont, Inc, 210 S. St, Boston, MA 02111. Telephone (617) 423-2020.

> Annual book, with quarterly and monthly reports. Provides financial information on open- and closed-end mutual funds. Offers short- and long-term statistics and performance evaluations. Price $120.00 per year.

Zweig Forecast. Zweig Securities Advisory Service, Inc, 747 3rd Ave, New York, NY 10017. Telephone (212) 753-7710.

> Newsletter published 18 times per year. Evaluates stock market trends and offers stock and other investment advice. Tables. Price $95.00 per year.

Index